MIRACLE

ON CORPORATION STREET

STEVEN SUTTIE

QUICK NOTE FROM STEVE;

I've been fascinated by the 1996 IRA bombing of Manchester for quite some time and I've also fancied having a go at writing something a bit different from the usual DCI Miller investigations, (even though I absolutely love writing them and plan to write many more.)

This book can be labelled under "Faction." (I know! I'd never heard of it either!) It's fiction, in the sense that the main characters who drive the story are not real. But it is factual in that everything that these characters get involved with after 9am actually happened.

Each scene in the following book is based around the actual events in Manchester on Saturday June 15th 1996, as they happened.

I have received lots of stories and memories from that day and I would like to thank everybody who has taken the time to send me their recollections of what went on. In particular, I'd like to thank the former Piccadilly Key 103 DJ Rick Houghton for sharing his memories of presenting his radio show that morning, and for allowing me to use him as a major character in the following, unbelievable story. Sadly, Piccadilly Radio is no more, but Rick can still be heard on Greatest Hits Radio, 7-10pm, Mon-Fri. (He didn't ask for a plug, but it is a great show.)

Let's wind the clock back 23 years now and see how dramatically modern life has changed in that relatively short period of time. I can assure you that it's quite an eye-opener...

EPILOGUE
Tuesday 11th June 1996. 9.35am

"Good morning, Peterborough Used Car Sales." The sales rep sounded really excited to be answering this call.

"Ah, yes, top of the morning to you. It's Thomas Fox, we did a wee deal on the Ford Granada last month, so we did."

The sales rep remembered the man's strong Irish accent well. He'd bought a car from the company the previous week. But it was the most peculiar sale that the company had ever made in that they had never actually met the man, despite over a thousand pounds changing hands in cash.

"Oh yes, I remember, Mr Fox. How are you?"

"Me, oh I'm fine, so I am."

"And the car? Everything's okay?"

"Oh yes, it's a grand wee motor, so it is."

"Yes, we don't sell anything that isn't of an excellent standard here, Sir."

"Very good. Well I'm interested in the Ford Cargo truck you have on your forecourt. I see it's two-thousand pounds?"

"Oh, yes, it's a very good vehicle that one, Mr Fox. Remarkably low mileage for its age as well." The sales rep was feeling quite excited about this call, he could do with a decent sale this early in the week and the 13 year-old Ford Cargo was the most expensive vehicle on the forecourt. "It's a very strong truck, I'd recommend you take it for a test-drive. You won't be disappointed."

"No, no, that's fine. I trust you. So please mark it as sold..."

"Oh, right. That's great news."

"Same deal as last time. Is that going to be okay?"

The salesman paused for a second. It had been weird enough the first time. But to ask for the same peculiar arrangement again was extremely odd. "Yes, of course. We're always happy to oblige our customer's wishes!"

"Grand. Well, I'll send the money in an envelope in a taxi like last time. Once you have the money, I want you to put the vehicle documents in the glove-box and drive it to this location. Have you a pen and some paper handy?"

"One second… er, yes. Okay, go ahead."

The Irish man gave the details to the salesman, who scribbled them down on his pad.

"Leave the keys behind the front wheel on the driver's side. Okay?"

"Absolutely Sir, not a problem at all."

"Grand. The taxi will drop off the envelope containing two-thousand pounds within the next hour, so it will."

"Okay, well, thank you Mr Fox. A pleasure doing business with you again."

"Good day to you."

With that followed the sound of the handset crashing down and the line went dead.

"Just sold the Cargo!" Said the sales-rep to his colleagues. The young man's manager looked concerned.

"Yes, I heard some of that. Is it the same bloke who bought the Granada?"

"Yes."

"And he's sending the money in a taxi again?"

"That's right. And I need to leave the Cargo at this address, with the keys behind the tyre, like last time."

The manager looked at the piece of paper he'd been handed. He didn't like the sound of this at all. It was very dodgy.

"Still, a sale is a sale! Tracey, what is five per cent of two grand?"

One of the ladies in the office thought for a second before replying. "A hundred pounds."

"So, my commission is a hundred quid!" Said the salesman proudly as he headed out to the forecourt to peel the price sticker out of the window of the red and white truck. "Happy days!"

15TH JUNE 1996

5:18AM

Andy Miller was in a great mood. The sun was shining, the birds were singing and he was off work for two days after today's shift. Best of all, England were playing Scotland later, one hour after he clocked off. Things could not be any better.

Miller closed the front-door as quietly as possible, he didn't want to disturb his parents who were asleep in the front bedroom which was right above the door. He unlocked his little Vauxhall Nova and got in, pulling the car door to very lightly. After putting the key in the ignition and pulling off the drive, he turned onto the main road. Once the car was a little further up the road, away from all the houses, he opened the car door and pulled it shut firmly. It was his daily ritual, he couldn't stand ignorant people who made loads of noise when they were going to work at dawn and he always tried his best to make sure that he wasn't one of them. The guy who used to live next door used to rev his motor-bike for five-minutes at half-five every morning, before setting off for work. Miller hated people like that.

"Let's have some tunes!" Said Miller as he flicked the radio on. Within seconds, the sound of "it's coming home" was playing through the speakers and Miller began singing along.

"Baddiel and Skinner and the Lightning Seeds there, and the UK's number one hit single, it's coming home! Is there a football match on today or something? Okay, good morning, it's Radio One, Kevin Greening here with the early breakfast show and well, there's only one thing on my mind this morning, and that is the exciting news that Britain is getting a brand-new TV channel next year! Channel 5 will launch onto our screens in March, and the owners are promising lots of exciting new soaps, dramas and films, and I personally cannot wait! So, we're asking you this morning, what kind of things would you like to see on..."

Miller switched the radio off. The DJ was far too cheerful for this hour and he didn't care if there was a new channel starting. His parents had Satellite TV and there were over 300 channels on that, and they were all crap anyway. The only thing Miller liked to watch was the X-Files, and that was only because he fancied Gillian Anderson like mad.

As he drove his car along the deserted roads towards Manchester city-centre, his mind wandered back to the football match. He'd been excited for this for months and the big day had finally arrived. Andy Miller literally couldn't wait to clock out at two, find a pub and then watch the match and hopefully, fingers-crossed, England would win.

5.45.a.m

"Morning Andy!" WPC Karen Ellis looked pleased to see Andy Miller as he stepped into work, it looked as though she'd been waiting for him by the staff entrance. This unexpected encounter really livened the twenty-three-year-old police constable up.

"Karen Jones... I mean, Ellis! As I live and breathe!" Miller's eyes widened as he stepped forward and hugged his colleague.

Karen and Andy had gone through training together a couple of years earlier and had completed their probationary period under the same sergeant. Karen had only been married for a month or so, and since coming back from her honeymoon, she'd been put on nights to cover sick leave. The two colleagues had really missed one another's company.

"Bloody hell, you look like you're in a good mood!"

"I am now I've seen you. When are you coming back on our shift?"

"Oh, God knows. Hope its soon though. I can't stand nights. It's just non-stop aggro with pissed-up girls, fighty-blokes and sted-head door-men."

"Well hurry up back. It's shit without you."

"I know, can't wait to get back on days with you and Cleggy. Where is he anyway?"

"He'll be here in a minute. Hey, don't say out, but he was out on a date last night!"

"Shut up!"

"He was."

"Who with?"

"Some bird he contacted from the lonely-hearts page!"

Karen Ellis laughed loudly and held her hand up to her mouth. Their colleague, Ian Clegg was a lovely lad, he got on with everybody brilliantly, but he went to pieces dealing with single females of his own age. This was great news, but quite unbelievable all the same.

The staff door opened and Cleggy walked through.

"Ah! Speak of the devil and he will appear!" said Miller.

"Bloody hell! Alright Kaz?" said Ian, looking equally as pleased to see Ellis as Miller had done.

"Alright Cleggy! So, what's this I've been hearing about you going on a date?"

"Aw, don't start. I asked you to keep it zipped Andy!" Cleggy was blushing, but he was smiling too. It looked as though the date had gone well, that much was clear.

"So..."

"So what?"

"Where did you go, what did you do, what's she called? Did you shag her?"

Miller laughed loudly at Ellis's outrageous line of questioning.

"Shut up!" Cleggy began blushing violently, which made his colleagues laugh loudly again.

"Come on Cleggy, spill the beans!" Said Miller when he'd got his breath back.

"Nowt... just, we met up in a wine bar..."

"A wine bar!" Screamed Ellis. The idea of Cleggy in any establishment with such a name was hilarious. "I'm guessing that was her idea?"

"Yes, it was her idea. Cost me a flipping tenner for two drinks!"

"So, then what did you do? I know for a fact that you won't have bought another round at that price!"

"I took her to the pictures."

"Aw, you old romantic Cleggy!" Ellis toy-punched him in the arm. "What did you watch?"

"Trainspotting."

Cleggy looked completely baffled as Miller and Ellis laughed loudly again, tears were streaming down both their faces by the time they'd stopped.

"You want your heads testing, you two."

"Aw, God, I love you Cleggy. Can't believe how much I've missed you both."

Cleggy just smiled, still trying to work out what was so funny about going to see Trainspotting.

"Well, anyway, I can't stand here all day, they'll be asking where I've got to! I just came to see what your plans were for the match?"

Ellis was talking about the biggest international football match in years. England versus Scotland in the Euro 96 tournament, which was scheduled to take place later that afternoon.

"No firm plans, me. I was going to clock out of here bang on two, no matter what, and head straight for the nearest pub. Probably Yates'." Said Miller with an unmistakable look of enthusiasm.

"I was just going to follow him," said Cleggy, pointing at his colleague.

"Why? Are you coming? Fancy?" asked Miller with a hopeful expression.

"Shut up! Have you seen the weather forecast for today? It's giving blue skies, bikini lines and ice-cold wines! I'm not standing in a pub full of yobs and knobs in stinking England shirts."

"And Scotland shirts! There's more Jocks in Manchester than there are in Glasgow these days!" said Cleggy.

"What's the plan, then?" asked Miller.

"Me and Bob have decided at the last minute to do a bring-a-bag-of-cheap-meat-barbeque, the salad and beers are free."

Miller looked at Cleggy and smiled. "That sounds mint!"

"Birds are invited as well, Cleggy!" said Ellis with a cheeky grin as she poked him in the ribs. The young constable's cheeks heated up again as he looked down at the floor. "Well, anyway, if you fancy it... you know where we are. Kick-off is at three!"

"Bloody hell Kaz! This is the most hotly anticipated football match in twenty years, since I was yay high!" Miller bent down and demonstrated how tall he used to be in the 1970's. "Trust me, I know exactly what time it kicks off!"

"Same goes!" said Cleggy.

"I just feel gutted for them that are on afternoons today though! My heart goes out to them. Imagine that, missing the match and then dealing with all the drunks and the fights afterwards!" Despite his words, Miller didn't look as though he gave a shit, really.

"Right, well, get yourselves finished here and get over to mine in time for kick-off. You'll probably be there for half-two, the roads will be dead, everyone will be in the pub or in the house."

"Awesome. Right, that's sorted. See you later."

"Yeah, nice one Kaz."

"Brilliant, see you later boys. I'd better get back to custody and finish my paperwork. See you in a bit."

6.a.m.

"Good morning team!"

"Morning Sarge!" Chanted the PCs as they sat down for the early-shift team briefing. It was Sergeant Ken Harris in charge of the city-centre's bobbies today, a very popular superior at Bootle Street, which pleased every police constable in the room. There weren't many popular sergeants at this nick, but Ken was definitely respected and loved by all of the constables that he managed, his supportive words, delivered in his soft Scottish accent and his friendly, laid-back manner was extremely endearing to the constables. All the other sergeants were much stricter and less personable, some of them even suffered from a bit of a "God-complex" and loved to remind junior colleagues that they were superior. But Sergeant Harris was a diamond, he wasn't interested in any of that nonsense. If you were right with him, he was right with you.

PC Andy Miller and PC Ian Clegg stood at the back of the room as all of the available chairs had been taken.

"Okay, I know that you are all eager to get today's shift out of the way and get home to watch the match..." Sergeant Harris looked up over his spectacles at the officers before him. They looked as though they weren't too comfortable with the tone in which the boss had made that introduction. "...but, I've been asked to let you all know that there is over-time available for everybody today."

There was a loud roar of laughter in the briefing room, Sergeant Harris laughed at the response, holding his hands up to calm his team. He had already anticipated that his officers would not be looking for over-time today when the biggest football game in decades was taking place just an hour after the end of their shifts. "Okay, okay. I said I'd ask..."

"Is this to deal with the drunks Sarge?" asked a PC on the front row.

"Yes Gregg, most of our pubs are showing the match on their big screens this afternoon. The fine weather that's forecast for today, plus a three pm kick off has all of the hallmarks of a busy tea-time!" Sergeant Harris looked over his glasses again and smiled. "I'm not doing any... if that makes any of you feel better!" The sound of laughter erupted in the room again before the Sergeant skilfully quietened his officers.

"Right, okay, so, as you will be aware, our rota is quite light on officers today. Due to the circumstances of the England Scotland game later, plus the Germany versus Russia game at Old Trafford tomorrow requiring extra policing, our rota is ten officers down for today's shift. Don't worry, it shouldn't be a problem, but I will warn you all that it's Father's Day tomorrow."

The police officers all looked at Sergeant Harris, wondering what that had to do with anything.

"As some of you might be aware, our teenagers tend to panic the day before Father's Day and present themselves in the city-centre looking for a last-minute gift. When they realise that their one pound-sixty-five won't buy them much, they tend to get caught trying to steal a bottle of Fahrenheit from Lewis's or Kendals."

The officers laughed loudly, the idea of some of scally young Manc presenting their loved-one with a stolen Father's Day present was hilariously believable.

"Or, the kids with no sense in taste try and nick those dancing plants, the ones with sunglasses on. So, just a warning there that the security guards will be inundating us with shoplifter calls today. I don't recommend any arrests today for shop-lifting, we'll need the cells for the angry, drunken England fans later, when Scotland the brave thrash the English!"

Sergeant Harris's comment received a good laugh. The senior officer had been extremely professional and had remained completely neutral until this point, but now, as the team briefing was coming to a close, he hadn't been able to resist pinning his team colours up for all to see.

"Whatever Sarge!" said one of the bobbies.

"I'm serious! If you want a good bet to put on your chitty, two-nil! Colin Hendry to score a penalty in the first-half and Ally McCoist to score in the second!"

The remark received another wave of laughter and sarcasm, but the Sergeant took the inevitable ribbing well.

"Now you should all be aware that we've got a lot of tourists in the city today due to the Euro 96 matches taking place at Old Trafford and Elland Road. There's a hell of a lot of Dutch, Germans and Russians especially. We're not expecting any trouble, the mood is very friendly, but just I just want to remind you all that control have got translators for all EU speaking languages on duty in the control room, so any difficulties that you might face will be easily rectified through control."

"How will we identify which translator to ask for?" asked another copper near the front.

"That's a fantastic question! But my advice would be, just look at what the badge says on their football shirt!"

The sergeant's razor-sharp reply attracted another good laugh from the officers. It was a pretty daft question, but Sgt Harris muttered an apology to the constable and added that he couldn't resist it as the laughter died down.

"Okay guys, off you go. Have a safe shift and remember, it's going to be a warm one, so make sure you stay hydrated."

6.32am

"Is that the stunningly beautiful and delightfully quick-witted Mrs Ellis?"

Karen Ellis had tried to let herself into the house as quietly as possible, but laughed to herself as she realised that she'd been heard.

Bob appeared at the top of the stairs. "Ah! It is! The most gorgeous police constable in all of Greater Manchester!"

"Erm, excuse me? I thought you said all of the north-west yesterday!"

"Oh, shit... yes, sorry..."

"What are you doing up, anyway?" She asked as she hung her jacket up.

"I woke up about five. Couldn't get back to sleep."

"Oh? Everything alright?" Karen was pulling the bobble out of her hair as she looked up the stairs as her husband of three weeks started coming down.

"Yeah, yeah, just, I can't sleep when the sun's out, feel like I'm missing out on something amazing! Plus, all the birds were singing a dawn chorus and they were getting right on my tits!" Bob kissed his wife as he reached the bottom step.

"Well to be fair, it is pretty amazing when the sun shines round here, just be thankful it only happens two days a year! Do you want a brew?"

"I've just done a fresh pot of coffee, it'll be ready to push down. I'm well excited for today, can't wait."

"Oh, yes, I saw Andy and Cleggy, they're coming straight from work."

"Brilliant."

"And don't say anything to him, but Cleggy was out on a date last night!"

"Was he indeed?" Bob raised an eyebrow. This was big news. "How did it go?"

"Don't know. He started blushing when we were asking for the details. But guess where he took her!"

Bob laughed, he already knew from the expression on his wife's face that this was going to be entertaining. "Go on."

"Trainspotting!"

The couple laughed loudly, with great affection. Only Ian Clegg would think that going to see a film about a group of Edinburgh's heroin addicts going cold-turkey would make for a romantic first-date.

"Where did he take her after? Sharing a kebab at the bus-stop and then for a shag on the canal?"

Karen was still laughing as she headed through to the kitchen. She pushed the plunger down on the Cafétiere, one of the couple's wedding presents from Bob's sister.

"Anyway, I'm sure we'll be able to get some more details out of him later!" Karen took a cup out of the cupboard and placed it on the work-top.

"Are you not having one?" asked Bob.

"Nah, I wanted to grab a couple of hours shut-eye. This stuff won't help with that. I'll have a glass of water with you in the garden though, before I go up."

"Good point. It's powerful stuff that coffee, it's about five times stronger than the jar stuff. Hey that reminds me, guess what I've got coming today."

"What?"

"A mobile phone!"

"No way! Really? Have you won the national lottery or summat?"

"No. Work have ordered it for me. It's being delivered today by courier. It's a good one as well, a Nokia. It's got games on it and allsorts. You can text message on it. It's costing them over eight-hundred quid!"

"Flipping heck!"

"I know. Still, it's good of work, isn't it?"

"Yeah, I'm jealous!"

"Well, don't worry. I'll let you look at it from time to time!"

"You'll be the only person on this street to have one. Make sure you walk up and down talking on it, so all the neighbours know!"

"Don't worry, that's my first priority!"

Bob had been with the same printing company since

he'd left school. He'd started on a £28.50 a week YTS scheme there and now, at the grand old age of twenty-five, he'd become one of the company's best sales-men. His success at work had been rewarded well, the owner had a real affection for Bob and had put him through his driving lessons when he was eighteen. He'd given him a company car when he was twenty-one. None of his mates could believe how well he'd done for himself, especially considering that he'd passed on the idea of going to college or university. Several of his old school-mates had gone through the education system, while he'd been climbing the career ladder. As his old school-mates were now starting out with their fledgling careers, Bob was very well established in his.

"So, apart from waiting for your mobile phone to arrive, what else have you got lined up for this morning?" Karen walked through the patio doors and placed Bob's coffee on the garden-table, before placing her glass of water down beside it.

"Well, I've done a list of stuff I need from Safeway. So as soon as my phone comes, I'll have a drive down and get all the stuff for the barbeque. I've invited my mum and dad as well. Have you asked yours over?"

"Yes, phoned mum last night. I think dad's a bit grumpy about it, he likes peace and quiet when the football's on."

"Well, don't worry, we'll shove him in the spare bedroom with the portable!"

Karen laughed loudly and snorted. "Don't even mention that idea to him! He'll probably take you up on it!"

"Well, anyway, there's no problem, everything's sorted."

"Lovely. Just hope this weather's going to stay nice."

Bob took a sip of his coffee and nodded appreciatively. "I've already checked on Teletext. It says it's going to be scorchio all day! There won't be a cloud in the sky."

"Well, soz Bob. I hate to go to bed when the sun's shining, but I'll have to get my head on the pillow for a few hours or I'll be shit-company later. I'll end up snapping at my dad!"

"Why don't you lie down in the garden? I promise not to block the sun-rays with a sock on the washing-line, so you get a big massive white patch right through the middle of your face!"

"Ha! For exactly that reason Robert!"

"How was work by the way? Any murders?"

"No, nothing happened really. We only had a couple of arrests last night. I think the yobs are saving themselves for tonight. I'm just glad I'm not working, can you imagine how pissed everyone will be by ten o'clock?"

"Well, you can thank me for that. I told you to book it off as soon as the fixtures were announced."

"Well, thank you Bob. I'd never have thought of that, what with me being a silly little woman and all that!"

"Exactly!"

Karen kicked her husband under the table.

"Ow! Karen! That's assault!"

"No witnesses, though. It's your word against mine. And I think the judge will believe the word of a serving police officer over a pamphlet salesman any day of the week."

"Hey, there's plenty of judges who want a good deal on bespoke top-quality business cards!"

Karen Ellis laughed as she stood, before leaning over and kissing Bob. "Night then."

"See you in a bit love."

8am

PC Andy Miller had spent the first two hours of his shift catching up on his paperwork. This was the best part of doing earlies, the two-hour "calm-before-the-storm" gap between the shift starting and the public venturing into town. This "quiet" period was perfect for ensuring that all of the straggling bits of paper-work and reports were all completed, present and correct.

Saturdays were always eventful in Manchester city centre, the prospect of tens of thousands of foreign football fans here as well just added an extra dimension to what was always a busy shift.

Groups of youths were a consistent problem in the afternoons, gangs of teenagers from the outlying residential areas of Hulme, Moss-Side, Beswick and Ardwick congregated in the city centre, close to the underground market on Market Street. They were generally okay, but it only took one or two of them to start getting lippy with members of the public and all hell could break loose.

The recent chart success of Oasis had had quite an effect on the city's impressionable youngsters. Many young lads were suddenly modelling themselves on Liam Gallagher, a young man from a council estate just down the road in Burnage, who had become one of Britain's most famous rock and roll stars practically overnight. The musical talent was arguably down to Liam's elder brother, Noel. But the swagger, the mod fashions and the punk-style, "couldn't-give-a-fuck" attitude all belonged to twenty-four-year-old Liam. And it seemed that every kid in the city wanted to emulate his obnoxious style and stroll through town pretending that they walked just like him, waving their arms at their sides as they walked with their bottoms as close to the ground as possible. In reality, most of them just looked as though they'd shat their pants.

Dealing with shop-lifting, muggings, drunken disorderly and street-fights were the bread and butter of Saturday city-centre policing, mixed in with telling members of the public where certain shops or bus-stops were and, surprisingly in this day-and-age of being able to buy wrist-watches for under £5, what time it was.

There was a notorious gang of teenage kids that regularly run amok in the Arndale Centre towards the end of the day on a Saturday, getting their kicks from running into shops and helping themselves to whatever they fancied, laughing and giggling as they ran away to the safety of the underground Arndale Bus Station, where they'd dive on the first bus they saw and hide from the chasing security guards.

The previous Saturday, the gang had gone into the Athena store and helped themselves to as many posters as they could carry. Staff had told the attending security and police officers that every copy of the famous 'L Enfant" man and baby poster had been taken and their shop's inventory records suggested that this amounted to more than thirty posters. It was a popular poster, but none of the staff, nor the police could work out why these youths needed thirty copies of it.

That kind of stupidity wasn't going to be PC Andy Miller's problem today. He would be miles away, at Karen and Bob Ellis's house with an ice-cold can of Castlemaine Four X in his hand, watching the match by the time that kind of daftness was taking place. The prospect filled him with excitement as he headed through to the police station's locker room and placed his uniform jacket in his locker and began rolling up his sleeves. Today was definitely going to be shirt-only weather. If only he could dump his police-helmet in the locker as well, he thought, as he considered how hot and sweaty his head would be today, inside that fibre-glass, reinforced headgear.

"Come on, Andy!" shouted Cleggy, as he appeared at the door. "How long does it take to shove a jacket in a locker?"

"Alright. Just making sure my sleeves are perfectly symmetrical in case we bump into a different sergeant!"

"Let's get going, we've got to attend a burglary at Stolen from Ivor on Market Street."

Miller laughed loudly. "Stolen from Ivor? What's been nicked, a hundred weight in shitty two-for-fifteen-quid jeans?"

"We need to go."

"Alright, keep your ginger hair on."

Miller closed the old, steel cupboard with a heavy clunk and looked down at his boots. They seemed shiny enough and his shirt was crisp and white, without a single crease. He felt happy with his appearance. Although he was two years into his service, he was still considered a rookie by the senior officers and as a result, they were still likely to pull him up on any aspect of his appearance that they could find a fault in. This always made him smile inwardly, as the officers guilty of this pettiness were always the scruffiest, slobbiest sergeants and inspectors in town.

Miller looked at Cleggy. "Please, make sure I'm the one who asks the manager what was Stolen from Ivor?"

Miller's colleague laughed. "Make sure you call him Ivor as well."

"Yes, game on! Let's see how many times we can slip Ivor into the conversation. Like, Ivor feeling that whoever did this has absolutely no sense in style!"

"Ha ha! Anyway, come on!"

"Alright..."

9 am

Miller and Cleggy left the burgled denim-wear shop after twenty minutes of offering the staff vague assurances which implied that every officer in the city was going to be working day and night on the case, which is what victims of crime always wanted to hear, regardless of whether it was true or not. The two young PCs were delighted that they'd managed to slip "Ivorganised a visit from the forensics team to come down and have a look for fingerprints," into the conversation, so the visit hadn't been a complete waste of time.

Market Street was extremely quiet, but for a few buskers setting up. The first wave of activity in the city-centre was beginning to calm down again now that thousands of shop staff had alighted their buses, trams and trains and had disappeared into the hundreds of shops all around the city-centre, where they would now remain until 5pm.

During the week, a hundred-thousand office workers would still be making their way into the offices, banks and call-centres. But weekends were completely different, and the city centre seemed deserted at this time in the morning, but for the odd person wandering around.

"Nice and peaceful, just how I like it," said Cleggy as the two police officers strolled up the busy pedestrianised thoroughfare which was packed with popular chainstores such as Toy and Hobby, C&A, Virgin Records, North-West Gas and Curries, as well as smaller, local chains like Stolen From Ivor and Rumours. Market street also serves as the entrance to the Underground Market, home to some of the most popular shops in the city, the busiest of which is Spin Inn records.

The Arndale Centre, the huge shopping complex which attracted the most footfall in Manchester thanks to its exclusive shops such as the Warner Brothers Store and The Sweater Shop has its main entrance facing the Underground Market entrance.

Market Street didn't always look like this. Twenty or so years earlier, before the Arndale Centre was built and had become the biggest shopping precinct in Europe, Market Street was a small part of the 282 mile-long A6 road, which links Luton with Carlisle. With the modernisation of Manchester in the mid-seventies, this major road which went straight through the city-centre was sent on a mini detour around the Arndale Centre, where the A6 was once again rejoined at Chapel Street and the long road to Carlisle continued on its way through Salford.

"It might be quiet now, but it'll soon liven up, so don't get too relaxed!" said Miller, smiling.

"Nah, I like this bit, it won't get busy now until about half-ten, eleven. All we need to do is hope it's a bit quieter than a normal Saturday because of the match and the weather, and we'll have the easiest day ever!"

"And a nice tan as well!"

"And clocked out at two on the dot!"

"And then over to Karen and Bob's!"

"And then watch Shearer score a hat-trick against the sweaty-socks!"

"I love it when a plan comes together!"

"Tell you what though, I'm sick of hearing Three Lions already, it's playing in every shop we walk past." Said Cleggy. "Part of me will be glad when Euro 96 is over and I'll never have to hear the sodding thing again!"

"I know. It's either that, or Killing Me Softly!"

"One time!"

"One time!"

"Oh, I knew there was something I was going to tell you. I've heard that Inspector who booked the Bernard Manning gig has been pensioned off!"

Miller was talking about a recent scandal that Greater Manchester Police had been at the heart of, which had been so big that it had resulted in the Prime Minister, John Major passing comment. The Manchester police force had hired the notorious local comedian Bernard Manning to appear at a function for senior officers, which was secretly taped by Granada TV's undercover journalism show, World in Action. Throughout the performance, Bernard Manning had made numerous jokes about "queers" and "faggots" and "niggers" and "coons" and "pakis" and "chinks" and "stupid fucking women."

The veteran local comedian was well known for his

outrageous and deliberately offensive show, so the language that he had used came as no surprise to the TV producers, after all, Granada TV had been instrumental in launching Bernard Manning's successful career. What had come as a surprise, however, was the fact that many of Manchester's senior police officials were seen on film, laughing and jeering at the unacceptable language used, particularly as the new political correctness directive was becoming a major part of police work, especially within areas with diverse communities such as Manchester. Weeks before the show, the GMP force had announced plans to drop the "WPC" title for female officers, as they "strongly believed that the role of a Police Constable was exactly the same, regardless of gender and it was out-dated, irrelevant and degrading to specify a police officer's sex in their job title."

The sight of these key police figureheads laughing enthusiastically at the very language and attitude that they were supposed to be committed to stamping out had become a major news story throughout the land.

"No way! Full pension?" said Cleggy.

"Apparently, that's what I heard. One of the lads from Middleton was on about it, the Chief Constable said somebody had to take the heat, so the Inspector was given a golden handshake!"

"Flaming Norah. Alright for some."

"I know, early retirement on a full wage 'til he dies!"

As the two young coppers headed up towards Piccadilly Gardens, wondering what kind of a punishment that was supposed to be, the radio crackled alive.

"Control to 616, over."

"616 receiving, over," said Miller into the radio strapped by his shoulder.

"616, GM Buses control have lodged a report of a disturbance in Piccadilly bus station, at the 192 stop adjacent to Piccadilly 21s. Officers required, over."

"616 to control. 616 and 712 attending now, we're just by Lewis's tram stop, ETA one minute, over."

"Received, thank you. Over."

Miller and Cleggy quickened their pace as they walked briskly to the bus stop of the high frequency bus to Stockport and Hazel Grove, which was situated by the side of Piccadilly Gardens, the huge green-space in the centre of the city-centre which proudly displayed bright and colourful flowers in neatly tended beds, surrounded by hundreds of benches which attracted shoppers and workers who were hunting a quiet rest from the hustle and bustle of the city, as well as winos, drunks and tramps who had nowhere else to go.

The dispute was still ongoing when the two constables arrived at the big orange double-decker bus.

"You're a fucking jobsworth, mate!" Shouted a young bloke, no older than twenty. He was wearing a pair of red Reebok Classic trainers with bright yellow Adidas popper pants and a black Naff Co 54 t-shirt. He looked furious, and not at his outfit.

The bus driver, dressed smartly in his camel coloured uniform was standing on the steps of the bus, refusing entry to the angry young man who was clearly worked-up and creating a scene.

"I'm not your mate!"

"Yeah, cos... I bet you haven't even got any mates you specky-four-eyed twat!"

"Hoi, watch your mouth, you!" Said Miller as he grabbed the young man.

"What's the problem here?" asked Cleggy of the bus-driver.

"This lad's trying to use a doctored Daysaver ticket. When I scratched the date, the number fell off." The bus driver handed the GM Buses ticket to Miller's partner for him to inspect.

"It's a common trick. They look on the floor for a bus ticket with today's date on, then cut the date off and stick it over the date on an out of date Daysaver ticket, using toothpaste."

Cleggy sniffed at the ticket and nodded as the minty-freshness hit his nostrils. "Where were you planning to travel to, Colgate?"

"This ones from the second of June," continued the

driver. "So, he's been getting away with this for the past fortnight. Little meff."

"Like it affects your life, Jimmy Jobsworth! You need to get a life! None of the other bus drivers give a fuck!" Said the aggrieved passenger.

"Hoi, I've told you! Shut your trap!" said Miller, increasing his grip on the young scally.

"Get knotted!" Huffed the young man.

The bus driver smiled smugly. "Anyway, thanks officers. I'm running five minutes late now thanks to this lob-on, so I need to get going."

"Alright, we'll deal with this."

"Cheers! See you later, ten-men!" Said the driver, waving at the youth as he opened the little door into his cab and pressed a button which closed the doors, making a loud "tsshhhh" noise as the bus pulled away from the stop. The passengers on board all gave a filthy look to the young man as he stood with the police officers.

"Wouldn't a Pritt-Stick be better than toothpaste?" asked Cleggy. "They're only fifty pence, you tight sod."

The young man wasn't in any mood for sarcasm. "No need. I need to get to Longsight, I'm meeting somebody."

"Well, if you walk straight down there," said Miller, pointing towards Piccadilly train station. "Keep going until you reach the Apollo, then take the right hand turning at the roundabout and you'll be there in about forty minutes." Miller released his grip and the youth straightened his t-shirt.

"Yeah, I know where it is, Sherlock."

"I don't think I like your attitude very much," said Miller with a look of utter disinterest.

"What's your name?" asked Cleggy.

"Mary Jane." Answered the pissed-off young man.

"Where do you live?"

"Down the grid."

"What number?"

"Cucumber."

Miller and Cleggy offered a round of applause to the cocky youth, which totally confused him.

"Seriously now. Where do you live?"

The youth shrugged and looked at the floor. "Irlam."

"Irlam? You call that living?" Remarked Cleggy.

"Right, you're doing my head in now Mary Jane. Off you go," said Miller, with a warm smile.

"Give me my ticket back, then."

Miller and Cleggy laughed loudly.

"Come on, don't be dicks. No need."

"Listen mate, you're lucky we're not arresting you, so stop being lippy."

"Arresting me? Yeah right, for a blag bus ticket. Whatever Officer Dibble!"

"Right, go on, see you later Alligator."

"In a while, paedophile."

Miller was becoming more and more irritated by this obnoxious character now. "Seriously mate, do one."

"I'm not going nowhere 'til you give me back my ticket! My property! Ten fifths of the law!"

Cleggy held the ticket out and ripped it up into little pieces, before handing it back.

"Aw yeah, nice one! I bet you're dead buzzing with yourself now!" The young man turned and stormed off in the direction that Miller had pointed him. He looked furious, which amused the two police constables no end.

"A very angry young man!" said Cleggy as they watched "Mary Jane" swagger out of sight.

"It's this spot, here," said Miller. "It attracts the lunatics."

"What, the 192 stop?"

"No, I mean, this whole area, Piccadilly Gardens, right down to China Town, this is where all the crazy people come to." Miller pointed over Piccadilly Gardens, towards Sunley Tower and the famous Piccadilly Hotel. "Don't you ever wonder why so many winos and homeless people doss around here?"

"Not really, no," said Cleggy as the two police officers began walking back towards Market Street, their "beat" for today's shift.

"Every bench in Piccadilly Gardens, every shop doorway

in the bus station has tramps and nutters sat there in a puddle of their own piss. Don't you ever wonder why its only here, that they sit?"

"Like I just said, Andy. No."

"Well I know why, it's their spiritual home!"

Cleggy laughed. "Right, so, sitting in the piss-stinking doorways of empty shops in Piccadilly Plaza is their spiritual home? Where do they go for a holiday? Gorton?"

"You can laugh all you want Mr Clegg. All this, where we're stood now was the site of the biggest mental asylum in Britain not so long back. Piccadilly, the Gay Village, China-Town, the whole area housed a massive asylum, filled with all the nutters from the north of England."

"Get out of it!"

"I'm telling you. It was only knocked down at the start of the century."

Miller was talking about the site of the former Manchester Mental Institution which was demolished in 1908. The site took up the entire area where the two officers were walking. It was an enormous space.

"You're talking bollocks!"

"I'm not. Straight up. Sergeant Birchall told me all about it when I was doing my probation with him. He believes in all that spirituality stuff and that. He said, that's why all the loons still hang about around Piccadilly."

"Bollocks!"

"Suit yourself. But tell me this, if he's wrong... why don't any of them hang about anywhere else in town?"

"I don't know."

"Think about it, you don't see them at Victoria, or down at the Town Hall, or down Deansgate or Oxford Road. There must be some reasoning in why they all congregate in Piccadilly."

"Okay, whatever Andy. It must be the ghosts of ye olde loony bin calling them home!" Cleggy was keen to dismiss the story but it didn't bother Andy Miller. He believed that there was something rather peculiar about it all and it interested him greatly.

"Anyway, I'm going in McDonalds for a leak. It's your turn to get the milkshakes in."

"Fair dos. Chocolate or banana?"

"Chocolate today I think. And get us an apple pie please."

Miller opened the door of the fast-food restaurant as Cleggy entered. He had a quick glance at his watch. Time was marching on, almost half of the shift was done already.

"It'll soon be two-o-clock!" He said cheerfully as Cleggy headed up the stairs to the loo.

9.15am

"Aw mum! Do we have to go? Live and Kicking's just starting. And Will Smith's going to be on it, talking about his new film!" Eleven-year-old Hayley Bradshaw was not impressed with her mother's suggestion of going to Manchester to do some father's day shopping. She was really excited about the new Independence Day film that was coming out soon, and the presenter Zoe Ball was promising lots of clips from the big movie, which was being promoted as the most expensive film ever made. Plus, she was absolutely, totally in love with Will Smith. The prospect of missing this to go boring shopping was quite literally the end of the world, and her face showed it.

"Hayley, if I've told you once, I've told you a thousand times! There's a video recorder there, and there's about five blank tapes next to it. Just push one in and press the big red button that says record!"

"Aw mum! It never works when I do it!"

Tina Bradshaw wasn't in the mood for any messing about today, but she knew the fastest and easiest way to resolve this problem was to do the job herself.

"Tell you what, stick a brush up my arse and I'll paint the wall," she muttered as she dropped to her knees in front of the TV and opened the smoked glass-doors. "Right, take one blank video, take the wrapper off, push it in the doo-dar, press channel 1 in, then press record. There. Done. I can't see how you can't do that but you can complete Sonic the Hedgehog."

"Is it definitely recording?" Asked Hayley, still disappointed that she wasn't allowed to watch it live.

"Aw Hayley! What's this?" Tina lifted a video out of the cupboard and held it in the air.

"Don't look at me!"

"Jumanji. I thought you gave that back to the video man last night?"

"I did!"

"Well if you did, you only gave him the box you dingbat! I'm going to have to pay double next week. Nice one very much!"

Hayley rolled her eyes to the ceiling as her mum closed the video cabinet doors and got to her feet.

"Right, come on."

"How come I've got to go but Robert gets to stay in bed?"

"Because Robert is a teenager Hayley. It's what they do."

"So, like, when I'm a teenager I won't have to go shopping with my mum like a little Joey?"

"Hayley Bradshaw, wash your mouth out with soap and water!"

"Well..."

"Listen love, all week I have been looking forward to us going out and spending a bit of time together and now you're just ruining it."

"Well, it's not fair."

"Get a life Hayley!"

Five minutes later, Tina and Hayley were in the family's Ford Escort and were pulling off the drive of their smart semi-detached house in Prestwich. The mood inside the car was frosty and Tina was beginning to feel sorry for herself. All she ever did was clean-up, tidy-up, wash, iron and cook for her kids and when she wasn't, she was handing them money or driving them here, there and everywhere and they just treated her like shit in return. Tina was surprised that Hayley was being such a cow today, especially as the trip to town had been discussed earlier in the week and she'd been really excited about it then. But Tina cast her mind back to what she'd been like at that age, and she knew that Hayley was just a chip off the old block. Tina had been a lot worse if she was honest, her dad had to pack her door frame with an inch of draft-excluder tape so it didn't bang as loud when she slammed her bedroom door. It had really annoyed her as a teen, slamming the door as hard as she could and it made a really soft sound. The thought of it made Tina smile.

"Sorry, mum," said Hayley, from nowhere.

"It's alright love. Thanks for apologising though."

"I just, like I really, really wanted to see the clips."

"Well you can, it's on video. You can put it on when we get back."

"I know, but Robert will stop it and tape the Chart Show. He always does it."

"Well I'll tell you what we'll do. When we get to town, I'll find a phone-box and I'll phone home and tell him not to. How's that?"

"Yeah."

"So, have you had any ideas about what we should get your dad?"

"Nah."

"What, none at all? God, you're worse than me!"

"Well he's got all the music he wants. I checked his tapes in his car and he's got Now 33, that's the latest one."

"I know. I bought it him for his birthday."

"And the new United shirt isn't out until next month."

"Aw, is it not?"

"No."

"He's got the Eric Cantona book."

Tina smiled and launched into her family-famous Eric Cantona impression. "When ze seagull follow ze trawler. Eet ees because 'e thinks, sardines!"

The mother and daughter laughed, it was good that the bad moods were now being forgotten about.

"See, you *have* been thinking about it!" Tina laughed loudly, she thought it was cute that Hayley had done all this thinking about her dad's Father's Day pressie, without even realising it.

"I checked his bottle of Jazz. It's still got most of it."

"Well, I'm sure we'll find him summat he'll like. If not, we'll get him one of those dancing sunflowers!"

Hayley laughed loudly. "There's no way he'll want one of them! He hates them!"

"Well, it'll serve him right for being so hard to buy for!"

"What about a video? Showgirls has just come out."

"Hayley!" said Tina, almost gasping.

"What?"

"You're not getting your dad a porno for Father's Day!

What are you like?"

9.20am

Corporation Street is the main road which cuts through the lower half of Manchester city centre between Victoria Train station and the banking district. It becomes Cross Street hallway along and the two roads cut straight through the western side of the city-centre to Manchester Town Hall, criss-crossing many major shopping streets, including Market Street, the area that Miller and Cleggy were patrolling today.

300 yards away from McDonalds, where the two police officers were waiting for their order, two men were sitting at traffic lights in a red Ford Cargo truck, with a white container section. The vehicle, which had "Jack Roberts Transport" written on the doors, looked just like any other heavy goods vehicle which was used to make deliveries to any one of the hundreds of shops in the area.

"Is this the place?" asked one of the two men sitting in the cab. He was wearing a hooded top, along with sunglasses and a baseball cap.

"A little further yet." Said the driver, dressed in exactly the same attire. "Just near the bridge."

The driver was talking about the elevated walkway between the Arndale Centre and Marks and Spencer. The glass walled, concrete "bridge" created a seamless walkway over the busy Corporation Street, connecting the two major shopping attractions high above the buses, cars and lorries which relied heavily on this busy street to navigate the city centre.

The traffic lights turned to green.

"Okay, nearly there," said the driver as he lifted the clutch and powered the vehicle forward. "Wire her up."

"Not until the engines off!" Said the passenger, a tone of panic very clear in his voice.

The driver laughed loudly, but it sounded forced. "Just testing."

The truck indicated, before pulling over on double yellow lines, close to the junction with Cannon Street, the depressing part of town that was nothing more than a road which predominantly served the Arndale bus station and gave access to the multi-story car park ramp. Cannon Street is widely regarded the roughest part of town, most of the street robberies and assaults which were reported to the police had taken place around here. It also stinks of piss.

The Ford Cargo driver switched the engine off and pressed the hazard lights.

"Right, nearly done. Attach the clock and let's get the fuck out of it."

One minute later, the two men stepped down from the cab, closed their doors very gently and walked casually away from the truck, heading down Cannon Street towards Deansgate. One minute after that, they were picked up on Cathedral Street by a man who was waiting for them in a burgundy coloured Ford Granada.

9.23am

"What the bloody hell..."

Traffic Warden Denise Cartwright was patrolling Corporation Street. She was amazed to see that some pillock had left a bloody big Cargo truck on double yellows, right next to a major junction. "If some folk had brains, they'd be lethal," she muttered to herself as she stepped closer to the vehicle.

After waiting a minute, to see if the driver came back with a lame excuse and an insincere apology, she started writing out a parking ticket. She began taking down the registration plate number, C213 ACL.

"I bet that's cheered you up, love!" said a man walking past as Denise filled out her parking ticket. She ignored the casual sarcasm, she was used to it and a lot worse besides. It was all in a day's work patrolling the city-centre. Denise finished filling out her paperwork and fixed the penalty notice to the windscreen, beneath the windscreen-wiper. But she wasn't happy, contrary to what the bloke had just said.

"Control, over," said the Traffic Warden into her radio.

"Control receiving, over."

"Hiya Carl, its Denise. Some total Dime-Bar has parked a ruddy big truck on Corporation Street, just near Marks and Sparks. Can you see it on the CCTV? Over."

"One sec... Yes, I see it. Has it broken down?"

"Not sure. The hazards are flashing, but there's nobody around. I think it'll need towing, it's blocking the carriageway. Over."

"Copy that. I'll keep an eye on it. If it hasn't gone in five minutes, I'll ring the recovery truck. Thanks Denise. Over."

9.30 am

Piccadilly Plaza, the huge concrete construction facing Piccadilly Gardens is home to Manchester's most popular radio station, Piccadilly Radio. The stars of this 22-year-old radio station are house-hold names in the region. Dave Ward and Umberto, Mike Sweeney, Phil Wood, Scott Mills and many other presenters are considered superstars in the city that the station serves.

These days, following a government shake-up of local radio stations using two frequencies, Piccadilly Radio has split into two stations, Piccadilly Gold on AM for the over 40's audience, and Piccadilly Key 103 on FM for the under 40's. This unpopular change in the late 80's was initially criticised by the station's one-million regular listeners, but now, after several years of advertising and rebranding, the station has never been so popular. This is a great result, especially as the two Piccadilly brands are now facing competition for the very first time, from two new radio stations in the city, Kiss 102 and Fortune 1458. Kiss were going after Key 103's listeners, whilst Fortune were chasing Piccadilly Gold's, with a broadcast schedule filled with former Piccadilly stars.

The studios have become one of Manchester's best-known buildings. You could ask anybody in Manchester for directions to the radio station, it's as well known as The Midland Hotel and the Arndale. The Piccadilly Plaza complex in which the stations are based has gigantic glass windows running the entire length of the building along Portland Street. These windows are used productively as the station's premier marketing device. With over one hundred and fifty thousand bus travellers seeing the bright, exciting adverts and posters every day as they enter or leave the bus station, Piccadilly has a huge visual presence in the centre of the city that it serves.

Piccadilly Radio has produced some of the nation's biggest broadcast stars in its relatively short life. The Radio 1 Breakfast Show host Chris Evans started here. In fact, he was sacked quite early into his broadcasting career on Piccadilly, for making upsetting comments about microwaving a cat. But before having his own show, Chris Evans was better known as a character on Timmy Mallet's show, a useless, jibbering fool called "Nobby No-Level."

Piccadilly Radio has produced plenty of other Radio 1 stars too, Gary Davies started at the Plaza, as did Mark and Lard's Mark Radcliffe. The biggest names at the station today are Steve Penk, whose infamous breakfast time "wind-up calls" have become legendary throughout the city. And in the evenings, former school-master James Stannage entertains the late-night audience with his deliberately argumentative and provocative radio phone-in show which attracts huge audiences on Piccadilly Gold, and regularly makes the local news headlines.

But it is relatively peaceful at Piccadilly Radio today. The office staff are never around at weekends and the newsroom operates on a skeleton crew, but despite the lack of staff, the station is usually buzzing with local bands doing live sets for Pete Mitchell and Geoff Lloyd's IQ show, their new music programme which has attracted and supported some of the biggest names in music throughout the Madchester years at the start of the decade, right up to today's emerging local talent including Puressence, Badly Drawn Boy, Audioweb and Oasis. But as Pete and Geoff were off today, the station was much quieter than usual. No bands had been prepared to miss the football, not even for free publicity on the number one station in the region.

Saturdays would normally see a lot of activity from the sports department, too, particularly during the football season when reporters switch between every game in the city, from the top flight, right through to the non-league teams. But as the football season was over, and the big Euro 96 football match was being shown on live TV later that day, Piccadilly Gold's output was nothing more than non-stop "golden hits and greatest memories" today with pre-recorded shows.

The two studios face one another, with a little booth in-between where the telephone calls were answered. The radio station is so popular that all 8 lines are regularly lit up with callers hoping for a request or a dedication over the airwaves. Callers were rewarded for their interaction with a carrier-bag full of free records and a car-sticker, which they could collect from reception. This is a popular feature which appears very generous, but in reality it costs the radio station nothing as they receive thousands of free records every week from all of the record companies and promoters who are hoping to get them play-listed on the biggest radio station in the north-west of England.

On Piccadilly Gold, Mike Sweeney was finishing up his weekend breakfast show, and was looking forward to handing over the CR1 studio to Darren Stannage, the son of the infamous late-night broadcaster, James. Darren was taking care of the 10am to 1pm slot which was pre-recorded. Facing Sweeney, in CR2, the Key 103 studio, Karl Pilkington was rounding up his early-morning slot, getting ready for Rick Houghton who was gearing up for his three-hour programme, much of which was planned around talking about the sunshine, a rare delight in Manchester, as well as the big match later in the day. The playlist included more than a few plays of this week's UK number 1 single, "Three Lions."

Mike Sweeney, one of the station's most famous DJs pressed his talk-back button, which carried his voice through into Karl Pilkington's studio.

"Where you watching the match Karl?"

Karl pressed his button to speak back. "I can't Mike. Just my luck, I've got to catch a train up to London."

"London?"

"Yeah, got a meeting with some comedian bloke who's looking for a producer for his radio show. It's been booked for a couple of weeks. Can't believe I didn't check the bloody footy fixtures before I agreed to it!"

"Hard luck Karl! If you find yourself near a phone-box, give me a ring and I'll tell you the score!"

"Yeah, nice one Mike, rub it in."

"Who's the comedian anyway? Anyone I've heard of?"

"Nah, doubt it. I've never heard of him. He's called Ricky Gervais."

"No, never heard of him."

"Alright, gotta go, on air in twenty seconds, Mike. Enjoy the match!"

"COME ON ENGLAND!" Shouted Sweeney, raising both fists into the air.

9.35am

"Excuse me love," said a sad looking man in his thirties as a pretty young blonde walked past him close to Our Price, the music mega-store a few doors down Market Street from McDonalds.

"Yes?"

"Aw, I was hoping you might be able to help me. I'm in a bit of a state." The man was smartly dressed, he was in his early thirties and he looked slightly embarrassed.

"Is everything okay?" asked the young woman. She was early twenties, if not late teens. She didn't sound local, her accent had a Midlands twang to it.

"It's a bit humiliating to be honest, but I've just had a phone call to say my wife's gone into labour."

"What, you... you're joking?"

"No, no, I need to get over to North Manchester General as soon as possible. But in my panic leaving the house, I've forgotten my wallet."

"Oh my God, that's... what, have you not got any money?"

"No, no, that's just it. I couldn't borrow one pound forty off you could I, for the bus? If you give me your name and address, I'll post it back to you when I get home." The man looked really sad and embarrassed.

"Oh, well... I'm really sorry. I haven't got any money on me."

"What, none at all? I wouldn't ask, but she's probably pushing now."

The young woman opened her purse. All she had in there was her Daysaver bus ticket. "Here, take my bus ticket. I can walk back to my digs." The young woman held out her bus ticket for the man.

"Nah, you're alright love." With that, the man turned suddenly and strolled off towards Piccadilly Gardens, leaving the young woman standing there feeling completely confused.

Two police officers were walking out of McDonalds, as the young woman placed her bus ticket back inside her purse.

"Hello hello hello," said Cleggy as he approached her. "Everything alright?"

"Oh, hi. Yes, I think so. Just had a really weird moment there, with that man." She gestured towards the retreating figure.

"Let me guess," said PC Andy Miller, smiling. "He's just had a telephone call, his wife's having a baby. And in the ensuing panic, he's come out without his wallet?"

"Yes, yes..." She looked quizzically at the smile on Miller's face and the penny began to drop. "Oh... okay..."

"He's a professional confidence trickster," said Cleggy. "We reckon he makes about a hundred quid a day."

"Really, that's so... disappointing!"

"Well, he's either a confidence trickster, or he's telling the truth and his wife is onto her four-hundredth kid!" Added Miller.

The young woman began blushing slightly as she smiled. "Right... so I'm the gullible one..."

"No, you're not gullible, don't be daft. That's what he does all day long. He knows that most people want to help somebody out in a crisis, and he exploits them. But he only approaches nice-looking people. There's no need to feel daft." Miller was trying to reassure her, this arsehole made a very good living from preying on people's good nature.

Tricky Micky, as he was known, wasn't committing any crime as such. He was just a very vile and manipulative liar who was earning more money from this scam than most of the people that he was conning earned. He was certainly earning more than the two police officers were, that was for sure.

"Yes, it's not as if you gave him a tenner for a taxi. That's what most people do!"

"Well... isn't there anything you can do?" she asked, now beginning to feel annoyed that this man was doing this all the time, and that the police knew all about him.

"No, there's no law in place to prevent it really, mainly because he's always so nice and charming. But the government are looking at introducing a new anti-social behaviour law that will cover nuisances like this. Once that's in place, we'll be able to ban him from the city-centre, fine him, stuff like that. But for now, we just try and disrupt him whenever we see him."

"That's why he disappeared so quickly when he saw us coming out of McDonalds." Added Cleggy.

"Oh... I get it now. I wondered why the conversation seemed to end so abruptly!"

"Loads of people are on to him now, a few of them shout 'has she had it yet?' to him as they pass him doing his little act, which knackers him up."

The young woman laughed enthusiastically. "That's hilarious! Right... well... thanks for letting me know." She said as the conversation came to its natural conclusion. Miller smiled warmly at her, and she returned the warmth.

"See you later. Oh, and watch out for the other guy on Oldham Street." Said Cleggy. "He says his mum's just been rushed into hospital. Suspected heart-attack!"

"Oh my giddy aunt! Okay, well, thanks. Have a lovely day."

"You too."

Miller and Cleggy started walking down Market Street, as the young lady walked in the opposite direction, the way that Tricky Micky had gone.

"Don't you dare turn around to check out her arse, Andy."

Cleggy laughed as he realised he'd said it too late.

"Nice girl." Said Miller as he returned his attention to where he was going. "No, I mean, proper nice girl."

"Should have given her your number, just in case she needs anymore advice about Manchester's slime-balls."

Miller smiled and looked back over his shoulder again. "I didn't even catch her name. Lovely girl!"

9.37am

"Hello, Cheetham Hill Auto Recovery."

"Oh, hiya, it's Carl at Manchester Traffic Control. Just wondered if you've got a vehicle available for a tow?"

"Alright Carl, it's Dave. Not got nothing for about half an hour. Where is it, city-centre?"

"Yeah, some spanner has left a big massive Cargo on Corporation Street. Right outside Marks and Spencers."

"What, just dumped it?"

"Well, we're not sure if its broke down or what. The hazards are flashing but nobody is with it, and no-ones been back to it in the last ten minutes. It's blocking the lane, buses are struggling to get past it."

"There are some dip-shits about, aren't there? Thing is Carl, we'd need to send the big truck for a Cargo, and that's attending a lorry breakdown on the M62 at the minute, won't be back for a good hour."

"Oh, alright. Well, I've done my bit, make sure you log the time of this down in case GM Buses control start giving us jip."

"Yeah, no worries. I'll radio the job through now. Are you going to be finished in time for the match, Carl?"

"Nah, on 'til five!"

"Gutted."

"I know! We'll have the little portable telly on in the corner though!"

"I'll be in the pub with a freezing cold pint of Carling Black Label, knocking off at twelve!"

"Alright for some."

"Shit for you! Anyway, if you have any more recovery jobs after twelve, don't bother phoning here because you won't be getting an answer!"

9:38am

Cleggy finished his milkshake and threw the empty carton into the bin and started laughing to himself.

Miller looked at his colleague with a raised eyebrow. "What you laughing at you div?"

"Aw, I was just thinking about something that Dave Phillips told me yesterday." Cleggy was talking about one of the afternoon shift officers who would be coming on shift at two pm. "They had a missing from home in Hulme the other night, this woman in her early forties who has a history of breakdowns, the call came in from a relative, regarding fears for her safety."

"Right?"

"So, Dave was saying that all of the officers were told to keep an eye out for her, she'd last been seen walking towards Manchester, from Hulme and she was quite inebriated. There was a description circulated, but," Cleggy laughed again as he recounted the strange story, "we were told that she should be easy to spot because she's carrying a candelabra." He laughed again as he said it.

"A candelabra?" Miller looked confused.

"Yeah, you know, those big things posh folk put on their tables with loads of candles in?"

"I know what it is. But why was she walking about with it?"

"Well, that was the big question, Dave reckoned it might have sentimental value, you know, maybe her Granny had left it to her in her will, or it was her dead husband's, summat like that. Anyway, he was in the meat-van with Sergeant Johnson and it was pretty quiet so Sarge decided to have a drive about the route from town, over to Hulme and back to town. He was pretty sure they'd soon find a vulnerable woman who was walking around with a bloody big candelabra." Cleggy started laughing again.

"Come on Cleggy, for Pete's sake. What are you laughing at?"

"Right, sorry. So, half an hour later, they find her, right, slumped on a bench near The Hacienda, just under the railway arches. She was leathered, and I mean totally, couldn't stand up, pissed."

"Right."

"So Sarge gets out of the van and looks around the bench. No sign of the candelabra, but she fits the description to a tee, height, physical profile, clothing and all that. Anyway, she's totally out of it, pissed as a fart. Sarge tells Dave to put her in the recovery position on the bench while he gets on the radio to control and tells them that he's located her, but there's no sign of the candelabra."

"Go on."

"There's this silence on the radio. Then the bloke in control says, 'candelabra?' So Sarge says, 'yeah, there's no sign of it.' There was another long silence on the radio, then control comes back on, Dave said you could tell he was trying not to laugh. He says, 'according to the report I've got, it doesn't say that she was carrying a candelabra, Sarge. It says that the missing woman was carrying a can of lager!"

Shoppers on Market Street gave the two policeman funny looks as they laughed loudly at the story, made all the better because Sergeant Johnson was the grumpiest bastard in Bootle Street nick.

"Aw, God, that's made my jaw ache!" Said Miller as Cleggy nodded with tears of laughter in his eyes.

9.39am

Granada TV studios are situated on Quay Street, on the outskirts of Manchester city-centre, close to the Salford border. The high-rise block of studios is another well-known Manchester landmark, its giant red GRANADA TV lettering on the top of the building can be seen from as far away as Bolton on a clear night.

Over the course of its forty-year history, Granada has become a giant of British television and is probably the best known of all the regional stations. This was the station that broadcast the first ever Beatles TV performance in 1962, as well as being the first to broadcast The Sex Pistols on Tony Wilson's "So It Goes" show and in turn, helped to launch the Punk-era. It is also the home to the world's longest running soap-opera, Corrie.

The Quay Street studios are a shrine to the north of England's overwhelming sense of self-belief. Indeed, Granada TV's bosses were so cock-sure of the station from the very beginning, that they pretended the building had 12 studios, installing signs on the corridors pointing to "studio 5 and 6" and "studio 7 and 8," as well as "studio 9 and 10" and of course, "studio 11 and 12." The only trouble with this was the fact that there were only four studios in the building. But this kind of cheeky, confident showmanship paid off brilliantly in impressing visitors and attracting advertising revenue and investment, which in turn, eventually funded so much more than 12 studios.

Although it is basically a regional broadcasting house like Yorkshire TV, Border, Central and all of the other 12 ITV regions, Granada TV has been so successful in its drama, quiz, children's entertainment, news and current affairs programming that it has gone on to become one of the world's best-known TV studio brands. This isn't through luck, it is thanks to Granada's incredible success in producing some of Britain's most popular drama and entertainment series.

Dramas such as The Adventures of Sherlock Holmes, Brideshead Revisited, Band of Gold, Prime Suspect and Cracker have sold to television stations right across the globe. The vast number of awards that Granada TV has won has, to some mild embarrassment, resulted in the fact that there are boxes upon boxes of them stored away in the basement, as there just isn't anywhere big enough to display them all.

Granada has become so popular that it is the only regional TV station in Great Britain that has seen so much interest in its programming that it was able to open up the studios as a major tourist attraction. Just eight years earlier, in 1988, the Granada Studio Tours opened and has since welcomed millions of visitors through its gates. Excited viewers from all over the UK and beyond are thrilled by the prospect of walking along the actual Coronation Street, posing for photos outside Alf's corner shop, having a pint of Newton and Ridley's Best Bitter in The Rovers, or riding down Baker Street in a horse-drawn cart. Others were attracted by the prospect of seeing how the TV shows are made and some visitors even got to sit in front of the TV cameras and try their hand at presenting Granada Reports.

But today, it was all quiet at the Quay Street studios site. Due to the football, most of the scheduled recording had been rescheduled. In fact, the only live broadcasting that was scheduled for today was the five-minute Granada Reports bulletin with Anthony H Wilson, due to air at 6.15pm after the ITV national news.

Security Guard Gary Hall was sitting at his desk in the luxurious, granite floored reception area. Normally, Gary, the TV studio's kindly, bald-headed friend-to-the-stars was kept busy escorting the celebrities, pop-stars and actors into the building from their limousines or keeping the queues of fans and autograph hunters in check outside the main doors. But not today, all was quiet at Granadaland and it was looking as though it would be a nice, easy day for Gary.

The only "work" that Gary had lined up for today was answering the telephone to people who didn't seem to have a copy of the Yellow Pages to hand. The phone rang every five minutes with people wanting to know if the studio tours were on today, how much it was, what time it closed and whether there was anywhere nearby to park for more than an hour that wasn't a rip-off. He glanced at the clock, it was 9.40am.

"Four hours and twenty minutes to go," he muttered under his breath as the telephone rang once again. "Hello, Granada Television, front desk."

The caller sounded calm and quite friendly as he commenced the call with a recognised IRA code-word, speaking with an Irish accent.

Gary felt his skin go cold and the hairs on his arms stood on end. He was momentarily lost for words as he jotted down the code-word on his notepad. He was used to answering hoax calls, there was usually at least one a week. But he'd never had one like this before.

"Are you there?"

"Yea... yes," said Gary, the panic clear in his voice.

"Good man. Listen now carefully. I've planted a bomb in Manchester city centre, it is situated at the junction of Cannon Street and Corporation Street. It will go off in one hour from now. Do you understand?"

"Yes, yes," said Gary, his forehead suddenly pouring with cold sweat.

The line went dead.

9.42am

"999 Emergency, which service do you require?"

"Police..."

"Putting you through."

"Police emergency?"

"Hello, yes, my name is Gary Hall, I'm the security guard on duty at Granada TV in Manchester."

"Hello Gary, what's the emergency?"

"Well, I think I've just had a bomb-threat."

Gary gave all of the information to the call handler, who didn't really seem too stressed, he thought. He imagined that they probably get loads of these calls. But he was glad that he'd phoned it in, regardless of how cool and collected the call-handler was being.

"A police officer might need to contact you, is there a telephone number..."

"Yes, I'll give you the XD number so they get straight through. Its 061..."

"0161?"

The call handler was being a bit anal about this common mistake, thought Gary. After all, he was phoning from the most famous address in town, so it was neither here nor there if he'd remembered the new dialling code correctly, or not. But he was still polite.

"Oh, its changed hasn't it, yes 0161 974 0471."

"Thank you Gary, stay by your phone."

*****

Within minutes of Gary's 999 call, all he could hear outside was the wail of police sirens as the red and white "jam butty" police vans and cars raced past the iconic building on Quay Street, heading up the road towards the city-centre at full speed.

A few moments later, with sirens still wailing all around, the thunderous roar of the police helicopter began drowning the sound of the sirens out. Gary stepped out of the building into the blazing sunshine and stood on the steps, looking up towards the sky.

As he saw India 99, the famous white and red police chopper overhead, he knew for certain that the authorities were treating this bomb threat much more seriously than the initial call handler appeared to have.

*****

"It sounds like it's all getting a bit fruity," said Cleggy as another police van screamed down High Street, past the Market Street entrance of Lewis's department store, heading in the direction of Shude Hill.

"I know. India 99's up as well. Shame they never tell us nowt though. We're akin to mushrooms, us. Permanently kept in the dark and fed exclusively on bullshit." Said Miller, as he returned his attention to the busker outside C&A. This one was Miller's favourite, the cool old Rasta who played all the Bob Marley and UB40 tunes. He was so good, he always attracted a large crowd of people around him and today was no exception. Miller and Cleggy tended to look the other way when he puffed away on his massive joint during the instrumental bits.

"He sounds even better in the sunshine!" said Cleggy.

Suddenly, the police radio burst into life. "Control to all city-centre foot-patrols. Standby, over."

Miller looked over at Cleggy and understood the expression of mystification which was glaring back at him.

"Standby for what?" said Miller. He'd never heard such a vague radio message before.

"Standby... for action!" said Cleggy, mimicking the old Thunderbirds intro with a hammy voice-over accent. But there was no time for fun, as the radio crackled alive again.

"All foot-patrols on duty in the city-centre are required urgently at the junction of Corporation Street and Cannon Street. Stand down from whatever you are currently engaged with and make your way there immediately. Repeat, desist from what you are presently doing and attend urgently. Over."

"Bloody hell. What's going on?" asked Cleggy. He

looked serious for a change.

"God knows. But we're about to find out," said Miller as he secured his radio to its holder and began running down the slight hill of Market Street. The sight of the two young coppers sprinting at top speed attracted lots of glances and comments from the early bird shoppers who were pouring into town.

"He went that way!" shouted one joker, pointing in the opposite direction.

In no time at all, the two PCs arrived at the location. The Chief Inspector, Ian Seabridge was standing with his hands on his hips, looking all around, as out-of-breath colleagues began appearing from every direction.

"Sir! Over here! I've got it!" Shouted one of Miller's and Cleggy's colleagues, PC Gary Hartley, standing beside his beat partner WPC Wendy McCormick. They were gesturing towards a huge red and white Cargo lorry. "This is it!"

The two PCs jogged across the road, weaving in between the big, noisy orange buses heading towards the Arndale bus station.

"Sir," continued PC Hartley, "I've just had a look in the cab, there are wires coming out of the dashboard, they trail over the seats and go into the back of the lorry."

The Chief Inspector looked shocked. He'd seen IRA bombs in the city before, he'd been on duty four years earlier, on Thursday the 3rd December 1992, when two separate 2lb bombs had gone off in the city centre, one at Parsonage Gardens, off Deansgate and the other close to Manchester Cathedral, which dates back to 1421. The second blast had destroyed the clock and the stain-glass windows of the historic building. That morning, 65 people were injured in the two explosions, which had been separated by almost ninety minutes.

But this big Cargo truck, something between the size of a Luton van and a HGV lorry was something else altogether. If that *was* the bomb, well, this was another level altogether.

The Chief Inspector seemed to jolt to life suddenly as the enormity of the situation registered with him. "Okay, I want this entire area searched again, bins, bushes, behind walls, manholes up, look down the grids, look underneath and behind everything, benches, flower pots, that Post Box…" The team of eight or nine officers were all nodding and listening intently. "You two – tape this entire area off, all the way back to Maxwell House, the bottom of Market Street and the same in that direction." He pointed up Corporation Street, beneath the famous, brutalist-architecture of the concrete bridge which connected the Arndale Centre to Marks and Spencers. "All traffic and public are prohibited to enter this area. Come on, let's move, the bomber has given us an hour, fifteen minutes of that hour has already elapsed."

The police officers who had surrounded Chief Inspector Seabridge set about their tasks with urgency as their boss lifted his radio to his lips to give the control room an update. "Oscar Charlie to control, over."

"Control to Oscar Charlie. Receiving, over."

"The bomb has been located, it's in a suspect vehicle we think, we're currently doing a further sweep of the immediate area looking for secondary devices. We need an urgent attendance from the bomb disposal team, I need you to alert them that the suspect vehicle is a large Ford Cargo truck, it has been left on double yellow lines and there are wires coming out of the dashboard and heading through the cab into the container section at the rear. Over."

"Received. Over."

"You need to contact the anti-terror team as well. Over."

"Received. Over."

"Standby. Over."

Whilst all of this was going on, dozens of people were casually walking past the suspect vehicle, completely oblivious of the danger that they were in. It took several minutes for the cordons to be set-up where the Inspector had instructed and for the members of the public who were already inside the exclusion zone to be moved on. At this point in time, the scene around the Ford Cargo was total chaos.

More police officers were appearing at the scene in their red and white police cars and vans as the officers from the mobile units joined forces with the foot patrol officers and got stuck into assisting with the thorough sweep of the area. The second search was quickly concluded, there were no other devices within 150 yards of the truck. The bomb was definitely in the truck. The thought gave the Chief Inspector a judder.

India 99 was patrolling the scene from 400 metres above, sending back constant updates to the control room at Chester House in Old Trafford, which was now filling with senior officers from the upper floors of the famous police HQ which overlooks Manchester United's stadium. The officers on board India 99 had initially been attempting to figure out an outer exclusion zone of three hundred metres until it emerged that the huge red and white vehicle close to Marks and Spencers contained the bomb. The exclusion zone was instantly upgraded to half a mile in all directions.

As the instruction came over the police radios on the ground, and the mobile officers got back into their vehicles to close all roads in the vicinity and prevent anybody entering the exclusion zone, there was a moment of panic. How were ten foot patrol officers supposed to flush all of the shoppers and the staff out of the busiest, most built-up square mile in the north of England, within 45 minutes?

But there was no point in wasting time moaning or cursing. The police officers were trained for these events, they knew what they had to do and began their work in earnest. People's lives were at stake here. Lots of people's lives.

The police control room had contacted the Arndale Centre and instructed their customer service staff to issue an urgent evacuation announcement, informing all shoppers and staff that they must head out of the Arndale immediately and do so calmly, heading towards the High Street exits, heading in the direction of Debenhams and Piccadilly Gardens. It was a "Code 1" warning, which told the shop staff that they weren't even allowed to grab their handbags or car-keys. Code 1 is the Arndale's strongest internal coded warning. It basically translated as for "get out now, no messing," but as it was a coded message, it didn't cause shoppers to panic and create a stampede. Every staff member inside the shopping centre followed orders as soon as they heard the announcement and the shoppers quickly followed.

Suddenly, this calm and peaceful Saturday morning shift had turned into the biggest and most stressful incident in Andy Miller's fledgling police career.

*****

WPC Wendy McCormick, who had discovered the bomb with her colleague PC Gary Hartley, headed back across the road to Marks and Spencers. She headed towards the nearest till in the busy supermarket and clothes store.

"We need to evacuate the building right away," she said to a shocked employee. The queue of shoppers looked quite scared as they instantly recognised the seriousness of the situation, helped by the no-nonsense attitude of WPC McCormick.

What happened next was a text-book evacuation. The M&S staff were trained regularly for events such as these, and it showed. The speed and professionalism of the evacuation impressed the police officer who'd instigated it.

"All staff, this is a code 1 request." Said the till-worker into a microphone on her till. Just seconds later, a voice boomed on the in-store Tannoy system and made a dramatic announcement.

"This is an urgent customer service announcement, can all shoppers please put down your shopping and head to the nearest exit immediately. This store is being evacuated." The person who was making the announcement repeated it again, from the beginning, as all staff members locked their tills or stopped stacking food and produce, and quickly moved around the store, advising all customers not to panic as they walked them to the doors. All the while, the Tannoy announcement was being repeated. The entire two-storey superstore was cleared of shoppers and staff inside two minutes.

WPC McCormick was impressed, she left M&S and headed quickly across the road to Pizza Hut. The restaurant was full of people with cups of tea, coffee and soft-drinks. She was surprised to see several customers were tucking into Pizzas at this time of day, in England.

"This area is being evacuated. Can I ask you all to leave and head up Market Street towards Piccadilly Gardens please?" She announced this dramatic news at the top of her voice. The reaction that she received in here was the polar-opposite to the one which had impressed her across the road. The customers just looked back in the direction of their drinks. The 34 year-old police officer was one of the most-experienced city-centre bobbies on duty. She had plenty of experience of dealing with bomb-scares throughout her eleven-year career. But the complete apathy which greeted her urgent request to evacuate shocked her.

"Please move out now! We are evacuating the area."

Still nothing.

"Where's the manager?" asked the WPC.

A young lad behind the counter shrugged. He didn't look as though he had too much going on upstairs.

"Everybody OUT! Now!" Adopting a markedly more assertive tone, the police officer finally received a reaction from one of the customers. It was a young mum with enormous looped earrings. She had two young kids sitting opposite her and their buggy was parked in the walkway.

"Hee-yar! Just a minute, keep your hair on, yeah! I've just spent seven quid there on pizzas and if you think I'm leaving here without my pizzas then you better give your head a shake love! See-ya!" The earrings were dancing as she spoke.

"The area is being evacuated! Everybody needs to leave urgently." The WPC was going red in the face. This was insane.

"I think she's got a point," said a young bloke sitting near to the gob-shite young mum.

Thank Christ for that, thought WPC McCormick, until the man continued talking.

"It's a bit shady asking her to leave without her pizzas, innit? Get them to give her the money back first, if you ask me! Innit?"

"Innit!" Said the young mum, shaking her hand so fast that her fingers began clicking, delighted to see that she had another like-minded person to back up her argument.

WPC McCormick made a snap decision. She realised that the young mum was the biggest dickhead in the restaurant, so walked across to her. Standing feet away from her, by the kids' buggy, she made a very harsh announcement.

"As a police officer, I am duty-bound to report you to social services if you refuse to move your children to a place of safety. You are refusing to move, despite several warnings that this area is being evacuated."

Suddenly, the young woman's attitude adjusted itself and it looked as though tears were forming in her eyes. That statement had hit the mark, and WPC McCormick could see it very clearly.

"Alright, no need to be like that," said the young mum, quietly as she picked up her children and began strapping them into the buggy.

"The rest of you. Out! Now!"

This seemed to have done the trick and the customers begrudgingly moved out of their seats and headed for the door, which was a relief.

"Hoi! Soft-lad!" Shouted the WPC to the young man behind the counter. "Out. Now!"

9:49am

"What's going on mum?" Asked Hayley Bradshaw as she walked with her mother.

"I don't know, love. There's a lot of police sirens about though, isn't there?"

The pair were walking along Deansgate, after Tina had parked her Escort in the multi-story car-park at the bottom of the trendy shopping street where Kendals department store was situated. There were quite a few people around, but it wasn't too busy. Tina liked to get into town early, she hated big crowds and long queues in the shops. She'd learnt a few years ago that it was heaven if you came shopping first thing.

"So, anyway, back to your dad. If we can get his present sorted out first, that will leave us free to shop 'til we drop!"

"Come on then, let's go to Pound-stretcher and get him a dancing sunflower!" The pair laughed loudly. Hayley was becoming so funny these days, she was developing a very quick sense-of-humour and she made Tina laugh all the time. It was definitely something she'd got from her dad's genes, Tina had always been rubbish at making jokes.

Another police van screamed past with its siren blaring and the blue lights flashing. The police man and woman inside looked as though they were really stressed out as the vehicle raced past them.

"God, I'm starting to feel right on edge! I hate sirens, they make me jump. What's going on?"

"Dunno. But dad always says that they must be late for their tea-break when they drive like that."

"The helicopter's flying around as well. Something must be going on."

"Oh, mum. Phone box. You said you'd ring Robert and tell him not to mess with the video."

"Oh aye, and there's nobody in it. Here, hold my bag."

A minute later, Tina appeared out of the call-box and took her bag. "He's not happy."

"Why?"

"Because I woke him up."

"Did you tell him though?"

"Yes, course I did. I said whatever you do, don't touch the video because it's taping something for your dad!"

Hayley's face lit up and it made Tina laugh. "Oh nice one! That is skill! He wouldn't dare mess with dad's taping. Good thinking mum!"

Tina and Hayley continued walking along the famous shopping street on the western edge of the city centre, both were smiling widely.

"Waterstones! Let's go in there, mum. There'll be something dad's after."

"Oh! You little genius! I remember now, he was dropping hints the other week about a book he wants. Aw, what was it now, I bloody wrote it down as well. It's about The Smiths."

"Let's just go in and ask, they'll know which one it is."

The mother and daughter stopped walking towards Kendals and stood to cross the road which was busy with taxis, buses and cars. Suddenly, all the traffic stopped and another police car came flying around the corner with its siren on full-blast, immediately followed by a police van.

"What in the name of God is going on today?"

"Search me, mum."

9.59am

The British Army's Royal Logistic Corps Bomb Disposal Unit is based in Liverpool, 34 miles, and almost an hour away from Manchester city-centre. They had been put on standby by Manchester police soon after Gary Hall had phoned them and alerted them to the bomb threat.

As a result, rather than sit on base waiting for the green light, the senior RLC officers had decided to set off and were already en-route to Manchester by the time that the Inspector had confirmed that there was a very suspicious vehicle parked at the location given to Granada TV. This speculative head-start had given them ten minutes, the worst that could happen, they'd reasoned, was that they would have to turn around if it transpired that this was a false alarm.

But the police in Manchester, and the highly-trained bomb disposal experts, hurtling along the M62 inside their truck, were all fully aware that if the bomb was due to go off in one hour, then they wouldn't be there in time. At best, they'd be twenty-minutes away when it was due to detonate.

To further complicate matters, Manchester's dedicated team of counter-terrorism officers, the very people who were fully trained and briefed on how to cope with an incident of this nature were presently in London. Today marked the public celebration of the Queen's 70th birthday and a huge tribute was taking place in the capital city, with key members of the Royal Family attending a series of public engagements.

All of the Royals, except for Princess Diana of course, were taking part. Relations between Diana and the Royals were at an all-time low following her candid, tell-all BBC Panorama interview with Martin Bashir last November. Following four years of separation from the future King, an invite to Her Majesty's official 70th birthday celebration, addressed to Lady Di, was extremely unlikely. Especially considering the recent news that the Queen had written to Diana, suggesting that a getting divorce from her son, would be a splendid idea.

As is often the case with these types of events, officers from the nation's various counter-terror departments were commandeered to attend and support the Met police's handling of the occasion. It was a busy diary, which was to include the annual Trooping of the Colour at Horse Guard's Parade, followed by a drive past tens of thousands of Union-Jack waving well-wishers along the Mall and around Buckingham Palace, before a public appearance of the Royals on the famous balcony to observe a ceremonial fly-past by the Red Arrows to mark the occasion in spectacular fashion.

As far as the potential for terrorism was concerned, all UK police forces were permanently on high alert as relations with the IRA had reached an all-time low. The peace-talks ceasefire which had been in place for seventeen-months had ended earlier in the year, resulting in the deaths of two people during the Canary Wharf truck bombing on February 9th. Relations had deteriorated even further between the IRA and the British government since that time following a series of attacks and threats.

Subsequently, today's major event in London was viewed as a prime target by the intelligence services and understandably, the Met police were keen to enlist the services of all of the major cities counter-terror officers to help them ensure that the occasion went without a hitch.

That was all well and good for Her Majesty and everybody who had travelled to London to wish her well for her 70th. But in the north of England, there was major disappointment amongst the senior officials at Greater Manchester Police as they realised that the one day that the counter-terror officers were desperately needed in their home city, they were all on duty 200 miles away.

But it wasn't all doom and gloom. As Manchester was one of the host cities for the UEFA Euro 96 tournament, there were key officers from the Operational Policing Unit not too far away, they were based at Chester House, overlooking the Old Trafford stadium which was hosting Manchester's fixtures. Despite the set-backs, there was still a very important job to do. There was a positive, optimistic attitude between Chief Inspector Seabridge and his team, that this wasn't over yet, and with that positivity, he encouraged his staff to stay calm, remain focused and do everything that they possibly could to ensure that every single civilian in the area is moved out of harm's way.

10:01am

The famous three-story black-brick building which houses the Manchester Evening News' offices are situated close to Deansgate, just inside the exclusion zone. This modest office-block in the heart of Manchester is the home to one of the most successful and well-known evening newspapers in the UK. The "evening news" as it is more commonly known in the region is one of the biggest selling local papers in the country, printing and selling almost half a million copies a day in its heyday in the 1960s.

As technology has moved on and local radio stations and TV news shows have provided an alternative platform for providing local news, the evening news' circulation has dropped quite a bit since the incredible print-runs of the 1960's, but none-the-less, it remains one of the UK's most profitable and well-regarded evening newspapers as any one of the army of thousands of paperboys and girls who have to deliver them every afternoon, to every street in the Greater Manchester area, can confirm.

As a result of the newspaper offices being situated within the exclusion zone, the famous building was being visited by a very frantic looking policeman.

"Hi, we are currently evacuating this area. Can you please activate your evacuation policy as a matter of urgency and get everybody out of here?"

The young lady behind the reception desk looked a little confused by this extraordinary announcement.

"I'm sorry, our estates manager isn't here today. He only works Monday to Friday."

The policeman didn't seem particularly interested in this. "That's nice, but I've not come here for a chat. Everybody must leave the building, right now."

"Yes, I get that, but what I'm trying to explain is that its Frank who looks after stuff like that. I can try and ring him at home?"

"Look. Who is the most senior member of staff in the building?"

"That's our Editor. Mike Unger."

"Can you get him for me please? I haven't got time to waste."

The receptionist lifted her phone and dialled the boss. "Mike, there's a policeman in reception. He needs to see you urgently." After a couple of seconds, she replaced the phone onto its cradle and looked up at the police officer. "He's just on his way down now."

The policeman looked stressed out, he was pacing up and down the floor beside the big, impressive looking desk which the receptionist was sitting behind. His neat white shirt was visibly wet with sweat.

"Hi, I'm Mike. What's happening?" The Manchester Evening News editor walked confidently towards the officer and extended his hand.

"We are evacuating the area, I need to clear this building now."

"Why? What's going on?"

"That's classified information, I'm afraid. All I can say is that the area is being evacuated for the safety of the public."

Mike Unger looked disappointed by this police officer's bearing. He smiled politely. "You do realise that I have the Chief Constable's home telephone number? I could just go and ring him and ask him the same question..." Mike held a sarcastic smile on his face for a couple of seconds longer than was probably necessary.

The officer suddenly lost a little of his confidence at this remark. He looked as though he felt a little stupid as he replied. "Okay, but this is not for public consumption."

"I'm quite familiar with the format, officer"

"There's a truck-bomb on Corporation Street. It's been parked at the junction with Cannon Street. A recognised IRA code-word has been issued and the bomb is due to go off in the next hour. Although that's more likely to be half-an-hour now."

Mike Unger was calculating this information as the policeman spoke. His news gathering instincts were heightened by this announcement, but his immediate thought process was regarding the location of the device. He spent a second or two considering the buildings that stood between his newspaper offices and the location that the policeman had specified.

"Okay. Well, I think we'll be okay here."

"As the most senior member of staff in this building, I am advising you to evacuate immediately. Your safety cannot be guaranteed if you ignore this advice."

"Okay, that's understood. Thank you. I'll inform all of my staff and pass on your advice."

"If you stay here, you will be doing so against police advice and you will be putting yourself and your staff in immediate danger."

"As I say, I will pass this on to my staff. Thank you." Mike turned and headed back towards the door that he'd appeared through less than one minute earlier. The policeman headed out of the doors and back onto Deansgate. It was clear to the receptionist that no seeds for long-term friendships had been sown here today.

Mike entered the office where all of his staff were working. "Okay, everyone, we need an urgent meeting. Shit, can somebody go and grab Gina off reception?" One of the reporters leapt off her chair and ran back the way that Mike had just come.

Mike went to his desk and phoned his colleague Bill Batchelor, the paper's photo editor who was in the office upstairs. "Bill, hi it's Mike, can you come down please, urgent meeting. Bring your staff down, oh and make sure none of them are in the dark room."

"Oh, right. We'll be down in a sec."

"Ta."

A minute after the policeman had stormed out of the building, Mike Unger had all of the building's workers gathered around him in the newsroom. The reporters, photographers, graphic designers and technical boffins were all waiting to hear what this extraordinary meeting was all about.

"Okay, guys, this is strictly confidential and cannot be shared with the public."

Mike's staff nodded their understanding.

"There is a truck-bomb about four-hundred yards away

from us, it's due to go off in half an hour." The faces before him looked shocked, some looked scared at this frightening announcement. "It's just near the Corn Exchange. We've just had a visit from the police and they are very eager for us to evacuate. This sounds very similar to the type of device that the IRA used to blow up Canary Wharf in February, which as you will all remember very clearly, killed two people and injured hundreds of others. So, everybody who wants to go should leave right now."

"What, are you not going?" Asked Tracey Thompson, one of the team's junior reporters.

"I've not decided yet. The first edition is ready to roll, so in theory, I could go home and we wouldn't miss publishing."

Mike's staff were eager to hear what was next, he was definitely leading up to a "but."

"But, there have been lots of false alarms in recent months as you all know. And the news is quite thin in the first edition, so all of this excitement will make for a great front-page splash for the second edition, whatever happens."

There was a great deal of tension in the newsroom. Mike picked up on it and continued. "So, the police advice is that we all go home immediately. I feel I have a duty to recommend that you all listen to this advice."

A couple of the reporters stood up and grabbed their personal belongings from their desks. This initial activity encouraged a few others to follow suit. One of them headed for the door, before turning back to face the popular editor.

"I think you should go too, Mike."

"Cheers. Like I say, I've not decided what I'm doing yet. But go on, off you go. I'll see you all on Monday."

Five members of staff left the office, it was quite apparent that they felt awkward about this. Mike guessed what was going through their minds and decided to press the message again, for the benefit of those who wanted to leave but hadn't yet got to their feet.

"First rule of journalism is trust your gut. I want you all to go with exactly what your gut is telling you, right now!"

This comment inspired a few more people to reach for

their belongings and head out of the door. Mike offered friendly farewells as they went, it was important to him to know that anybody who remained here was doing so entirely by choice and free-will, not because of a sense of coercion.

Once the door was closed behind those who were going home, Mike stood up and faced the remaining members of staff.

"Seriously, if I thought that we were in real danger, we'd all be out of here a couple of minutes ago. But think about it, even if that bomb did go off, we're quite a distance away, and we're protected by dozens of buildings between the Corn Exchange and here, not least the Royal Exchange. That said, the policeman who came to evacuate us said that it is due to go off in half an hour. So at twenty-five past ten, I want anybody who remains in the building to go down to the basement. Okay?"

"Yes Mike."

"No problem."

"Good, right, I'm going to go and send the first edition to print. I want all photographers out there, getting shots of the action on the streets, police, cordon lines, all that type of stuff. Reporters, can you start putting this story together for the second edition, based on what we know so far? And don't forget, twenty-five past ten, we go to the basement. Understood?"

"Yes, Mike."

"One hundred per cent Mike!"

"Great. Let's get to work on this!"

10.05am

The people of Manchester are well renowned for their laid-back, easy-going nature. It can be a very endearing quality. But when their city-centre is being evacuated and they are leisurely strolling around, and saying things like "there's always fuckin' summat," or "I'm not going anywhere 'til I've got me dad a present, I'm telling you now," the people of Manchester can be a bit of a pain in the arse.

Miller and Cleggy had been given the task of clearing Market Street. Starting at the bottom end, their first job was clear the shops of customers and staff, as well as to liase with the Arndale security staff to lock the exits from the gigantic shopping mall that led out onto the street that they had been given the responsibility of clearing. This sounded like a relatively simple task, but with all of the panic and confusion, it was turning out to be a much more complex task than it first appeared. Hundreds of people were racing out of the Arndale and onto the bottom of Market Street, where Miller and Cleggy could only point them all towards the top of the street and prevent them from heading down towards Corporation Street, which was all taped off with POLICE LINE – DO NOT CROSS tape.

Mancunian people are naturally very chatty and inquisitive and as a result the two police officers were soon surrounded by a crowd of concerned shoppers and shop workers who wanted to know what was going on.

"There's no need to panic," said Miller to the growing crowd. "Just head up Market Street and the officers up there will give you more information."

This carrot and stick approach worked well, the promise of detailed gossip 200 yards up the road did the trick in encouraging the nosey-parkers to get a move on.

"Sack this," said Miller, as a sea of heads continued to gravitate towards the two officers through the Arndale's main entrance. "You stay here and point them up there, I'll go in all the shops and make sure they are all evacuating."

"Good call." Said Cleggy, as another person approached him for the low-down. "Just go up to the top of Market Street, officers up there are giving everybody free balloons and leaflets with all the information inside." The woman looked at him as though she suspected that he was being sarcastic, but turned and headed the way that he'd directed her anyway.

Miller jogged back down to the bottom of Market Street and began looking in the shops, there were still plenty of people inside them. JJB Sports and the smaller, annexe HMV store which specialises in T-shirts and posters were both still packed full of customers.

"Right! Everybody leave this store immediately!" Shouted Miller as he entered the Sportswear shop. "Have you got an intercom?" He asked of the young lady behind the counter.

"Yes, why, what's going on?"

"The area is being evacuated. Can you tell everybody to leave right now and head up to Piccadilly Gardens?"

"Yes, no problem," said the shop-worker, looking quite scared by all of this sudden drama. She repeated Miller's message over the store's intercom system and her voice began booming around the store. Miller was astonished to see that people were still looking through the rails and at the vast display of trainers on the back wall. It was surreal.

The shoppers laid-back reaction to the young woman's dramatic announcement frustrated the police constable so he considered his options. He knew that he had to clear these shops, and that a bomb was waiting to detonate just around the corner, a bomb that wouldn't just kill these knobheads, but him as well. This was no time for politely heading over to the shoppers and asking them to leave. Miller decided to act proactively and took his truncheon out of its holster on his belt and walked across to the wall where he smashed the fire-alarm glass.

Suddenly, the deafening shrill of the fire alarm began blaring throughout the shop. This tactic paid-off brilliantly as the shop began emptying instantly, the loitering shoppers couldn't stand the ear-piercing shrill of the alarm.

"Come on, everybody out," shouted Miller, the instruction could barely be heard above the monotonous ring of the fire-alarm bells. "You too," he shouted at the girl behind the counter. "Out!"

The young woman stepped across to him, proudly wearing her JJB sports uniform. "Can I just go and get my stuff out of my locker?"

"No!" said Miller, without hesitation. "You need to get out! Now!"

Within seconds, the shop was cleared of people. Miller decided to employ the same tactic at the other shops down this end of the street. He ran into Wimpy's fast-food restaurant and smashed the fire alarm glass and stood back and watched as the staff all ran out of there within seconds. Next, he sprinted across to the shop opposite and smashed the alarm in HMV's smaller store at the bottom of the street, which also worked in clearing the shop in record time. Realising that he had chanced upon an excellent method for evacuating the stores, he continued zig-zagging across this dark and gloomy section of pedestrianised shopping area at the bottom of Market Street, which was situated directly underneath the upper floor level of the main Arndale Centre. He went about his business as quickly as he could, smashing the fire alarms at each shop as he went, shouting at the top of his voice, "everybody out, right now, head up towards Piccadilly."

Outside The Works bookshop, a couple of Spanish football fans approached Miller. They were trying hard to speak English and were doing quite a good job. They made more sense than most of the local teenagers did, anyway.

"Hello, excuse, need to travelling to football game in Leeds. Where?"

Miller read between the lines and realised that these football fans were more concerned about where to catch their coach to Elland Road for the France and Spain game which was taking place at tea-time, than they were about the city-centre evacuation. The young constable didn't have time to mess about with this.

"Up there, hurry." He said, pointing them up Market Street.

"Oh thank you, thank you, gracias."

10:07am

One of Manchester's finest buildings was currently in the process of being evacuated. Luckily, due to the time of the day – there wasn't very many people to get out of the imposing, stone-built classical-style Royal Exchange Theatre, which stands less than a hundred metres away from the Ford Cargo truck, on the next block along Corporation Street from Marks and Spencers.

Within the complex is a shopping centre which consists exclusively of high-end, expensive clothing, jewellery and accessories from the finest designer chains in the world. As a result, very few connoisseurs of JJB Sports or Stolen from Ivor tend to visit this uber-posh arcade of stores which sit directly beneath the theatre.

Although the Royal Exchange is one of Manchester's most famous and well-loved buildings, it is one of the youngest theatres in the country, in September it will be celebrating its 20th year after being officially opened by Laurence Olivier in 1976. To most Mancs, it is generally taken for granted that this impressive structure has always been a purpose-built theatre for all the posh folk from Cheadle and Worsley.

But the building has a very rich and impressive history, dating back to 1729 when Manchester Royal Exchange was the place which put Manchester on the world map, and earned this region its nickname "Cottonopolis." It was in this building, or at least the first version of it, that the trade in cotton which sparked the Industrial Revolution, began.

Traders from all across the world travelled to this site to examine the finished cotton products that Manchester and the surrounding Pennine towns had to offer, striking up deals which saw the locally manufactured products being exported to places as far away as Africa, America, India and Europe. This incredible new trade quickly turned the north-west of England into one of the richest places on earth, a fact testified by the region's fantastic town halls and market buildings which were built like palaces to unapologetically celebrate and demonstrate the wealth and prosperity which was around at the time,

Manchester town hall itself being a fine example of this, but only one. There aren't many naff town halls in the north.

The demand for the "Cottonopolis" goods only increased throughout the following century and as such, a bigger trading floor was required. By the end of the century, version two of the Royal Exchange was under construction, which facilitated the deals and the trade which would see Manchester through its most prosperous century, during Queen Victoria's reign.

The current building, which was currently in the process of being evacuated was the third version of the trading hall, the biggest and most elaborate yet. Built between 1867 and 1874, the emphasis on the design was to impress. This was the building which was designed to inspire confidence in Manchester's goods and it certainly lived up to this brief, becoming the biggest and grandest trading hall in England, well-lit by the three grand domes which provided the natural light into the building.

The building was badly damaged in the Manchester Blitz, taking a direct-hit from a German bomb during an air-raid at Christmas in 1940. Much of the Royal Exchange had to be rebuilt, for a fourth time, and a smaller trading floor was designed as the "boom" era was by now slowing down dramatically as modern technology, such as electricity, was spelling out the end of the Industrial Revolution in the north-west of England following two extraordinarily successful centuries of teaching the rest of the world how to manufacture things.

By 1968 trading had ceased here altogether, this iconic building was falling into disrepair and serious conversations were taking place about demolishing it as plans for the Arndale Centre redevelopment scheme gathered momentum. Luckily, for the Royal Exchange, a theatre company took an interest in the building and took residence in 1973, and in 1976, the Royal Exchange Theatre Company was founded and the stunningly beautiful building has never looked back after being given a new lease of life in the profitable world of the arts.

"Come on, everybody out, move it!" Shouted the police

officers who were in charge of clearing the area.

"Is everybody out of here, now?" Asked another policeman of the building's manager.

"Yes, yes, the cleaners have evacuated. There are no other staff due to arrive yet."

"Great stuff, lock the doors and let's get a pigging move on."

The police-officer doing the ordering about looked surprised by the panicked expression on the manager's face.

"I thought the manager of the Royal Exchange Theatre would be pretty used to a bit of drama! Come on!"

10.10am

"The Most Music, this is Piccadilly Key 103, Rick Houghton here with your Saturday morning soundtrack in the sunshine. The lines are red-hot this morning, lots of callers getting in touch today on 228 6262, on the line right now is Shelley in sunny Rochdale. Morning Shelley!"

"Morning Rick!"

"So, come on, tell us, what are your plans for today?"

"Smothering myself in sunflower oil and sunbathing in the back-yard, listening to Piccadilly Key 103!"

"Hold on! Wait a minute, I thought that when the sun came out, everybody round your way goes to Hollingworth Lake? I was led to believe that was the law in Rochdale?"

"Nah, sack that! I'm happy enough in the back yard with my tunes on!"

"Well that sounds good to me! You have a great day Shelley. We'll play this one just for you. A brand-new song from a brand-new band, and let me tell you Shelley, these girls are going to be massive! I guarantee you're gonna love this in the sunshine, it's The Spice Girls, with their debut record, Wannabe."

"Aw cheers, Rick!"

The twenty-three year-old radio presenter pressed play on the CD. He hated this song already, more mass-market crap from the big record companies. But he was paid well to play it, so he did. He turned the volume down in the studio whilst it was playing though.

It was an incredible achievement to host a show on one of Britain's most popular local radio stations at such a young age, so Rick wasn't about to complain about the music he had to play, like some of the older presenters did. He realised that it was much easier all-round if he simply turned the volume down whilst the most annoying songs played.

Piccadilly's two radio stations had eight phone lines each. The phones didn't actually ring, the calls fed into a small light panel in the studio, which lit up red when a call was coming in. It wasn't uncommon for all sixteen red lights to be flashing as the people of Manchester tried to get on the air and talk to the DJs.

However, it was unusual for the seventeenth light to be flashing. This light on the panel was the ex-directory studio number, which was only known to staff and VIPs. Rick pressed the button and answered the call.

"Hello, CR2?"

"Is that Piccadilly Radio?"

"Yeah, who's that?"

"Right, it's Chief Inspector Ian Seabridge calling, from Greater Manchester Police."

"Oh..." This was a shock. Rick had expected it to be his colleague, Scott Mills, asking him why he was playing this crock of shit record.

"We need your help I'm afraid. We're dealing with a major incident this morning and we are currently in the process of evacuating the city-centre."

Rick's mind began racing. He'd not worked here for long and he wasn't exactly sure of the evacuation procedure. He was thinking of the next steps, where the emergency tape was kept, who else was in the building, whether the incident was nearby, whatever it was. All kinds of things were rushing through the young DJ's mind as the police chief continued to speak on the line.

"Do you have a pen and paper?"

"Yeah, yeah, sure."

"Okay, good. I need you to put an important message out on your airwaves. I need you to tell the public not to come into the city centre under any circumstances. Can you do that?"

"Yes, of course." Rick was feeling quite stressed by all of this, it was so bizarre and out-of-the-blue.

"The last thing we want to do is alarm the public, so all you need to say is that the police are presently dealing with an incident and that the city centre is closed until further notice. If any member of the public attempts to enter the city-centre, they will be turned around at our road-blocks which are covering every road into the area."

Rick was scribbling the details down on a scrap of paper

on the mixing desk. His hand was trembling. "So... out of interest... what's the incident?" He asked, as curiosity got the better of him.

"This is strictly classified, it is not for broadcast..."

"Sure."

"We've had information that a bomb has been planted on Corporation Street, by the junction with Cannon Street. As I've said, at this stage, we do not wish to create panic. So, we're not making that information public."

"Okay, understood. I'll get that message on air straight away."

"Thank you. I'm just going to phone GMR and Kiss Radio now. I think that between you all, you'll soon get the word out."

"Have you phoned Granada?"

"No. They phoned us. They are the ones who took the warning call."

"Oh, right..."

"So, I'll leave that with you."

"No problem. If there are any further updates, don't hesitate to call this number, I'll keep an eye out for your call."

"Thank you. Over and out."

Rick was too stunned by that dramatic call to notice the bizarre way that the police chief had ended it. Nothing like this had happened whilst Rick had been on air before. Here he was, sitting at the controls of the biggest radio station in Manchester, feeling sick with nerves as he had to switch from his fresh, fun, energetic and care-free radio style, to that of a serious news reporter. With his hand still trembling, he pushed up the red fader for his microphone and waited for the current song to finish so he could relay this important message to the shops, café's, factories, homes and vehicles of half-a-million listeners who were tuned in as always to the station.

"I wanna really really really wanna zig-a-zig-ah."

"It's Piccadilly Key 103, live from the heart of Manchester and some important information to tell you about this morning. We've just been informed by the police that Manchester city-centre is currently closed while officers deal with an incident. So, listen, this is really important. If you are on your way into town right now, you need to turn around because you won't get in. If you are planning to visit town later, the advice is to change those plans. We'll give you more information as we get it. But to repeat that advice, Manchester city-centre is currently closed and the police are advising the public to turn around if you were planning to visit this morning. If you come anywhere near the city-centre, you'll be sent back home by police officers."

Rick started the next CD and pulled down the microphone fader. "Fucking hell." He said to himself as he stood from his seat and walked around the studio equipment and headed for the door. He walked out of his studio and along the tiny corridor to CR1, the Piccadilly Gold studio, where Darren Stannage was looking after a pre-recorded programme which was playing out on reel-to-reel tape.

"Alright Rick? What's up with you?" Darren could see that his colleague was stressed.

"Mate, I've just had the weirdest phone call." Rick relayed the details to Darren, who soon looked as shocked as Rick had done when he'd entered the studio. "You'll need to make the announcement as well!" Said Rick.

"Yeah... but... it's going to sound a bit weird, butting in on somebody else's show. The listeners don't know its pre-recorded."

Darren and Rick wondered what to do for the best. It was true, it would sound really weird talking over another DJ's show. Especially if this turned out to just be another hoax. There had been loads recently, since the IRA had ended its ceasefire in February when they bombed London's financial district. If it did turn out to be a hoax, and the DJ on the recorded show heard the announcements, it could make life awkward for Darren. Some of the presenters had massive egos and could easily put his fledgling broadcasting career in jeopardy, through no fault of his own.

"Ring the boss, see what he says."

"Can't. All the chiefs are at Alton Towers on a jolly."

"What about Danny? He'll know what to do." Darren was talking about one of the station's other presenters, Danny

Matthews, who managed the radio station at weekends and in the evenings. He knew everything that there was to know about the place.

"He's gone with them."

"Aw for... Have none of them got a mobile phone?"

"Doubt it."

"Shit."

*****

"This is GMR, I'm Phil Trow, and we're broadcasting live from the NEC in Birmingham today."

GMR is the BBC's local radio station for the city, an acronym of "Greater Manchester Radio." The station is largely speech based and most of its broadcasts are aimed mainly at the over 40's audience. Their studios are based within the famous BBC building on Oxford Road on the outskirts of the city-centre. The well-known presenter sounded uncharacteristically flat today.

"Some news that's just coming in from the police, we've been asked to tell you about an incident in the city-centre this morning. Sarah Collins is in our newsroom on Oxford Road and has all the details."

"Yes, thank you Phil. Greater Manchester Police have asked us to let our listeners know that they are currently dealing with an incident in Manchester city-centre and as a result, the entire area is presently closed to members of the public. If you had any plans to travel into the city, the advice from the police is to stay away."

"Thank you, Sarah. If you get any further updates on this incident, please let us know."

*****

Paul Webster was presenting his show on Kiss 102, relatively oblivious to what was happening half a mile away at the Arndale. Kiss, the dance music station aimed unapologetically at the under 30s audience is based on Portland

Street, just a hundred yards or so away from its main competitor's base at Piccadilly Plaza.

Kiss won the broadcast license after Manchester's first "community" station, Sunset Radio, lost its license a few years earlier. Sunset's closure was met with great sadness from its listeners, who loved its "rough-edged smoothness." Many listeners compared its unique, raw sound to that of a pirate radio station, but without the swearing. Although occasionally, particularly on the 808 State show on Tuesday nights, Sunset Radio even had swearing.

But Kiss 102 was turning out to be a different kettle of fish altogether. At just two years old, the dance-music station has established itself as a very professional and structured radio service, boasting some of Manchester's biggest-name club DJs on its schedule as well as a number of well-known local voices from Sunset, Piccadilly and Stockport's KFM Radio.

Paul Webster opened his microphone and presented a very unusual link. "Okay, shut up. I need to be serious for a minute. I've got some important news for all our listeners, Manchester city-centre is currently closed down to the public. The police are dealing with an incident right now and are not letting anybody into town. So, if you were planning to visit the city-centre, you are being advised to change your plans. We'll have more on this developing situation soon. Keep it Kiss."

10:12am

Hayley and Tina came out of Kendals department store with a few additional Father's Day pressies. The Smiths book had been easily sorted at Waterstones, and now he had a new bottle of after-shave moisturiser and some posh socks. That seemed enough.

"Right, love, I'm not happy with all this that's going on at all. We've got dad's presents now so shall we just get out of here and go back home?"

"Yes, I don't mind. We'll probably be back in time for Will Smith anyway."

"Are you sure you don't mind?"

"Nah. Straight up."

"Okay, well, I've just got a bad feeling about it today, I don't feel happy. Come on, we'll stop at McDonalds on the way home."

Hayley clenched her fist and raised it as she said "yessss!"

As the mother and daughter walked back towards Deansgate car park, they walked past lots of people who were standing in small groups, gossiping. Tina slowed her pace down considerably, to try and hear what was being said. What she overheard turned her blood cold.

"No, it's all of town they're evacuating. My husband heard an announcement on the police helicopter."

"No, I heard it was just the Arndale. It'll just be a practise drill."

Tina interrupted. "Sorry, hiya, sorry to interrupt. But what's going on?"

Hayley looked down at the floor, her mum could be so embarrassing sometimes.

"There's a bomb-scare. Police are making everybody leave town." Replied a security guard who was standing in the middle of the group.

That one detail was all that Tina was interested in. She grabbed her daughter's hand and started running up Deansgate, back towards the car park. She didn't have the time to wait for any more details, she'd heard more than enough.

A minute later, Tina saw that there was a problem. Police tape was flapping right across the street and a couple of police officers were sending people back in the direction that Tina and Hayley had just come from.

"Er, hiya, sorry, I've just heard about the bomb. I want to get my car out of the car park." Tina had a stressed, frightened look on her face.

"I'm sorry, this area is out of bounds."

"Yes, I know, but my car's in there and I want to go home."

"I appreciate that, but nobody is allowed past this point. I'm sorry."

Tina looked at the police tape which was stretched right across Deansgate where it meets with Market Street. The entrance to Deansgate multi-storey car-park was literally twenty-five metres away from where they were standing, opposite the Ramada hotel.

"Aw please, just this once?"

"Sorry, nobody is permitted beyond this location, it's for your own safety."

Tina could feel tears of frustration burning her eyes. She leaned over the tape and looked down the street, over the bridge which carried the road over the River Irwell. There was no traffic at all on this normally busy road which would usually be filled with buses and taxis making their way out of the city. As she leaned further to see what was going on, she saw a police car was blocking the road at the traffic lights at the bottom of the road. Her idea of walking around and gaining access to the car park from the Salford direction was already snookered.

"Well what am I supposed to do? You're evacuating the area, but you're not letting me evacuate!"

The police officer was starting to get a bit irritated now and began walking away from Tina and her extremely embarrassed looking daughter, Hayley.

"Unbelievable!"

10.15am

The reason that Manchester had so few police officers in the city-centre this morning was due to a rota change which had been made many weeks earlier in anticipation for the England versus Scotland match. The senior police chiefs had insisted that the afternoon and night shifts would be top-heavy with additional officers, to cope with any drink or hooliganism issues which were always predictable for a game of this nature. Any high-profile international game would undoubtedly involve excessive drinking over a long period, something which habitually led to difficulties for the police, ambulance staff and hospitals. As a result, many officers had been swapped from earlies to afternoons for today's shift and it all came down to good old sod's law that the biggest police incident in Manchester's modern history should come about on the only shift of the year that had an unprecedentedly low number of officers on duty.

Despite this exceptional coincidence, the police were getting on with it and were doing a sterling job in handling the extraordinarily complex task of evacuating the city-centre, there was no point in moaning about it. Many of them were familiar with the old Lancashire saying, "you've got to piss with the cock of you've got."

Evacuating the Arndale Centre had been the easiest task, thanks to the in-store Tannoy system. The security and customer services staff had managed the situation calmly and professionally and were helped greatly in the task because all of the shop staff were regularly trained and briefed on evacuation procedures as a matter of course. Europe's biggest shopping centre had always seen viewed a potential IRA target by the authorities, ever since it had been built. The Arndale Centre complex was constructed during a time when the Irish Republican Army had started shipping their bombs to England, determined to cause the same kind of murder and mayhem here which had plagued Ireland for the previous decade.

Indeed, whilst the Arndale's foundations were still being laid, the IRA had carried out an atrocity not too far away from this site, on the M62 motorway between Batley and Rochdale which killed twelve people and injured fourteen others. As the roof was being constructed, a wave of pub bombings terrorised cities across England, killing 28 people and wounding more than 200. An IRA bomb had always a major threat to this place, and a threat which had always been treated extremely seriously throughout its twenty-one-year life.

With the Arndale now cleared of shoppers and workers, the 10 police officers on foot patrol had been joined by the Arndale Centre's team of security staff who had volunteered to help with the task of clearing the rest of the shops, offices and salons within the exclusion zone, rather than move away to an area of safety. The assistance of the security guards was greatly appreciated, there was still a great deal to do. The police radio was constantly alerting the officers to developments, and it came as a great relief to many of them to hear that a number of Fire-fighters were preparing to get involved in the evacuation process as well.

Added to all of this, the biggest star of the evacuation was currently India 99, swooping high above every street, ginnel and road within the exclusion zone, delivering a deafeningly loud and goose-bump inducing message. It was harsh, and straight to the point, and it was working very effectively.

"EMERGENCY! Leave the city-centre NOW!"

The public, in the main, followed instructions and went where they were being pointed towards without much fuss. There were some, however, who weren't quite as obedient and these people were testing the patience of the police and security officers who were risking their own lives, in an effort to protect theirs.

"There's a fucking bomb-scare every week!" Announced one of the more awkward ones, a news stand owner on Deansgate. "There's no way I'm leaving my shop, just to be given the all-clear in half an hour and get back here to see all my fags and Maverick bars have been robbed. Not on your Nelly mate!"

These people were, gladly, few and far between. But the police officers didn't have time to mess about. If one or two people were determined to stay put and refuse to act on the very loud, unavoidable and dramatic calls for them to evacuate, then there was little they could do but just leave these people to it, sadly.

The bigger priority was to ensure that everybody who had a fully working brain got as far away from the area as possible. A major concern was the maisonettes on the Arndale Centre roof. Hidden from view of the public, there is a housing development just above the shopping centre, an avenue of flats and bedsits which were mainly occupied by elderly people.

There was so much chaos and panic around, and the police officers were so thinly stretched that these residential properties had initially been overlooked in the evacuation process. It had taken an Arndale Security guard asking a police officer if the maisonettes had been cleared, before anybody went up there to alert the residents that they were in great danger and start helping them to clear out of their homes.

As the time went on and the area around the Ford Cargo was becoming deserted but for the emergency services personnel, the tension was building.

Miller and Cleggy were still on Market Street, double-checking that all of the shops were cleared of people. One or two people were still emerging from the escalators which served the underground market. It seemed that these people were the last, or at least that's what the two police officers hoped anyway. They were both eager to get out of here and as far away from this location as they could.

"Up there please, straight up towards Debenhams. Quick as you can!" Cleggy's patience was wearing thin and his instructions were becoming a lot less friendly as the time wore on.

One of the men began walking across towards Miller and Cleggy.

"Straight up there please, Sir!" Barked Cleggy but the man continued walking towards them. As he got a little closer, both of the young constables recognised him.

"What's happening?" He asked.

"We're evacuating the area, everybody needs to move

away from here. Urgently."

"Yes, yes, I'm becoming increasingly aware of that. I'm more intrigued by the rationality of all this. Just what is going on?" The man was a very familiar face from Granada Reports, Anthony H Wilson. "I work in TV. Have you guys phoned Granada? Are they aware of what's happening?"

Miller and Cleggy were slightly taken aback. This man was one of Manchester's best-known characters. Not only was he a TV personality, he was also the owner of Factory Records and the Hacienda nightclub. His well-publicised enthusiasm and interest in all things Manchester had resulted in him gaining the nickname "Mr Manchester." It was surreal that he was standing here, talking as though this was just an ordinary Saturday morning. It was far from it.

"Sir, can we talk as we walk please, we need to get away from here as a matter of urgency?"

"Of course, yes, let's walk. But please don't call me Sir, call me Tony. So, what's happening?" The man began walking casually up Market Street, as requested.

Cleggy and Miller looked at one another. This was mad. The presenter of Granada Reports was trying to get the information that they weren't permitted to reveal. Miller decided to break the awkward silence as the three men walked.

"Okay, but you've not got it from us, okay?"

"Who said that?" Said Tony, with a glint in his eye.

"There's been a bomb threat, we've got to evacuate the entire area up to Piccadilly Gardens."

"Bomb threat? And... so where are people being evacuated to at the lower end?"

"Victoria train station."

"So, you guys are taking it seriously? I mean, forgive me. It goes without saying that you are obviously taking it seriously, but what I mean to say is, there have been a number of bomb scares in recent weeks. What's different about this one?"

"We've seen it!" said Cleggy.

"The bomb?" Tony Wilson didn't seem too stressed, just interested in what was occurring in his beloved city. His journalism instincts had kicked in and he was treating this conversation like an interview in front of the region's news cameras.

"Yes, well, what we believe to be the bomb. It's in a truck, just down there, between Marks and Spencers and the junction with Cannon Street. It's by the post box, under the bridge. There was a coded warning given to Granada."

"IRA?"

"Apparently. It was an IRA code-word that was given."

"And this was given to Granada you say?"

"Yes."

"Nobody has phoned me." Tony Wilson looked confused as he took an enormous mobile phone out of his tan leather satchel. "See? I've not had a call." He raised an inquisitive eye-brow at the coppers. "How curious. I'm on air later, I'm reading the tea-time bulletin, straight after the ITN news."

The three men were reaching the top of Market Street and were approaching several other police officers, all of whom were still barking orders at people, instructing them to head towards Piccadilly Gardens, where the exclusion zone had been extended to.

"Okay, well, let's hope it's a false alarm. Stay safe guys."

Miller and Cleggy watched as Mr Manchester, the man who had given the city so much, from Punk and Joy Division to The Happy Mondays and The Hacienda, walked casually away from them. He was heading in the same direction as everybody else, only at a much more laid-back pace.

10:16am

The Bomb Disposal Unit was zooming up the M62, its blue lights and siren blaring as the white truck, ironically very similar to the vehicle that the team inside it were going to disarm, was making steady progress. But the tension inside the vehicle was evident. It wasn't the prospect of tackling a bomb which was causing such anxiety. The RLC officers were extremely calm and collected about things like that. They were less relaxed about the fact that they were probably not going to be on site in time to disarm the bomb.

Brigadier Williams was the senior officer on board the unit, accompanied by two of his best Technical Ammunitions Officers. He was talking on the radio-phone to Ian Seabridge, the Chief Inspector in Manchester, who was on Cross Street, close to Mr Thomas's Chop House, one of the city's favourite dining venues. Frustratingly for the bomb squad officers, the Chop House was 25 miles and about 300 metres away from the Ford Cargo.

"I'm keen to build up a mental picture of the scene," said Brigadier Williams. "Are any of your officers close to the device?"

"Negative. All police officers are guarding the inner cordon line, at least one hundred metres away from the vehicle." The Chief Inspector sounded very nervous and stressed. He was well trained on how to cope with these types of incidents, but it was all theory. He didn't have very much "hands on" experience of evacuating one of Europe's busiest city-centres on one of the busiest shopping days of the year.

Brigadier Williams on the other hand was calm, collected and sounded as though he was discussing something far less serious, like a faulty windscreen wiper. This was perfectly normal in the Chief Inspector's experience of soldiers, the greater the potential for disaster, the calmer they tended to be.

"I'm not comfortable with that inner exclusion zone. Widen it, immediately, to a minimum of 300 metres and no officers are to be positioned in line of sight of the device. Is that understood."

"Yes, Sir. 300 metres, no line of sight."

"Good. Issue that instruction now. I'll hold."

The Chief Inspector repeated the information into the police radio, as Brigadier Williams listened.

"Instruction issued, Sir"

"Good. We've seen a similar device to the one you describe. It was the one which devastated Canary Wharf in February. Two dead, scores seriously injured, several buildings destroyed."

"Yes Sir, I remember it well."

"So, if this device is made up of the same Semtex and ammonium nitrate composition, based on the size of the vehicle in question, we are looking at an incredible force which will bring buildings down. Are there any vulnerable buildings in the vicinity of the device?"

The Chief Inspector had to think quickly. "No, Sir. Nothing that I would describe as vulnerable. To either side we have the Arndale shopping centre and Longridge House facing it, an eight-story office block."

"What about above it?"

"Either side of the road the buildings are at least twenty metres in height."

"Okay. If this device goes off, it will destroy those buildings, these bombs are designed to cause the maximum amount of damage. Is that your helicopter I can hear?"

"Yes Sir."

"Instruct the pilot to stay at least one kilometre away from the device at all times."

"Understood."

"If there are any developments, contact me immediately. Our ETA is thirty-one minutes. Over and out."

10:17am

Miller and Cleggy had been sent down to the Corn Exchange to assist with the evacuation, which was proving to be problematic due to the nature of the building. Work on the grand Edwardian construction had begun in 1897, replacing the previous corn market which dated back to Medieval times. Today, the impressive, triangular shaped renaissance-styled building looks like a rather tired palace from the outside, whilst inside, it resembles a bright, airy market-hall. Its roof is made up of 1700 square metres of glass, the centre-piece of which is its famous glass dome.

Built before electricity was available, the need for light from the roof was a crucial requirement in the building's construction and as such, the architects tried to utilise as much of the natural light as possible, to aid the building's purpose, which was the sale of corn and food produce. The light flooded in from above as planned when it opened in 1903. At the time it was widely regarded as the finest building of its kind in England, attracting traders, farmers and representatives from across the north-west region to buy and sell their produce.

93 years on, the building has survived two world-wars, the Manchester Blitz and numerous planning applications, and still attracts thousands of enthusiastic visitors. It is no longer corn merchants and farmers who frequent the Corn Exchange, though. This rather eccentric market-hall now deals in produce aimed at the youth market. Record stalls, second-hand books and comics, skate-boards, tattoo parlours and piercings stalls sit alongside Harry Hall's bikes, tarot-card readers and jewellery makers. It is a thriving, noisy, exciting place which offers something for everybody, from indie kids to goths, reggae fans to soul-boys with an overpowering aroma of pot-pourri and lavender joss-sticks.

"What's going on?" asked Miller as he entered the Corn Exchange with Cleggy. The place was still filled with people, even though it had already been evacuated once.

"No idea. But you can see the truck from the front-doors so I'm not hanging around here for long!"

It quickly became apparent that the people inside the Corn Exchange were the traders, who had returned after the initial evacuation because of fears for the safety of their goods.

"We don't mind going outside, if the doors are going to be locked. But there's no way we're leaving all our stock unattended while the doors are wide-open!" Explained one despondent stall-holder.

"Where's the caretaker?" Asked Cleggy as Miller stepped over to another group of people who were standing in a huddle a few metres away.

"He doesn't come back 'til four. So that means we're all stood outside while God knows which little meff is in here, helping themselves to all our stuff."

This was a problem. There were only two police officers here, facing twenty to thirty traders, all of whom were determined to stay put. Miller was receiving a similar response from the group that he began talking to.

"Listen mate, it's alright for you to say get out, but its not your gear that you're leaving behind. Is it? I've got five grands worth of records there and you just want me to leave them while people are still walking around in here. I'm not going nowhere until the doors are locked up. So put that in your pipe and suck it."

Miller nodded sympathetically as he lifted his radio to his mouth. He turned away from the small group of traders as he explained the issue to the control-room. "We're going to need some extra bodies to clear this location, over."

"Received. We are struggling at the minute for obvious reasons. I'll try and get some other uniformed support for you. Over."

Miller went back to his colleague and nudged him away from the angry traders who were still going on with themselves about the security of their goods.

"Just been onto control. They're trying to sort some uniformed support!" Said Miller, with a raised eye-brow.

"What's that supposed to mean?"

"Well, there's no police officers available. So, I'm not entirely sure."

"Well if they send in a Traffic Warden, I'm out of here mate."

A few tense, awkward moments passed. All Miller and Cleggy could think about was the fact that the glass roof above them could come crashing down on their heads at any moment, if that bomb went off. But they couldn't really tell the traders that as they were prohibited from creating panic or alarm. It was a difficult situation to manage but fortunately, help was soon at hand.

Twelve fire-fighters marched into the Corn Exchange and their presence changed the mood dramatically.

"Everybody out! NOW!" Shouted the first of them. His voice boomed around the building and the tone was deliberately intimidating. Another fireman shouted a similar message, in an equally aggressive manner.

"But we're..." One of the traders tried to make the case for staying put but was quickly shut down.

"OUT! NOW! There's a massive fucking bomb outside this building and if you stay here you will die. GET OUT! NOW!"

This no-messing approach, from a gang of massive fire-fighters, worked like a charm. The traders, men and women of all ages silently submitted and began walking off the trading floor, heading for the exit.

"Come on," said Miller to Cleggy. "Let's get the hell out of here!"

"Cheers," said Cleggy to the fire-fighters as he stepped past, himself feeling slightly intimidated by them.

"How come they're allowed to say there's a bomb, but we're not?" Asked Miller as they went outside, back into the hot sunshine.

"Dunno. But its good that they did, I'm glad to be out of there!"

As they walked quickly away from the building and across to Victoria railway station, Miller radioed control and cleared himself and Cleggy from the job. They were very quickly allocated a new one.

10:18am

The mood in Piccadilly Gardens was difficult to describe. There was a broad mix of panic, tension and concern, ranging all the way to excitement and giddiness. A number of young shop-workers seemed quite animated as a result of all of this unexpected drama and activity, and quite delighted that this extraordinary evacuation of the city-centre had resulted in them being sent to sit in the blazing sunshine.

"Do you think we'll still get paid?" A young lady asked her Top Shop colleagues sitting on the grassy embankment.

"Yes. They can't exactly dock you for being evacuated."

"Depends where you work. I know for a fact that Kwik Save dock you, me mam works there. Once, they had a fire in the storeroom and the bosses docked her wages whilst she was on the car park!"

"Chinny reckon!"

"Shady as!"

"Swear down. On my nan's life."

"I thought you said your nan died last year?"

"No I didn't."

"Yes you did, you took the day off for her funeral. You little liar!"

"Pants on fire!" The lad who said it flicked his can of Tab at the girl, which made her scream as the rest of the group laughed loudly.

The mood wasn't so relaxed and carefree with everyone, though. Piccadilly Gardens was filled with people of all ages and professions, several of whom were senior managers and owners of the businesses which had been evacuated. The older ones watched the police helicopter's activities with an unmistakable expression of concern and shock. They talked quietly in hushed tones as the roar of the helicopter, and the booming, amplified voice of the police officer on board continued to repeat the scary, shocking message.

"EMERGENCY! Get out of the city-centre! NOW!"

"All we can do is hope and pray that it's a hoax. There have been several in the past few months." An elderly looking man was talking quietly to two of his staff members. His small jewellers shop at the bottom of Market Street was just yards away from the area that the police had been taping off and his shop was one of the first to be evacuated.

"I doubt it's a hoax, Roger. I've never seen this much panic on the police officers faces before." Margaret, one of Roger's assistants was talking just as quietly as he had.

"Well, this situation with the IRA is becoming intolerable. Why break a seventeen-month ceasefire? How will that help their cause?" Roger looked lost.

"We don't know that it is a bomb, yet. Just try and stay calm Roger. We might get the all-clear in a minute."

All around Piccadilly Gardens, an area no bigger than a couple of football pitches, people were just standing, watching the police constables at the top of Market Street. People were still coming along from the direction of the Arndale, they all looked scared and shocked.

The sun was beating down and the mid-morning temperatures were soaring. Several people began moving towards the trees which surrounded Piccadilly Gardens, just to stand in the shade. Every time a police-van screamed past with its siren blaring, there were mutterings and observations from the people who were stuck here, in no-mans-land.

"Oh, here we go."

"Something must be happening!"

"Which way did that one go?"

Nobody knew anything, and that was the most frustrating part of it all. Plenty of people had theories and had voiced their opinions on what was happening. But none of the police officers were giving any clues away. Dozens of people had stories about conversations they'd had with the officers. The same information had been given to all of them, which was;

"Please make your way to Piccadilly Gardens and await further instructions."

*****

Rick Houghton was continuing to make the

announcements on Piccadilly Key 103. After every song, he repeated the police advice to stay out of the city-centre. The phone lines were blinking at him non-stop and he tried to answer as many calls as he could. Each call was the same.

"Hello, Key 103."

"Hiya, er... I've just been listening. Do you know what's going on?"

"I've no idea," lied Rick. "All I know is what I've been saying on-air."

"Oh... right..."

"I think there's going to be more information about it on Ceefax in a few minutes."

"Right. Nice one, I'll check on there then. Oh by the way, what was that song you played before, something about I wanna cig or cigar?"

"It's a new band called The Spice Girls. Do you like it?"

"No. It's shit."

As Rick ended the call, he saw that the line was instantly lit up again as another caller tried to get through. It was only natural that people were inquisitive about the warnings that the DJ was repeating on his show, Rick totally understood the reasoning, but he knew that he couldn't reveal the reason behind the announcements, the Chief Inspector had been very clear about that.

*****

The same thing was happening at the Kiss 102, GMR and Fortune 1458 radio stations. The public were desperate to know why such a dramatic statement was being announced on the radio. If it was a bomb or something, why not just come out with it and say it?

Many of the callers were nosey-parkers whose interest had been piqued by the vague warnings. But some of them were terrified mums, dads, wives, husbands or grandparents of people who worked in town and they wanted to know what the hell was happening. They'd already tried ringing their loved-one's workplace, but there was no answer, they'd explain.

"I'm really sorry, but we have no further information. Have you tried looking on Teletext?"

The vast majority of people were being absolutely brilliant about the evacuation. They were following orders from the police respectfully and politely, going where they were told and in most cases, in good, Mancunian humour. There was lots of talk of "another bloody bomb-scare?" and such like, but the police officers were not at liberty to confirm or deny this, they just had to get on with getting everybody away from the area.

Some people weren't happy to go, as Miller and Cleggy had found out in the Corn Exchange, and now they were being sent to see another business-owner who was flatly refusing to evacuate. As they made their way down the now deserted Market Street, to the next job, the two PCs noticed a couple of blokes working.

"Hoi, lads, you need to come down from there, we're evacuating the area." Cleggy was shouting upwards, to two young builders who were at the top of scaffolding affixed to the Norweb showroom.

"Are you jesting mate? We've got to get this sorted and this scaffolding packed away by half-one if we're going to catch the match." The young bloke was pleading with the officers.

"You need to come down right now, or I'll make sure you never get a works chitty in the city-centre again," said Miller, opting for the worst-case scenario option for these blokes. They took their work-gloves off and threw them down onto the scaffolding platform that they were standing on.

"Absolute fucking piss-take." Said the first one as he stepped off the roof and onto his ladder.

"Hey, there's no need to be grumpy. Its an early finish, isn't it?" Cleggy was trying to keep things cordial.

"It's double-pay on a Saturday mate. And we've not got the job done so we won't get paid a fucking penny. So cheers!" The builder wasn't in the mood for anymore conversation as he reached the bottom of the ladders.

"We'll be back in two-minutes. Make sure you're not here," said Miller as the second builder began to make his way down the ladder. He turned to Cleggy. "Right, where's this hair salon?"

Cleggy pointed to the small street behind his colleague. "Pall Mall."

They walked briskly away as the builders muttered things under their breaths about "jobs worths" and "getting lives."

The officers were soon outside the salon. Cleggy opened the door and was hit by the hot-air and the smell of freshly drying shampoo as he stepped inside. Miller was just behind him as the owner saw the two visitors enter the salon in his mirror and threw a towel over his face in an extremely over-the-top manner. The lady whose hair he was doing chuckled loudly.

"Oh, for heaven's sake!"

"Sir, are you the owner of this business?"

The hair-dresser walked across to the police men. "Yes, I am. And as I've already explained to your colleagues, we can't leave this shop for another ten minutes! At least!"

"And would you mind explaining why that is, please?"

"I've already told your colleagues. Ask them on your walkie talkie thingy." The hair-dresser was acting stressed and exacerbated but he was actually coming across in a very endearing way. Cleggy and Miller smiled warmly at him.

"It's been a very busy morning. Would you mind just explaining the situation to us?"

Rolling his eyes as dramatically as was humanly possible, which earned him another chuckle from his client, the business-owner set about explaining the situation.

"I have two ladies with dangerous chemicals on their hair. If I rinse it out too soon, they'll be as ginger and frizzy as Mick Hucknall with a bottle of poppers!"

"Yes, I quite understand..."

"But if we leave it on and evacuate the salon, like you want, their hair will fall out and they'll both look like George Dawes off Shooting Stars!"

The lady chuckled again and Miller and Cleggy couldn't help but suspect that she wasn't one of the ladies that was facing the prospect of such a traumatic hair-do. She looked as though she just came here to be personally entertained by the flamboyant owner.

"Seriously though, I know you've got a job to do, but if I leave it on, the chemicals will burn their scalps off and they'll look like Freddy Krueger's ball-bag. So as you can totally appreciate, my hands are tied behind my back on this one. I'm up shit-creek without a paddle. I've already told the other police folk."

"Can I speak to you outside for a moment, Sir?" Asked Cleggy. He opened the door and gestured the hair-dresser outside, who huffed and raised his hands in the air as though he had a gun pointing at him as he followed the request to step outside. Once again, the two police officers smiled widely at this character, despite the tension they were feeling.

Cleggy decided to adopt the fire-fighter's no-bullshit response to this situation. "Sir, I don't know what the other officers told you about the evacuation."

"Not a right lot in fairness, they just said we have to get out. I'm not being funny, but I've got a bloody business to run."

"Okay, well that's because we've all been told that we're not allowed to say anything. But I'm going to tell you anyway... just around the corner, parked outside Marks and Sparks, there's a truck-bomb. It's due to go off at any moment, and if it goes off while your ladies are still in there, it will kill them, and you as well."

The hair-dresser raised his hand to his mouth. After a couple of seconds of processing this extraordinary announcement, his attitude changed dramatically.

"Well, why didn't they just say that? I'll give them a quick rinse now, I'll be two-minutes!"

"You need to be a bit quicker than that." Said Miller as the funny hair-dresser ran back inside, waving his arms around dramatically as he went.

"Mags, Wilma, come on ladies, let's get those caps off you at the double!"

10:27am

Tina and Hayley Bradshaw were back at Kendals, standing in a large group of people who had been pushed back to this location by the police officers. Every person in the group was complaining about the fact that their vehicles were trapped inside the exclusion zone, or their keys and money were in their lockers in work. Practically everybody who was standing on the pavement at the side of Kendals had a hard-luck story about how they'd been trapped here.

"Try not to worry, these things happen all the time! They'll give the all-clear in a minute and you can all get back to what you were doing." Said an elderly chap, who seemed as though he thought that all these complaints and moans were a waste of time.

"No, you're missing the point!" Said Tina, once again forcing Hayley to blush. "I went back to get my car and they forced me back here! If the police had just let me go in my car, I'd of been home by now!"

"Well they know what they are doing. Just be patient for pity's sake!"

Tina turned to Hayley and rolled her eyes. "I'm going to swing for him in a minute!" She muttered, but Hayley just looked down at the floor, feeling thoroughly fed-up that she was missing Will Smith for all this nonsense.

"Mum, let's just get the bus home. We can come and get the car later. There's no point standing here all day!"

Tina thought about what her daughter was saying. It was a good suggestion, but half of these people were saying that it will all be sorted in a few minutes. She was stuck, thinking that it would be a good idea to go home on the bus, but also thinking about how much of a hassle it would be to have to come all the way back again later on the bus, just to pick the car up. Plus the parking would end up at silly money if they stayed that long.

"Let's just give it a tiny bit longer eh, love?"

10:30am

Miller was standing by the outer cordon at the top of Market Street, waiting for Cleggy to finish speaking to three young girls. They were in their early teens and were in floods of tears, the police and security officers they'd encountered had been shouting at them and telling them to "move it!"

It had all become a bit overwhelming and this aggressive method had resulted in them panicking and getting worked-up. So Cleggy, with his experience of younger sisters being at a similar age had volunteered to settle them down. After a couple of minutes, whatever he had said seemed to have done the trick and they were laughing and smiling and were soon on their way towards the evacuation point.

Cleggy walked briskly across the road, back to where Miller was standing. "It's always women who cause all the trouble!" He announced.

"You what?" asked Miller, completely at a loss.

"Those young girls. It was the female security staff and female police officers who'd got them all stressed out. Anyway, I've sorted it. Told them that the people who shouted at them are silly bitches."

Miller smiled. "I dare you to say that to Sergeant Jenny Fitzgerald!"

"Yeah, right. Can you imagine? I'd be eating my dinner through a straw for the rest of my days. Anyway, where's this old tramp that won't move?"

Miller nodded along Fountain Street, towards the Army careers office. An old homeless guy was sitting in a doorway, refusing to budge, despite several conversations with numerous officers.

"Come on, let's see if my charm tactics can extend to two happy endings today."

Miller checked his watch as he walked. If the timings that were being reported were accurate, the bomb was due to go off in about ten minutes. He'd rather be a bit further away from here if he was honest, but he kept that observation to himself as he stepped along silently beside Cleggy.

They were soon with the man who was refusing to leave.

"Ey up Charlie. Fancy seeing you here!"

The old man looked up, his eyes didn't seem to focus too well. He muttered something inaudible in response to Cleggy's cheerful greeting.

"I normally see you in Piccadilly Gardens, don't I? And now, the only time we ever want people to go there, you come and sit here. You're a right character you, Charlie!"

"Not my problem!" Muttered the old man, as he took a sip from his Thunderbird bottle.

"Well, thing is mate, it will be your problem if Lewis's falls down on you."

"Couldn't give a rats arse, me. You're born alone..." Charlie paused as he thought about the next sentence. "... Born alone. And then you die alone. That's all it is. That's all."

"Hey Charlie," said Miller, realising that Cleggy's effervescent charm had definitely been lost on this one.

"Yeah, what?" Charlie was looking down at the pavement, he looked thoroughly depressed.

"Have you seen that guy in Piccadilly bus station giving away free samples of Golden Virginia baccy? It's the biggest packets too, half ounce."

"Eh? You what?" Charlie looked up in Miller's direction, trying to focus his yellowing, blood-shot eyes. But the combination of the Thunderbird wine and the blazing sunlight made him struggle.

"You know where the information office is in the bus station?"

"Yeah..."

"He's there. You better go now though, he said he's going home soon. He gave one lad two packets."

"Right, right," said Charlie, planning his strategy for standing up. His first job of putting the bottle in his jacket pocket was almost complete.

"Come on Charlie, let's help you up mate. You don't want to miss the free baccy."

Cleggy and Miller held out a hand each and Charlie

accepted them both, gripping tightly as the police officers pulled him up to his feet. Charlie wandered off along the deserted street, mumbling something as he went. The two police officers stood and watched him, keen to make sure that he kept walking, and turned the corner at Marble Street. At one-point Charlie paused and looked as though he was having second thoughts, but he got going again, presumably remembering the free tobacco deal.

As Charlie disappeared from view, Miller and Cleggy headed back towards the outer cordon. As they walked, their radios burst into life.

"Control to 616, 712."

Miller pressed the button on his radio and confirmed that he and Cleggy were receiving.

"What is your location? Over."

"Top of Market Street, by Lewis's, over."

"Received. We have reports of an elderly man failing to respond to requests to evacuate. Can you attend, over?"

"Received. What is the location? Over." Miller was thinking that this was probably about old Charlie. He was about to confirm that the well-known street-dweller had been moved on now.

"It's the council-flats above the Arndale. All of the other residents are out, but we've not been able to get a response from a Mr Danny O'Neill. His caretaker won't leave the address until he's out. Can you attend urgently please. Over."

"Received. On our way, over and out."

The two PCs began running up High Street, past Debenhams and the Metrolink tram stop towards Cannon Street, and headed into the stinking concrete stair-well which led up to the Arndale car park.

Racing up the steps three at a time, they soon reached the entrance to the small and quite bizarre housing development called Cromford Courts. The electronic gates were open, so that saved some time messing about trying to gain entry.

"Over here!" Shouted a middle-aged man. He was waving his arm frantically and he looked quite scared. Miller and

Cleggy sprinted across towards him.

"Thanks for coming," said the old guy. "I'm trying to get Danny out. He's not so good, he's got flu. He won't answer the door or his telephone, I've been banging on for ten minutes."

"He's definitely in?" asked Miller.

"Yes. He only goes out on Sundays and Wednesdays. He's very particular about things. He's an RAF veteran, served in the war." The caretaker was clearly concerned about the old man's welfare and the police officers were touched by the fact that he was putting his own safety in jeopardy in trying to alert his resident.

The Cromford Courts development is made up of 60 bed-sits, one-bed flats and two-bed "apartments" which covers much of the Arndale Centre's roof-space. It was named after Cromford Street, the old Victorian slum area which had made up part of Manchester's Soho district before it was cleared in the 1970s to make way for the Arndale complex.

The ultra-modern council flats were considered "futuristic" when they were completed in 1981, not only because it was a perfectly normal cul-de-sac of homes, built in a completely alien setting on top of the biggest shopping complex in Europe, but because hardly anybody lived in Manchester city-centre at that time. One of the earlier residents of this peculiar little place was Mike Pickering, the one-time Hacienda DJ who went on to form the hugely successful dance and pop group M People.

The flats are about 200 yards away from where the Ford Cargo truck was parked, and directly beneath the towering Arndale House office block, which stands 20 storeys tall. This place was an extremely vulnerable location, there was no question about it and this fact was acknowledged on the faces of all three men who were standing by Danny O'Neill's front door.

"Have you not got a key?" asked Cleggy. The caretaker looked at him with an unmistakable look of "what a stupid question." He politely shook his head.

Miller began banging on the door, as loudly as he could.

"Hello! Police! Can you answer the door please? THIS IS THE POLICE."

There was no way that Danny couldn't be aware that something quite remarkable was happening outside his modest address, the police helicopter was roaring overhead, its Tannoy making non-stop, frightening announcements about the evacuation, at top volume.

But still, there was no response at the front door.

"Can we boot it in?" asked Cleggy. Just as he asked the question, all three men heard the faint, muffled sound of activity behind the door. A few seconds later, the door opened slowly, and the face of 77 year-old Danny O'Neill appeared. He didn't look well at all, he was shivering, despite being wrapped in a blanket.

"Danny!" said the caretaker. "Come on, we need to get you out of here, the whole place has been evacuated."

"Listen to me now. I'm not going anywhere, except back to my bed!" Said Danny, quite forcefully.

"Sir, you are in great danger if you don't come with us now." Miller was trying to be nice, but equally assertive at the same time.

"I've already told you. I'm not going."

"The area is being evacuated. Everybody else has gone. We can't tell you how dangerous it will be if you stay." It was the caretaker, trying to talk some sense into his resident.

"You can overdo this danger business." With that, Danny closed the door quietly and shuffled off back to his bed, leaving the three men standing at his door speechless.

10:35am

The emergency services phone-lines were facing unprecedented demand as members of the public dialled 999 to try and find out more information about the scary warnings which were being broadcast on all four of Manchester's radio stations.

"Police emergency?"

"Hello, I'm just wondering if you know what's going on in town?" asked the caller.

"Is this call regarding an emergency?"

"No, well, it is and it isn't. It's just my husband works in town, and I don't know what's going on?"

"Well, I'm sorry but this line is for emergency calls only. I am now terminating this call."

As soon as the call-handler had kept her word and terminated the connection, the next call was waiting to be answered.

"Police emergency?"

"Hiya, I was just wondering what's going off in town?"

The calls were all quickly terminated as the call-handlers tried to keep the lines open for genuine emergencies, but this "cutting-you-off-now" tactic did nothing more than heighten the anxieties and concerns of the callers. All they knew was that the radio stations were saying that Manchester is closed, that nobody is allowed into the centre. Other than that, there was no information and it was creating a sense of panic, particularly amongst the tens of thousands of people who had loved ones in the city.

It wasn't just radio stations and emergency services that were being inundated with calls. The public were trying other key organisations to try and get a clue as to what was happening. Another in-demand service was the bus enquiries hot-line and its team of four call-handlers who were based in offices overlooking Piccadilly Gardens. The most cunning callers tried to play dumb, in the hope of extracting the information.

"Hello, GMPTE travel-line?"

"Oh, hiya. I was thinking of going into Manchester city

centre in a minute..."

"I'm sorry, all bus and rail services in and out of Manchester central zone are currently suspended."

"Oh, right. I didn't know. Why's that then?"

"The police are dealing with an incident."

"What, the whole city-centre is closed?"

"Yes, that's the situation at the moment. Is there anything else I can help you with?"

"Yes, er, right so all of town is closed because of a police thing. What is it?"

"I'm sorry, I don't have access to that information. Is there anything else I can help you with today?"

"Oh, you know and you just won't tell me! Tell you what, love... Get knotted, big time!"

Manchester's telephone network was taking an almighty hammering and huge numbers of people in the city couldn't get a connection on their phone-lines. For these people, there was no dial-tone, no engaged tone, nothing. The line was completely dead. The phone exchanges in the Greater Manchester area were working at maximum capacity and as a result, were completely overloaded as the people of the city tried to call friends and relatives to see if any of them knew anything about this mysterious situation in the city-centre. Others were frantically trying to find out information about loved ones who had gone off to work just a few hours earlier.

One thing was certain, this very vague and menacing information which the radio stations and Ceefax were putting out was causing a great deal of panic and concern, and these feelings were only heightened by the wall-of-silence that was coming from the authorities.

*****

India 99 had now ceased executing the circular swoop that it had been performing high above the city-centre for the past thirty minutes and was now hovering at a specific spot. Despite the aircraft remaining stationary, the deafening warning from its powerful Tannoy continued to be repeated over and over again. To the thousands of evacuees in Piccadilly Gardens, the helicopter appeared to be somewhere above Boddingtons Brewery or Strangeways Prison at the north-west of the city-centre. It appeared to stay perfectly still, a good distance beyond the Arndale House tower-block. The sheer noise of the aircraft's rotor-blades chopping through the hot summer air was startling, despite it being at least half a mile or so away.

Onboard the aircraft, the TFOs had completed their task of scanning the streets and buildings, looking for any people who may still – inexplicably - be within the danger zone and having somehow missed the message that central Manchester was a no-go zone. As is always the case with any India 99 operation, its work had to be carried out as quickly and as efficiently as possible in respect of its one hour and fifty minutes maximum flying time. It was satisfying for the three crew members on board to see that their primary objective of helping with the clearing the area had been a swift and effective success.

It all looked quiet and peaceful, eerie almost on the streets below. The helicopter crew on board India 99 would expect to see Manchester city-centre looking this deserted at dawn on a Sunday morning in the height of summer. But today, at 10.30am on a Saturday morning, this "ghost-town" looked very sinister and foreboding indeed.

All around the outer cordon zone, tens of thousands of people were assembled in the locations that police officers, fire-fighters and security guards had pointed them towards. These locations included Piccadilly Gardens, Victoria railway station, Manchester town hall and the G-Mex centre areas. In between these official evacuation points, thousands of people had opted to gather at other locations, such as the exclusive shopping arcade along King Street, or down the side-streets around Kendals department store on Deansgate. Other than these locations, the city centre was completely deserted. No people, no traffic, nothing. It was like something out of a film.

The TFOs were training their state-of-the-art video recording equipment on the Ford Cargo truck, zooming in as far as their lens would allow, anticipating an explosion at any moment. The IRA had given an hour's warning, thankfully. And now, that hour was almost up.

A dozen fire engines were queued all along the road by the side of the new Nynex Arena, just beneath the location where India 99 was hovering. The fire fighters were all standing beside their vehicles, their eyes were all trained on the Arndale House tower-block, beneath which they'd been informed, was the bomb.

10.39am

With no official information being revealed to the public, the mood within Piccadilly Gardens was becoming volatile. Now that the gargantuan task of evacuating one of Europe's biggest and busiest shopping locations was complete, several police officers were taking advantage of the opportunity to have a breather. If that bomb went off, none of them knew when their next rest might present itself.

But the stranded workers and shoppers in the Gardens weren't concerned about the police officer's rest-breaks. Now that there were finally a few bobbies knocking around, dozens of concerned and frustrated people surrounded them. They wanted answers as to what the hell was going on.

Miller and Cleggy were standing by the Queen Victoria statue, opposite Piccadilly 21s night-club, when the first wave of concerned citizens spotted them and headed across. The young constables felt quite overwhelmed by the barrage of questions.

"Is it right that it's a bomb scare?"

"Someone said this is a practice drill. If it is, can you just tell us so we can go back to work?"

"I heard that a building is collapsing."

"No, I've heard that the sewers are releasing a poisonous gas. Someone's been rushed to hospital apparently. Fumes off shit can kill, you know."

"Is it a bomb? Everyone here is saying that it is, planted in the Arndale."

Miller and Cleggy couldn't answer even if they tried, as the questions continued.

"There's a bloke over there who's been listening to all the local radios and they are all saying that the city centre is closed because of a police incident. But look at all the police, stood there doing sweet F.A!"

Eventually, the rabble died down, the concerned faces were finally beginning to realise that this was turning into a lost opportunity. If they wanted to hear what the police officers had to say, it would be an idea to shut up and let them answer.

Miller decided to try and smooth things over. He

considered that since the area was now clear, and that the bomb was due to go off any minute now, he might as well try and calm these people down with some sort of a plausible explanation for the bizarre situation they had all found themselves in. "We are dealing with a suspicious device, and more information will be released in due course. Might be something, might be nothing, that's all we can say at the moment. But it's better to be safe than sorry."

"So, is it a bomb then, or not?" asked one man as the rabble started up again. Another barrage of noise was shouted at the officers, sounding more like statements and opinions than actual questions.

"That's all we can say for now. Just stay here for your own safety until further notice. Come on," said Miller, tapping his colleague. "Let's go back down there." They began walking away from the crowd, as further questions and a few insults were shouted at their backs.

"We pay your bloody wages you know!" Shouted one woman.

"I don't blame them for feeling pissed off, but they don't have to take it out on us, do they?" Said Cleggy as they crossed the road and headed onto Oldham Street, heading towards Affleck's Palace. They stepped into a ginnel and took a deep breath as they removed their helmets. Both of their heads were dripping in sweat.

"Shall we have a fag? If that bomb goes off, we might not get another chance for a bit." Miller pulled his packet of Regal cigarettes out of his pocket. He handed one to Cleggy, along with the Focus Point. Cleggy was saving the reward tokens for a Head bag for his football gear.

"Cheers."

"You do know that your bag is going to have ended up costing me about seven hundred and fifty quid, don't you?"

Cleggy leant back against a graffiti piece and lit the cigarette. He blew a big plume of smoke out of his mouth and nostrils before replying. "I resent that, Andy."

"Go on..." said Miller, smiling widely at his partner's ridiculous statement.

"What?"

"What do you resent? I'll tell you what I resent, buying your cigs, and your fucking Head bag!"

Cleggy didn't say anything. He knew that he had a good deal going here. He decided to change the subject. "Weird isn't it? How quiet it is. It's giving me the creeps."

"I know. Proper strange."

Normally at this time on a Saturday morning, Oldham Street would be a noisy, smelly, bustling place filled with cars, big orange buses, black cabs and hundreds of excited shoppers heading towards Afflecks Palace or Piccadilly Records, or any one of the indie shops and retro boutiques along this popular stretch, referred to locally as Ancoats and before that "Little Ireland" due to the high numbers of Irish immigrants who had settled here during Queen Victoria's reign.

Up until 50 years ago, this place had been the industrial heartland of Manchester city centre. Stretching out from here, all the way along to Piccadilly train station, the area was filled with mills, warehouses and storage yards for as far as the eye could see. All of these industrial units had sprung up during the Victorian era, their locations favoured because of the canal junction which offered the vital transport links with Leeds, Liverpool, Huddersfield, Macclesfield and Halifax throughout the industrial revolution, and Manchester's economic heyday. But as the original, industrial purpose for these tall, imposing buildings slowly died between the 1930s and 60's, the area had become quite run-down and derelict. By the late 70's and early 80's, it was a very disappointing part of the city.

The new shops which began emerging over the course of the past decade were filling the buildings and breathing a fresh lease of life into the former "no-go" area. Taking advantage of the cheap rents on offer, these "junk but not junk" and specialist shops fast became the most exciting and vibrant part of Manchester, particularly with the youth market. These shops sell everything from horror videos to import dance music records and home hydroponics kits, to vintage 1970's and 80's fashion items, retro toys and magazines, old Grifter and Chopper bikes, Raleigh Burner BMXs and just about anything that has a bit of nostalgia or character about it. The area also boasts dozens of shops which provide the brand new, quirky fashions that are too underground for the mainstream chain-stores in the Arndale.

Cleggy was right, it was weird, seeing this normally thriving part of town so quiet and deserted, it was surreal. If it wasn't for the monotonous hum of the helicopter and the shrill of the emergency services sirens in the distance, it could almost feel apocalyptic.

"Any road, what time's this bomb supposed to go off?"

"Any minute now I reckon. They gave an hour apparently, and that was at 9.40."

"What time is it now?" Said Cleggy to himself as he checked his watch. "10.40."

"Right, well. If it does go off, I think we can forget all about clocking out at two."

"I know, that thought has crossed my mind as well. You've bloody jinxed it!"

"Me?"

"Yeah Andy, you! You said it's going to be the easiest day ever. As soon as you said it, I thought you'd fucked everything up!"

"Well, okay, I accept that. But if there wasn't a bloody big truck bomb outside the Arndale centre, it would have been the easiest day ever!"

"It's all going tits up. I bet Scotland win this afternoon as well, just to top it all off. They played like a bag of shit in the first match. And Gazza's had them all getting pissed up in the bloody dentist's chair all week!"

Miller took a long drag at his cigarette and smiled at his colleague's gloomy disposition. "Cheer up, Cleggy."

"I'll cheer up if control give me permission to punch the next gob-shite who blames all of this on me." Said Cleggy as he sucked the last drag out of his cigarette and threw the butt onto the cobbled floor, causing orange sparks to fly everywhere.

"Get on your radio and ask Sergeant Harris!"

*****

Six fire-engines were parked up outside the Nynex Arena, the new concert and sport venue that had only opened last year. This exciting new building was the biggest indoor concert arena in the UK with an incredible 22,000 seats and home to the Manchester Giants basketball and Manchester Storm ice hockey teams, with plans for major boxing matches to be staged here as well. Already, the Arena had attracted the biggest names in the UK music industry. Amongst those who had already appeared at the venue were Wet Wet Wet, Oasis, Eric Clapton, Rod Stewart and David Bowie. Local boy-band heroes Take That sold out a 12-night run at the Nynex shortly after it opened last July.

The Nynex, as it is best known, is named after its main sponsor. Nynex Communications are the American company who have spent the past few years causing millions of road-work problems around the city as they installed every corner of Greater Manchester with their exciting new cable TV and phone network, offering up to 200 channels and a free-phone line at half the cost of the satellite broadcasters, Sky.

The opening of the Nynex Arena heralded an exciting new period of redevelopment in Manchester. There are plans for hundreds of millions of pounds of investment in the city, all thanks to money generated by the Commonwealth Games award which was announced the previous year. The prestigious sporting competition was due to be held in the city in 2002, and it was an incredibly exciting opportunity for the region, not least because Manchester had managed to beat London in the competition to host the event, something that has accentuated the us and them, north and south rivalry. Nobody could quite believe that Manchester had won over London and the achievement was instantly recognised as an astounding opportunity which would see the capital of the north receive a major make-over before the world's TV cameras descended on the city to cover the games in six years-time.

Dozens of exciting new developments were planned, including a sport-city village close to the newly completed velodrome in the east of Manchester, an area that had fallen way behind and was in desperate need of regeneration.

The exciting plans included the UK's biggest aquatics centre which would boast two fifty-metre Olympic sized swimming pools, an athletics stadium, a netball centre of excellence and the jewel in the crown was the City of Manchester stadium which would host the opening and closing events, as well as the most high-profile sporting events throughout the three-week event, promised to be delivered in spectacular style. It was a big deal.

It was all plans on paper at the moment, but the way that the TV reporters were talking it up, Manchester would soon be seeing so much investment in the area that it was hard to believe that this forgotten place, with its "grim up north" slogan was soon going to be one of the UK's most heavily invested-in areas, the likes of which had not been seen by any living Mancunian. Things were certainly looking up in the city which has produced so many incredible sports stars through the years.

But not today. The only excitement at the gigantic arena which had been built above and around Victoria railway station was the sight of the fire-engines which were waiting along the side of the building, opposite Boddingtons Brewery, it's famous black chimney with distinctive yellow lettering towering high above against the rare backdrop of a clear blue sky.

"Hoi! Fire-bobby. What's going on?" Asked a cocky teenage-girl as she approached the lead appliance with her giggling friends following close behind. She was wearing an unmissable hot-pink Kappa tracksuit and the badge looked a bit wonky, suggesting it was a Cheetham Hill special edition.

"You what?" Asked one of the crew, sitting high above the girls in the fire appliance.

"I said, what's going on? Cloth ears!" The young girl's friends giggled again.

"You're a bit nosey aren't you?" Said the fireman with a smile.

"Aw come on, don't be sly. Tell us why you're all here. Is there a fire or summat?"

"Where are you going?" Asked the fireman.

"Arndale."

"Oh, well you won't get in. It's all closed, there's been an evacuation. You can't get further than the bridge around the corner. The best idea is to go and visit your dad in Strangeways and come back in an hour." This comment made the rest of the fire-fighter's colleagues laugh enthusiastically in the cab.

"Why are you saying my dad's in Strangeways? My dad's in Wakefield."

The fire-fighter was silenced by this remark. He looked down at his feet as a hush filled the cab.

"Ah! Had you going then!" Said the teenager as her friends laughed loudly. "Right, tell us what's going on or we'll pop all your tyres."

The fire-man was becoming slightly bored of this gobby girl now so decided to answer her questions and hopefully she'd piss off and take her giddy mates with her.

"There's a bomb squad dismantling a bomb near the Arndale. Town's shut for the next hour at least. So, you might as well go and do your shop-lifting in Eccles today."

"Ha! You're well funny you! Cheers big ears!" The girls began walking away, laughing loudly as they headed down the road, towards the area that they'd just been advised was closed.

"Oi! Listen a minute!" Shouted the gobby one, as they reached the corner. "My mate thinks you're fit! She wants to go with you!"

10:44am

Not far from the cordon line, close to Manchester Town Hall, 30 year old Franklyn Swanston was standing in his wedding suit outside Manchester Register Office. He looked stressed, his bride-to-be should have been here by now. And now that all these cordon lines were going up, he was worried that his special day was going to be cancelled.

"Which way will she be coming?" He asked his best man, who shrugged. "There'll be a way through though, won't there? She won't have to miss it will she?"

There were no answers to Franklyn's questions. He kind of knew that as he asked them, he was just thinking out loud.

He and his bride, Amanda Hudson had been together for four years. They met at work, they both had jobs at Bowlers Nightclub in Trafford Park and had been saving for this day, and the honeymoon, for ages. And now, the big day was finally here and Amanda wasn't here, and the city centre was closed down.

"I can't believe this!" Said Franklyn, as he looked again at his watch. "It could only happen to us, this!" He smiled widely at his friends, but it was clear that he wasn't feeling very happy.

The Registrar came out of the building and walked across to the anxious looking groom.

"Any news?"

"No, no, nothing."

"Okay. Well, try not to panic too much. There's still a little time."

"I know... I'm trying not to panic. But it's not easy!"

"I've just had a telephone call from the next wedding's groom. He has said that he's not prepared to risk it today, so they are going to hold the wedding function anyway, and I'm going to reschedule the ceremony for another time."

Franklyn didn't look too interested in this other guy's problems. He had enough of his own to think about.

"So, what this means is, if Amanda is just stuck in traffic, we should still be able to go ahead."

"Oh, right, I see."

"So, fingers crossed! But this gives us an extra forty

minutes."

This news clearly came as a relief to the groom, his shoulders relaxed noticeably. "Oh, oh… that's great. Thank you."

The registrar headed back inside and left the groom standing in the sunshine with his guests.

Franklyn's photographer looked quite edgy.

"Is it going ahead then?"

"Well, I hope so. If she comes soon!"

"It's just…"

"What?"

"I've got another job at one, in Cheadle."

"Well, you were booked to be here until twelve, so it's not a problem. Is it?" Franklyn had enough to worry about without this photographer doing his head in as well.

"I don't know. Look at the traffic, nothing's moving. If I wait here, only to find out that it's not happening, well, I might end up losing two jobs in one day because of all this."

"Look man, just wait a bit longer. She's just stuck in the traffic. It'll be fine, it was her idea to get married so it's not like she's having second thoughts." Franklyn smiled widely but the photographer just looked down at his camera. He looked thoroughly stressed out and frightened.

10.45am

Roy George was a laid back, happy-go-lucky type of bloke. He had to be with a name like that. Ever since Culture Club had first hit the charts 14 years earlier, Roy had been teased endlessly at his work. He worked at Senior Service, the cigarette factory on the border of Hyde and Dukinfield and had done since leaving school aged 14.

Now in his early 50's, Roy had worked his way up the ladder and had become shift-supervisor on the packing floor. His staff were forever pulling his leg because of his name. On one memorable occasion, he'd been driving a fork-lift truck and had accidentally reversed it close to where a colleague was stacking boxes. The worker had turned around, dropped the box that he was stacking and shouted. "Watch where you're going Roy! Do you really want to hurt me?"

This had the staff in stitches and the incident was still mentioned several years later in the staff canteen. Luckily, Roy saw the funny side, and always got a laugh when he remarked on the incident with his own come-back. "I don't know how I didn't hit you! It's a miracle."

But today, Roy wasn't in his usual care-free state-of-mind. He'd been sitting in his house at the top of Dukinfield, doing his Guardian cross-word and listening to the radio when suddenly, he felt as though his life had been turned upside down. The weird announcements which were being made on the radio sent a shiver down his spine. Something very serious was happening in town, but he had no idea what. His mind was filled with troubled thoughts.

Roy had walked his daughter Caroline to the bus-stop at eight o'clock, wishing her well for her first day of her new Saturday job at Mark One in the Arndale Centre. She was so excited, working in one of her favourite clothes shops. She even qualified for a staff discount on all the latest fashions. He'd felt a tear well up in his eye as the 221 bus pulled away from the stop and Caroline waved shyly through the window at her dad. He was so proud of her, she'd done brilliantly at school, and was achieving great results at Tameside College. The plan was for her to go to University and eventually become a maths teacher. The first person in Roy's family to go to Uni. He couldn't be any more proud of the lass.

Roy had felt sick since he'd heard the first announcement and had retuned his radio to all of the local radio stations to try and find out what the hell was going on. They were all saying the same thing, just that Manchester was closed to the public and that there was an ongoing police incident. As far as Roy was concerned, that could only mean one thing. The IRA had planted a bomb. And the likelihood was that it would have been planted in the Arndale Centre. Where Caroline was working. What else could it be?

Then another awful thought crossed Roy's mind. He was quickly reminded of the awful events from a few months earlier, in Dunblane. A lone gunman, a local odd-ball with a very dubious reputation had driven five miles from his home to a primary school on March 13th and had walked around inside until he reached the gymnasium where he was met by 28 five and six-year olds. The gunman opened fire on these innocent children, killing 16 of them and their teacher, and injuring 15 others, many of them very profoundly. The gunman then demonstrated the utter pointlessness of it all by killing himself. It was such a traumatic event, the deadliest mass-shooting in British history. What if another evil, fucked up cunt had done something similar in Manchester, wondered Roy. You heard about these copy-cat crimes, what if it was something like that?

Roy's mind was running away with awful ideas and he tried to make it stop. But he couldn't. He was gripped by fear and panic, he needed to know what the hell was going on in Manchester. He'd tried everything he could think of to try and find out more information. He'd dialled 192 and asked directory enquiries for the phone-number for Mark One, but the phone was just ringing out. He'd dialled GMR to see if the local BBC radio station had any more information, but they wouldn't tell him anything. He'd even phoned the bus enquiries line, after all they were based in Piccadilly Gardens and they'd surely be aware of what was happening. Despite all of his anxious efforts, Roy wasn't getting anywhere fast.

When Roy still had his dog, Shep, he used to love walking over the hill at the top of the Golf Club. He could spend hours standing there, just looking out at the amazing view, gazing down onto Manchester city centre in the distance. He loved it there, and Shep loved it too, he got to run up and down the hill chasing his ball like he'd gone berserk, while Roy took in the incredible view and the fresh air at the bottom of his street, sometimes watching the sun setting behind those famous buildings on the horizon.

Sadly, Shep had passed away two years earlier, and Roy hadn't been back to his spot since. He knew that it would make him feel too sad to go there without his little pal. But today, with everything that was going on, he really felt that he needed to go across and take a look at the city-centre and see if that would give him any clues as to what on earth was happening seven miles down the road.

Roy hastily pulled his walking boots on and headed out of the house, walking down his neat little avenue until he reached the clearing onto the top hill. This was one of the best spots in Manchester for its view. You could see as far away as Fiddlers Ferry power station near Runcorn from here and even out to the coast at Blackpool on an especially clear day. But he wasn't interested in studying any of those views today. All Roy wanted to see was Manchester, and hopefully try and work out what was happening, and most importantly, if Caroline was okay.

As he made his way along the path, through the trees and bushes, he could feel his heart-rate quickening even further. That horrible, nervous, sick feeling in his guts was getting stronger as he reached the last tree which obscured the view. Roy broke into a little jog as he reached the small grassy hill that elevated above the trees which were swaying slowly in the pleasant breeze. He was desperate to look beyond the towns of Denton, Audenshaw and Droylsden and see the city-centre.

He felt emotional as his eyes focused on the view. Manchester was very easy to spot in the distance. The huge skyscrapers of Sunley Tower, Arndale House and the CIS tower marked the spot very clearly. They looked like dinky toys, it always amazed him how tiny and insignificant those enormous skyscrapers looked from up here.

Everything just looked normal, just as it had every other day that he'd stood here and romanticised about the view, often cursing the loss of another mill chimney as the view slowly but surely modernised over the years and Manchester's industrial heritage was slowly wiped away from the sky-line. Roy could hear old Harry's words as he stared down at the horizon.

"Every time one of them chimleys is pulled down, a thousand men have been laid off. You'd just better hope and pray that our chimley never has to come down!" Harry, his old charge-hand at Senior Service, had said the same thing practically every-day for twenty-odd years. "There's only one winner when those chimleys come crashing down and that's Fred Dibnah!"

This idea of Roy's, to come over here and see if he could work out what was going in the city-centre suddenly seemed like a stupid, idiotic idea. From here, nothing looked any different than it did any other day. Except that the skies were blue and the sun was roasting, that was certainly a change. Other than that, there was absolutely no difference to that skyline since Roy had last stood here with Shep. Good old Shep, daft as a bloody brush he was.

A tear broke free from Roy's eye. He'd lost his wife Jean, four years earlier. Then he'd lost Shep, just as he was starting to come to terms with his life as a widower. It was just him and Caroline after that. As the tears filled his eyes and his chin began quivering, an awful thought was terrorising him. He knew that he just wouldn't be able to bear it if he'd lost Caroline. He couldn't take that. That would be the final straw. That young, kind-hearted lass had everything to live for, the world was her oyster. He couldn't face another day of this life if anything had happened to her.

Roy turned quickly, wiping angrily at his face as he stepped down from the overgrowth and back onto the path. He started jogging back towards his house, he needed to get back on the phone, find out what in the name of Jesus Christ and Moses was going on. Find out if Caroline was alright.

10:46am

The RLC Bomb Unit screamed into Manchester with its sirens blaring. The jam butty police cars and vans which formed the road-blocks on the outskirts of the city were reversed out of the way before the huge white vehicle thundered through. The vehicle, loaded with millions of pounds worth of state-of-the-art kit and the very best ammunitions experts in the land looks like a cross-between a fire-engine and a delivery truck, a bright yellow stripe adorns its sides along with the bold, black lettering which says "BOMB DISPOSAL."

The unit pulled up close to Mr Thomas's Chop House on Cross Street and within seconds, the four soldiers were releasing the ramp at the rear and were reversing the robot down onto the street. The "bomb doctors" as they are known within the British Army had their plan ready, long before the driver had switched the engine off. The police officers, including Chief Inspector Ian Seabridge watched on in awe at the speed and co-ordination of the bomb squad, who had pulled up and had their robot heading towards the Ford Cargo, 300 metres along the road, in under a minute.

"We've got a chance now," said the bomb doctor who was driving the robot with a hand-held joy-pad. He was talking calmly into his helmet mounted radio, not a hint of excitement or apprehension was detectable in his voice. It was almost as though this was nothing more than somebody playing the most expensive computer game in the world. As the robot headed steadily towards the danger zone on its caterpillar tracks, the two remaining officers were in the back of the vehicle, scrutinising the activity via the video cameras which were relaying the visuals to them.

The robot continued on its journey along the deserted road, it looked very small and insignificant as it slowly became smaller in the eyes of its operator. The traffic lights changed to red. It was surreal to see the traffic lights operating as normal when the roads were completely devoid of vehicles and pedestrians but the robot carried on regardless. It was making sustained progress on its journey that, if successful, would end with it turning back around and making the same trip back to its transporter within the next few minutes.

In the back of the Bomb Disposal Unit, the specialist ammunitions officers were already assessing the vehicle that was parked outside Longridge House, close to the junction that their remote-controlled robot was approaching. The hazard lights were still flashing, which wasn't great news. The repetitive, simultaneous winking of all four indicator lights told the bomb doctors that the battery still had power. It was most likely that the vehicle's battery made up an integral part of the bomb's detonation device. It would be much better if the battery had drained, which was the first possibility that was being explored since the bomb had been due to detonate some ten minutes earlier according to the coded warning.

As the robot inched closer to the Ford Cargo truck, its acceleration power was reduced to minimum, before it was stopped altogether. With the tiny vehicle stationary by the side of the driver's cab, the remote-control operator began moving one of the boom arms which contained a video camera up towards the cab. Another soldier in the back of the vehicle then began controlling the camera, zooming in and focusing on the interior of the cab.

As had been reported by the police officer who had first discovered the vehicle an hour earlier, there were wires coming out of the dashboard, which trailed over the passenger seat and led through into the huge container section behind the seats.

The camera operator was talking into his headset as he examined the scene. "Battery is live, clear visibility of lights on dashboard. The cable which trails from inside the dashboard and travel into the rear of the vehicle look as though they are connecting a tamper-trigger. I suggest that the detonator is independent of the vehicle's power source. We'll need to open her up and observe the internals. Over."

The tamper-trigger which was being referred to was an additional detonator, attached to the primary device. Should anybody try to enter the vehicle, the device would have been triggered instantly. It was definitely the lucky day of the policeman who had first identified this as the suspect vehicle.

Had curiosity gotten the better of him and he'd attempted to open a door, the vehicle would have exploded, taking PC Gary Hartley and hundreds, if not thousands of innocent civilians with it.

The remote-control officer spoke into the microphone attached to his helmet. "Permission to activate the cutting arm."

"Permission granted. Over."

Within the blink of an eye, another boom arm began to rise up from the robot at the same time as the tiny buggy moved slowly along Corporation Street, being positioned by the side of the huge white container section. The boom arm held a cutting tool which was now skilfully being controlled to cut away the side of the vehicle. It took several, tense minutes for the cutting arm to make its first low abrasion cut, a horizontal slice down the side of the sheet metal which was thankfully very thin and relatively easy for the robot to cut away. Once this crude cut was completed from the top down to the bottom, the arm was pulled back momentarily while the robot was repositioned one metre further along the side of the truck.

Once in position, the operation was recommenced, the cutting tool made an incision at the top of the panel and began cutting down, slowly through the metal work. This was a delicate operation and took time as the last thing that the robot handler could afford to do was create a spark from the metal work, so slow and steady patience was the virtue, despite of the intense level of urgency.

Several more minutes passed as this incredibly delicate work was carried out by the robot, via the bomb doctor, who was controlling its every move 300 metres away, not far from Manchester town hall.

It was hugely ironic that the robot device which was being used here on the streets of Manchester was first invented as a result of IRA car bombs in the 1970's. Nowadays, most of the world's leading Armies have invested heavily in the development of their own bomb disposal robots as their impressive capabilities have been proven time and time again. No army would prefer to knowingly send a human being into a dangerous situation when a remote-controlled robot could do the job just as well. If the worst were to happen, the army could build a new robot.

In the late 1960's, the troubles in Northern Ireland quickly escalated into a very dark period. Both for the people of Northern Ireland and the British Army. Several soldiers were killed trying to diffuse crude car-bombs in the early 70's and these deaths were seen as a victory by the terrorists, who saw an easy opportunity to bring death and destruction, and hastily organised more bombs. The Army urgently needed to come up with a solution to this growing problem. Within weeks of being given a brief to find a safe way to diffuse these car-bombs in 1972, Lieutenant Colonel Peter Miller created the world's first "remote-controlled" unit. Its design was incredibly crude and basic, but it was instantly hailed a success.

A car bomb had been identified in a heavily populated district of Belfast and the area was evacuated. Where the responsibility to disarm such a device had previously fallen to a bomb disposal expert to take "the long walk" to the vehicle and try to diffuse an improvised explosive device by hand, this new invention changed all of that. Peter Miller's brainchild was built around an electrically powered wheelbarrow which had a large, heavy-duty hook attached to it. The "remote control" aspect was incredibly low-tech, the operator of the wheelbarrow had to control it by using long-ropes which were attached to the steering, the brake and the throttle.

Despite its basic technology, the "wheelbarrow robot" as it was nicknamed, could be driven towards a suspect vehicle and its hook could be attached underneath the vehicle. It would then tow the car away to a safer location. Usually, this would consist of a hastily constructed bay the size of a domestic garage and was erected by soldiers using sandbags. Once safely towed inside this rapidly built bunker, it would then be blown up by rockets being fired at it.

This may have seemed quite basic and amateur, but the wheelbarrow robot had undoubtedly saved the life of its operator on its very first outing. As a result, tens of millions of pounds have since been invested into the development of these robots by the British Army. The one which was currently pulling apart the Ford Cargo on Corporation Street belonged to the fortieth generation of that basic electric wheelbarrow which had been driven by ropes on the streets of Belfast 24 years earlier.

With both diagonal cuts now completed, the robot operator was now rotating the cutting arm to a ninety-degree angle so that it could begin the task of cutting a line horizontally between the two vertical cuts.

In the rear of the BDU truck, the bomb disposal experts were watching on nervously. It was now 11.10am, exactly half an hour after the bomb was supposed to have detonated. The ammunitions officers didn't show it, but a sense of tension was growing as the time went on and the robot went about its painfully slow work of removing the truck's side panel.

11:11am

"Good morning, this is Piccadilly Key 103, I'm Rick Houghton with you until one. If you've just tuned in, we have some important news regarding Manchester city centre. The whole area is currently closed due to an ongoing police incident. So if you are planning a trip into town, the advice is to make alternative plans because you won't get anywhere near the city centre this morning. We'll give you more information as we get it. Now here's the former Pepsi Network Chart number one from a few weeks ago. It's Mark Morrison, and a Key classic, Return of the Mack."

Rick closed his microphone and looked across at the phone-in panel. The red lights were still flashing non-stop on both the Key 103 and the Piccadilly Gold numbers. But there was still no activity on the XD line, which only staff and the emergency services had the number to. Rick had stopped answering the calls from the public now, he saw no point in taking the calls as he couldn't provide answers to any of the questions. He was only repeating the information that he was permitted to reveal on the air.

Out on the streets of Manchester, the rumour mill was still running at full capacity. The Bomb Disposal Unit had been seen by thousands of people who were stranded by the police road-blocks and it hadn't taken long for the word to spread around that this really was a bomb scare. The information hadn't taken long to reach the thousands of shoppers, shop staff and weekend office workers who were assembled in Piccadilly Gardens. For many of them, this information was all they needed to justify a long walk home. Getting out of the danger zone, with the prospect of an unexpected afternoon off work, on a gloriously sunny Saturday when the hotly-anticipated England and Scotland game was taking place seemed like a fantastic proposition.

Not long after the rumours about the Bomb Disposal truck had spread amongst the folk in the Gardens, a mass exodus of people suddenly began. Hundreds of them began walking, some of them jogging, towards Ardwick, down Piccadilly

Approach and towards the British Telecom building on the very outskirts of the city centre, heading for the main roads, Ashton Old Road, Hyde Road, Stockport Road out of town. Hundreds of others had headed east, opting to make their way out of town along Rochdale Road, Oldham Road and Cheetham Hill Road. The same thing was happening along all of the major routes out of town, Bolton Road, Eccles New Road and Trafford Road were suddenly filled with hundreds of walkers. It was quite a spectacle.

Piccadilly Gardens was suddenly looking a great deal calmer, the sea of heads was thinned out considerably as the numbers decreased. It quickly became apparent that it had only needed one solid piece of information to achieve this result and many people were criticising the police officers for their tight-lips policy. There were still thousands of people staying put, though. Many of them were nosy-parkers loving the drama, keen to see what would happen next. Many were business owners who would have to wait and then go back to lock their premises up properly after the all-clear. The others were a mixture of shop staff who were unclear of the procedure and bus-drivers who were stranded here with their double-deckers parked up silently in the bus station.

The helicopter was still hovering at its static position, just beyond Arndale House tower, which told the crowds that this incident was still ongoing, many of whom were beginning to think that the sudden thinning of the numbers of evacuees signalled a down-grade of the situation which had resulted in them all standing here.

At the city's railways stations, all services in and out of Manchester had been suspended. This was straight-forward enough to organise at the main stations of Piccadilly, Victoria and Oxford Road. But the decision to suspend all rail services that were destined for the city centre was causing a great deal of frustration from the passengers on the trains which had been prevented from advancing on their journeys into Manchester. Dozens of trains were standing at commuter-line stations, their engines switched off and the doors closed.

Bearing in mind the weather, these trains were

becoming increasingly hot and stifling for the passengers sitting inside the carriages, all of whom were unclear of the reason for the delay. The guards and drivers were staying out of the way, up front in the cab. The only information that any of the sweaty passengers were given came over the train's intercom system.

"Good morning, this is your driver speaking. I apologise for the delay to our journey this morning, this delay is due to an incident further along the line. Hopefully we will be on our way soon and I'd like to thank you for your patience as we wait for clearance to proceed."

Despite the pleasant message, as time wore on, the passengers were becoming more and more unhappy with the situation. Babies were screaming due to the heat, elderly passengers were feeling faint and the younger passengers were becoming increasingly vocal about their unhappiness.

On one train, which made up the 10.05 Bolton to Manchester Victoria service, the passengers had been stuck on board the train at Farnworth railway station for almost an hour and tempers were beginning to fray. A man who was taking his wife and two daughters into Manchester for a few hours of shopping, before returning back to Bolton to watch the football was starting to see his day's plans going to pot.

"Hee yar! Hee yar!" He shouted, as he banged on the train window, trying to attract the attention of the guard and driver who were standing further along on the platform. The railway workers ignored him at first, but the constant banging and shouting convinced them that this passenger wasn't going to sit down and shut up anytime soon and that his actions were likely to be causing distress for the other passengers.

"I'll go," said the guard, to his colleague and walked along the side of the train to the trailing carriage where the commotion was taking place. As soon as the guard reached the carriage, he could see that the man was extremely worked up.

"Hee yar! You better let us off this train now mate."
"I can't, sorry. We might be on our way any minute."
"Listen to me, open the doors now, its too hot in here."
"Just calm down. We'll be on our way soon."
"It's alright for you saying calm down while you're

stood out there in the breeze. Open the doors now or I'll put the fucking window through! I'm not jesting!"

Inside the carriage, the man's wife was saying "Lee, leave it, leave it, Lee." But he was oblivious as he continued shouting out of the window. Another passenger came across and backed the man up.

"You need to let us off. It's like gas mark 8 in here mate!"

"I can't open the doors as the train is still in service."

"Are you taking the fucking piss? We've been sat here for nearly an hour. Open the doors now or I'm going to smash the windows out." It was clear on the face of the man who was causing all of the commotion that his fuse had blown.

"Wait here," said the guard as he walked back to where the driver was standing at the front end.

"Wait here? Is he taking the fucking piss?" asked the man who'd come to assist Lee with his request to leave the carriage.

"Tell you mate, I'm gonna boot that window out."

Several other passengers got involved in the discussion, all of them were in agreement that it was ridiculous that they all had to sit inside the carriage when the train was clearly not going anywhere. The fact that the guard and driver were standing outside the vehicle just rubbed it in.

A minute passed before the guard came back. "I've spoken to the driver, he's just trying to get an update from control. If it looks as though we are staying here any longer, I've decided that I will let any passengers off who don't want to remain on board."

"Right. Listen," said the angry man, Lee. "Let us off now or I swear down I'm gonna smash this window, then I'm gonna punch your head clean off your shoulders."

The guard opened his mouth to speak, but it looked as though he was having second thoughts. He walked back to the cab and opened all of the train's doors, before locking himself in the driver's cab whilst the frustrated, hot and bothered passengers made their way off the train and up the ramp out of the station.

Lee still looked angry. He banged on the cab window as he went past and shouted, "dick-cheese."

11:13am

The Bomb disposal robot was continuing to make good progress of its job of cutting away the side panel on the Ford Cargo. The final horizontal cut that it was making into the metal sheeting which made up the wall of the truck was around 80% through. There was a growing sense of confidence amongst the bomb doctors that this worrying situation would soon be resolved, without any more fuss. The coded warning which had been given to Granada TV had said that the bomb will detonate in one hour.

Over an hour and a half had now passed and there had been nothing. This was positive news as it meant that there was a very good chance that there was a fault with the detonation device, which wasn't uncommon with IRA bombs. They were generally built by amateurs rather than people with any serious expertise in ammunitions and IEDs.

The sound of the police helicopter hovering half a mile overhead was literally the only sound that could be heard in the "ghost town" which surrounded the Ford Cargo. The exclusion zone was over half a mile in most directions and with the exception of the bomb doctor who was driving the robot, there wasn't a single person to be seen in the area.

Finally, the robot's cutting arm had made the last cut through the van's side panel and the huge piece of sheet metal crashed against the small machine which had cut it away. The operator reversed the robot back so that the panel would fall flat on the floor. He then drove it back to its spot, now parked on top of the large white metal sheet. The cutting arm was folded down and as it was collapsing, the video camera arm was activated and rose up from the main chassis of the vehicle.

Within seconds, the bomb disposal team were viewing footage of the interior of the truck's cargo bay. The first thing that they noticed was that the entire space was filled with huge bags which looked like cement bags. From the base to the ceiling, pallet after pallet of these bags was stacked up in such a way that it looked as though whoever had loaded this vehicle had struggled to get every last bag into it.

Not only was this unusual, and extremely troubling, it presented a significant problem. The bomb doctors, at this stage in the operation, would normally be using the robot to try and locate the device's detonator, or at least any wires feeding into it. But because of the way that this truck had been stacked, it was going to be an impossible job for a camera on a boom arm to identify where it was.

"It looks like they want to blow the whole north of England up, not just Manchester," remarked Brigadier Williams, the man who was in charge of this mission. He was shocked by the sheer quantity of the explosives which had been packed. He could tell that this was a classic IRA bomb, made up of Semtex and ammonium nitrate, which is basically an agriculture fertilizer, but is also useful for its explosive ability and is used widely in mining and quarrying, as well as by the IRA for making bombs. There was no doubt about it, this truck had been left here to cause an extraordinary amount of damage.

"There is no sign of a wire. We will have to snip the wire in the cab. If that doesn't disarm it, then we will have to review the strategy. Over."

The robot controller understood the message loud and clear, and estimated the risk involved. He pulled the camera boom back towards the robot and drove the expensive piece of hi-tech machinery forward a couple of metres, until it was level with the driver's cab door. He moved the cutting tool arm back up so that it was level with the window and then he took several steps back and positioned himself behind the BDU vehicle. He leaned around slightly, so that he could see the Ford Cargo and his robot, ensuring that he had enough cover should the next action from the robot cause a detonation.

The cutting arm was deployed once again. This time, its objective was to break the cab's window. Once it was smashed through, the RLC officer paused to see if this activity would activate the tamper trigger.

He was very quickly made aware that it had done.

11:17am

Manchester's Traffic Control department, based at Bootle Street police station was much busier than usual. This small office which housed the closed-circuit television camera feeds of the city-centre's main roads didn't usually have more than two or three people inside it. But today, in light of the events on Corporation Street, the room was packed out with police-officers, civilian staff and a few top-ranking officers who were desperate to hear the news that the bomb had been defused. They had all been watching silently as the strange little robot on its caterpillar tracks went about its business at the side of the Ford Cargo truck.

There was a sudden, loud gasp as the TV monitor screen suddenly turned white for a second, before turning black. All that the monitor was displaying now was the date and time and the camera location details in white characters at the margin of the screen.

A frightening, loud rumble shook the room, and the screen violently moved on its bracket. The staff inside the room continued to stare at the screen as the whole building vibrated as though an earthquake was tearing the city in half.

*****

Jean Farrant was pegging her washing out in her back garden in Droylsden. It was such a lovely day for drying, she'd decided to give the living room curtains a wash. There was a lovely, gentle breeze flowing and the sun was really warm considering it was still morning. As she pegged the laundry to her line, she was thinking about what else she could wash and get dried today.

Jean jumped as she heard a sudden loud thud, it sounded like it had come from the front of the house. This frightening boom sound shook her up and she felt quite shaky. One minute she'd been lost in her own world thinking about laundry, and now her heart was beating fast in her chest. She rested the curtain on her washing line and dashed around the side of the house, she was pretty sure there'd been an accident on the main road. She stepped as quickly as she could, keen to see what had happened and phone for an ambulance if necessary. It had been such a loud bang, she had visions of a van on its side. Or a truck that had rammed into a bus at the traffic lights.

But as she rounded the corner of her house, she saw that the road was clear. There'd been no accident, the traffic was flowing just as smoothly as normal. Jean checked the road both ways. Nothing. Whatever that sound had been, which had given her such a start, it wasn't a road accident. Then the thought occurred to her that it might have been a gas blast. She began looking behind her, over the backs to see if she could see any smoke. Again, this theory drew a blank. After a minute or so, she began to get her breath back and headed around the back, and got on with her job, wondering what the shocking loud bang could have been. Whatever it was, it had given her quite a start.

*****

"Listen love, I've said it a thousand times. I'll do the barbeque, all you've got to do us just go and fetch the stuff." Dave Fitzpatrick was sitting in his back garden in Gorton, trying to read his paper. But his missus, Julie had different ideas.

"Dave! For the last time! Get off your fat, useless, pimply arse and get down to Kwik Save. I've done you a list and there's a tenner on the side. If you don't go now, I'm going out on the lash with Mad Carol, and that never ends well. You've been warned now, you lazy…"

Julie's words were cut short by a loud, reverberating thud in the distance.

"… what the hell was that?"

"Sounds like thunder. Always the same, couple of nice days and then it starts thundering!" Dave didn't look up from his paper.

"That was not thunder. Sounded more like bonfire night. When the kids put an air-bomb in an empty wheely-bin!"

"Well, if it is thunder, it means we can't have a

barbeque, which means I don't have to go for your dossy shopping! Bliss!"

"Chinnies if you think you're sitting there all-day Dave! Thunder or no thunder!"

"Chinnies back if you think I'm going to be seen in Kwik Save buying dosser burgers. It's all eye-lids, lips and arseholes in their stuff. No Frills my arse, Julie. I won't be seen dead in that shop!"

*****

Phil and Susan Cartwright were enjoying a pleasant walk in the bright sunshine at one of Manchester's prettiest beauty spots, Hartshead Pike. This spot, high on Hartshead Hill above Ashton is a popular place for weekend walkers who flock here during the good weather to take in the incredible views across the region.

Up here, on a clear day, you can make out all of Greater Manchester's neighbouring counties, Lancashire, Yorkshire, Merseyside, Cheshire, Cumbria and even North Wales. But with the heat today, there was a haze which obscured much of the view. The best time to come up here was a fine, sunny, crisp winter morning with a good ground frost. On those days, the view seemed endless.

Despite the fuzzy haze in the distance, the view of Manchester city centre was still impressive today. Although it was six miles away, you could clearly make out the Arndale building, the CIS Tower and Sunley House, the skyscraper which rises up from Piccadilly Gardens, and all of the thousands of houses and shops and farms and factories in between this rural location close to the Yorkshire border, and the heart of the city.

Suddenly, a strange dull bang resounded from the place that Phil and Susan were gazing it. It was a clear but faint sound and it seemed to echo for several seconds.

"What the flaming hell was that?" Asked Susan. Phil was about to reply that he had no idea. But he didn't get the chance. It quickly became apparent what that sound was, as a huge, menacing cloud lifted into the air above those tall buildings six miles away.

The hill that Hartshead Pike sits on top of was filled with hundreds of people, all gazing down at this enormous grey cloud which began filling the blue sky over Manchester.

"Jesus!" Said a man who had been walking with his dog as he suddenly froze on the spot, captivated by the troubling view.

"What the hell is it?" Asked Susan, already knowing the answer. The scene before them looked just like the sketch on the front cover of Raymond Briggs' popular book 'When the Wind Blows' from a few years earlier. The cloud was developing into a mushroom formation and the speed in which it rose up into the sky confirmed that it had been formed from an explosion. That's what that dull, reverberating thud had been, there was no question about it.

The silence which followed was strange. Nobody on the hill made a sound as they all looked on, with shock, fear and sadness etched on their faces. Even the dogs stopped running about, they sensed the seriousness of the situation and sat quietly, looking to their owners for reassurance.

Every single person on that hilltop knew somebody who was likely to be there, somebody who might be caught up in this terrifying situation. The eerie silence lasted for a good minute, as the cloud continued to swell, now turning a good shade darker as it dwarfed the distinctive buildings which marked Manchester on the landscape.

*****

Trish Talbot was cleaning the windows of her top floor flat on the Salford Precinct housing estate. The brilliant sunshine had illuminated how filthy the windows were, so she'd decided to give them a quick once over with the Windolene, before going off to catch the bus to her son's house where she was minding the grandkids whilst the adults went off to watch the football. Trish was really looking forward to it, playing in the garden with them, she'd even been down to the Shopping Giant when it opened to buy some water pistols along with crisps, pop, toffees and a handful of packets of stickers for their albums. Kieron was collecting the Euro 96 stickers, whilst Chantelle was getting close to filling her Toy Story album. Trish was hoping that the grandkids wouldn't want the football on, she hated the sport with a passion.

"What's the point in twenty-two men running around chasing a bag of bloody wind?" She'd say if anybody mentioned the blasted game. Trish was a rugby fan, a Salford Reds season ticket holder at The Willows. That was a proper game, played by proper blokes, not these Nancy boys who earn about a million quid a year and roll around screaming if they trip up.

Trish was in her own little world as she smeared the white powdery solution onto her windows. She loved the smell, it always brought back happy memories and it made her laugh to herself. "What a life!" She said with a smile as she realised how ridiculous it was to feel a warm sense of nostalgia from cleaning windows. All she had to do now was wait a couple of minutes for it all to dry and then she'd be able to wipe it off and go and get on the bus with her big bag of treats and the water-pistols.

Suddenly, there was a deafening boom, and Trish felt the whole block of flats shake. She was standing on top of a chair and she almost fell off it, it had rocked that much.

"What the…" Trish realised that she couldn't see anything due to the white smears on her window. The whole building was still rumbling beneath her feet and her ears felt weird, a high-pitched ringing sound was piercing through them. She stepped down shakily from her chair and hurried to the sink, where she grabbed a duster from the cupboard.

When she wiped the glass, she couldn't make sense of what she was seeing.

*****

Rick Houghton was sitting on his chair in the Piccadilly Key 103 studio, preparing to present another link about the city centre closure when his chair suddenly began to wheel back along the carpeted floor. The whole room shook violently causing CDs and the jingle carts to crash down from their shelving units. Apart from the sound of smashing CD boxes, there was no other sound inside the sound-proofed booth which he was sitting in. The CD which was playing suddenly stopped as the station's power supply flickered for a few seconds.

Rick just sat there, a metre away from his broadcasting equipment, expecting the whole place to collapse on top of him at any moment. After all, he was sitting directly beneath the gigantic Piccadilly Hotel and the biggest skyscraper in Manchester, Sunley Tower. After several, panic-stricken seconds of sitting there in shock, Rick began to realise that the station was off the air. He wheeled his chair forwards along the carpeted floor using his feet and pressed play on the CD player, starting the song which had been playing, from the beginning.

He couldn't believe that a bomb, on the other side of Manchester city-centre, had created such a vibration here, in a concrete building half a mile away. As he began to pull himself together, he was beginning to think the building that he was in had been bombed. He leapt up from his seat and ran through to CR1 where his colleague, Darren Stannage was working.

"I think they've bombed the plaza!" said Rick, with a look of complete terror on his face. He was having visions of the two men being trapped by fire, two storeys above street level.

Darren stood and walked out of the studio. "Come on," he said as Rick followed. They walked along the maze of corridors to the presenter's offices, the only place where they could see outside of the enclosed building.

What they saw as they peered through the giant windows did nothing to calm their nerves. There were hundreds of people standing in the middle of Portland Street, looking up at the sky. Many of them had tears in their eyes. Others were being consoled by their partners. The look of shock and sheer disbelief on all of their faces told the two radio presenters that whatever it was that these people were staring at, it wasn't good.

Frustratingly for Rick and Darren, they couldn't see what the crowds of people were looking at, as it was all happening behind them and there were no windows on that side of the radio station's building.

"What do we do?" Asked Darren.

"No idea." Replied Rick.

*****

Tina and Hayley Bradshaw were feeling hot and bothered, and very frustrated as they stood waiting with forty or fifty other people outside Kendals department store. Tina had been promising her daughter that they'd be allowed to go and get the car any minute now, for the past half-an-hour. It was red hot in town today, and Hayley was so bored standing here with all these old biddies waiting for something to happen. Tina was annoyed enough about the situation, but Hayley wasn't helping with her constant complaining about being "too hot" and "bored" and "missing Will Smith" whilst repeating her view that "it's not fair."

And then something did happen. Quite unexpectedly, as the oldies were all talking rubbish amongst themselves, the floor began rumbling violently beneath Hayley's feet and then a deafening, massive bang followed which made her feel quite dizzy. The window that she had been looking at her reflection in seemed to bulge inwards for about a second, before the bulge was released and the huge 10 foot-tall plate of glass exploded in the twelve-year girl's old face, knocking her off her feet as the tiny fragments of glass flew straight at her at forty-miles-an-hour.

*****

The gleaming white Jaguar wedding car had been crawling in stop-start traffic for almost 45 minutes. It wasn't the driver's fault, he'd tried every single route to get his passenger to Manchester Register Office. But whichever road he had tried to get down, he found himself trapped in queues of traffic. Now, he was on Deansgate, just at the back of Marks and Spencers which was on the next block up. Taxis, buses and vans were blocking every route, many of them had their engines off, quite a few of the drivers had got out of their vehicles and were enjoying the sunshine and gossiping with other drivers about what was going on. Other car drivers were beeping their horns, which was completely pointless and was greeted by others beeping back sarcastically.

The mood inside the car was tense, to put it mildly. It was starting to smell a bit iffy in there as well, the heat inside the vehicle was increasing minute-by-minute. The windows were all rolled down, but there was absolutely no breeze at all.

The bride, 26 year-old Amanda Hudson was fighting back tears as her dad held her hand and tried, without success, to reassure her that everything was going to be okay.

"I don't think we're going to move any further now," said the driver. "I think you'll have to walk the…"

The driver stopped talking as an immense bright flash blinded the occupants of the car. As the flash drowned everything in white, a sound, louder than anything any of them had ever heard before, boomed so deafeningly that all three occupants in the car felt it rattle in their bones. The car lifted-up from the road and crashed back down onto the tarmac. The bus in front of them was shaking from side to side as its windows popped and rained glass down onto the road all around it.

Amanda watched in disbelief as the gigantic windows in the shops looked as if they were breathing in for a second or two, before exploding into millions of little pieces, showering the pavement beside the car. The terrifying sound was echoing all around, it got quieter as each reverberation travelled further away. It was the most disturbing and distressing sound that she had ever heard.

This was a far-cry from the fairy tale day that Amanda had been planning since she was a little girl. She started crying as she saw the look of complete bewilderment on her dad's face.

11:18am

The truck bomb that had exploded on Corporation Street had given off such a powerful blast that windows up to a mile away from the seat of the explosion had shattered and thousands of tons of glass began raining down on the streets all around the city-centre.

The unbridled power of the blast projected masonry, glass and shop fittings as far as half a mile away from the bomb's location on Corporation Street. The energy and the heat twisted metal girders and smashed through concrete pillars. It lifted the concrete bridge which served as a passageway between the Arndale Centre and Marks and Spencers, dumping it back down half a metre away from its foundations. A deep crater which would comfortably fit a family car inside it was all that was left of the road where the Ford Cargo had been parked with its hazard lights flashing for the previous 117 minutes.

The raw energy from the blast had been trapped inwardly by channels between the Arndale Centre and Longridge House, the green-tiled office block which faced the shopping centre and Cannon Street. The power of the blast was contained within this channel, throwing debris around corners and into the Arndale bus station and up Market Street, where the sheer force of the detonation had snapped the six-inch thick marble benches in half, as though they were made of polystyrene. The unyielding thrust of heat and debris had to escape somehow, and the fallout from the explosion turned 90 degrees around corners, bringing concrete, glass and shop signs with it as it continued on its unrestrained journey in all directions.

An enormous mushroom cloud had been created by the explosion and it pushed high into the sky, 1000 metres above street level, a plume of smoke which could be seen from all across Greater Manchester. This bomb was like nothing that had ever been seen before to most people in the city, not since the second world war, anyway.

Windows had exploded in people's faces, and shop signage had fallen from above, crashing down on the people beneath. People of all ages had fallen to the floor, lying shocked and helpless amongst the billions of tiny shards of glass which covered every pavement and road.

At the bottom of King Street, close to Kendals department store just outside the police cordon line, a jeweller's window had exploded onto the floor and a handful of people had run across to it and began filling their pockets with watches, rings and bracelets. Nearby, people were lying on the floor, blood squirting out of their faces and others were trying to help them as this small group of individuals paid no attention to the casualties, but opted instead to raid this shop window of its prized possessions. People were too shocked and distressed to speak, or challenge this outrageous activity. They just looked on, speechless, struggling to believe their eyes as the looters ran away laughing, heading up King Street towards Manchester town hall with as much of the stock that they could carry.

Across the road, a small girl was lying in a pool of blood, her mother was screaming, trying to wake her up. Her small body looked lifeless and was covered in thousands of pieces of broken glass. A crowd of people, all covered in cuts and injuries themselves were trying to help the girl and calm her mother who was screaming with an unnerving, guttural shriek which was coming up from the very bottom of her soul.

The woman was on her knees, staring up at the sky as though she was begging God to help her daughter. It was a most distressing sight for everybody who was present. Her disturbing screams continued, "No! Hayley! No, PLEASE! Wake up!"

11:19am

The bomb had exploded two minutes ago. The deafening blast seemed to have lasted for ten or fifteen seconds, as it reverberated against every flat surface that the city centre had to offer. The shockwaves took out the windows of almost every shop and office and had even shattered bus-stops up to half a mile away, in all directions.

Once the sound of the blast had faded, and the energy slowly subsided, it was replaced by the sound of glass falling from windows and smashing into tiny pieces on the pavements below. Then, for a few seconds, there had followed a dark, foreboding silence. Everything seemed to have stopped. But this eerie, troubled silence didn't last for long. The next sound started within seconds, filling the streets and car-parks with the sudden and overwhelming, ear-piercing ring of fire alarms and burglar alarms. The monotonous shrill tone of thousands of car and shop alarms delayed response to the drama added an extra layer of menace to the already incomprehensible situation.

Another sound soon followed, the screams and the cries of hundreds of people who had been shredded by the flying glass. Some were crying for themselves, others were shouting for help. With the sound of the alarms coming from every direction, a sense of panic and terror suddenly gripped everybody in the vicinity of the police cordon zone as the quiet, dumb-founded shock gave way to noise, panic and chaos.

One of the worst affected areas for injuries was King Street, by the side of Kendals department store at the junction with Deansgate. Dozens of people had assumed they would be safe here, under the canopy. But the blast, which had turned corners, had showered them all with shards of glass and lumps of debris, as it made its rampant way through the city-centre.

For these people, the initial shock of that almighty explosion which had rocked the ground beneath them, was being replaced by the realisation that they had somehow been caught up in the middle of it, despite being outside the cordon zone. The sudden smog and smoke which had reduced visibility considerably couldn't disguise the fact that the pavement was covered in blood and glass.

Another location which was seeing a high number of serious injuries was the concourse of Victoria railway station. Hundreds of Saturday shoppers had been evacuated here and told to wait until the all-clear was given. It only became apparent that this was possibly the dumbest place imaginable to assemble people during an evacuation, when the bomb exploded and hundreds of square-metres of glass which made up the station's roof shattered, raining millions of shards of glass which came crashing down onto the people who'd been sent here for their own safety.

Dozens of people were sitting on the floor, trying to come to terms with the shock of what had just happened, many of them with huge spikes of glass sticking out of their heads. One elderly lady was lay on the floor, blood pouring from a severe cut on her wrist, a crowd of concerned people surrounded her, tending to her injury and trying to keep her calm, completely ignoring their own cuts and injuries which were bleeding profusely. Others with less serious injuries were trying to make sense of the scene before them, wondering how to even begin working out who to try and offer help to first.

Railway workers were running out of the offices, eager to help the injured. As they ran onto the central concourse, several of these good Samaritans quickly learnt of the hazard of trying to run on the fallen glass, the first-aid kits they'd been carrying flew out of their hands as they slipped, falling over and subsequently sustaining their own cuts and injuries as they landed on the razor sharp fragments which covered the entire concourse.

Confused, stressed and anxious people looked at one another, wondering what to do. Is it okay to pull a three-inch razor-sharp chunk of filthy glass out of somebody's skull? Where was the first-aid equipment? How much blood had the old lady lost? The pool of blood around her was getting bigger and darker with each passing second. People were silently trying to take all of this in as glass continued to fall from the roof, 25 metres above them. Each piece landing with a menacing, shattering sound which echoed all around the place.

This was what terrorism looked like. The fear and panic, confusion and helplessness that was etched on every single face in the crowded railway station said so much more than any words ever could.

11:20am

"Emergency Service, which service do you require?"

"Ambulance. Fire. Everything!"

"Is this in relation to the explosion in Manchester?"

"Yeah, yeah... I'm here, it's... you need to send people down to help us."

"I can assure you that help is on its way. What is your location?"

"Me? I'm in Manchester..."

The caller was evidently in shock. Adrenaline and panic were clearly disrupting the conversation. It was very common and the emergency operator recognised the signs.

"Where exactly are you in Manchester?"

"Me? I'm at, er... I'm in the train station."

"Okay, well stay there, help is on its way, I'm clearing the line now."

Three miles away, the ambulance control room at Belle Vue was receiving most of the calls. The phone operators had all heard the blast and had swapped opinions on what it might have been for a minute or so over a brew and a Wagon Wheel. But then, all of the emergency services lines suddenly became jammed as callers dialled 999 to request ambulances for strangers or for relatives or for their friends.

This had all come as a major shock to the ambulance control staff, who sent out the initial couple of crews to reports of a gas explosion at Marks and Spencers. That's all they knew about it. But as the calls continued, relentlessly, a clearer picture was beginning to emerge about exactly what had happened.

The nearest ambulance station to the scene of the blast was Plymouth Grove in Longsight, which was just over two miles away. All available crews at this station, known amongst the staff as "central" were despatched to the city-centre. There were too many calls coming in, all of which were requesting urgent help from the same general locations. In no time, the senior staff at Belle Vue realised that this was a critical situation and the event which had triggered all of these calls was quickly escalated to a major incident. Within minutes, all available crews from every ambulance station in Greater Manchester were headed for the city-centre, awaiting further instructions as they neared the incident.

The first ambulance to arrive on the scene was a central crew, from Plymouth Grove. They arrived shortly after the blast as they were situated nearby when the first call reporting a gas explosion came through. The dust was still settling as the ambulance screamed along Fountain Street, round the back end of China Town and Piccadilly Gardens.

On board the ambulance were two experienced paramedics, Les Birkhead and Norman Thurrell. Neither could quite believe what they were attending as their blue-lights and sirens headed towards King Street. People were just walking around in a daze, blood covered their ripped clothes, an inch of shattered glass covered every pavement, burglar alarms and fire sirens were wailing as a thick, dense dust-cloud made visibility much harder with each yard of progress. Les and Norman suddenly found themselves driving into a war-zone, just minutes after discussing where they were going to pick up their lunch from. Neither of the men could quite take in what was happening all around their ambulance. As they progressed to the location that they'd been sent, they were under no illusion that this was a major incident and they were preparing themselves for the very worst-case scenario. From what they saw as the vehicle advanced towards Kendals, they felt sure that there would be numerous fatalities. Double-figures, at the very least.

Les was driving whilst Norman, the older and more experienced crew member was reporting back to base. It was very difficult for Norman to continue with his running commentary to the control room. His first instinct was to treat these people who were lying around in pools of blood. But Les continued driving, following orders to provide an initial assessment for control. The mood was horrendous inside the ambulance and a row broke out between the two men. Norman couldn't stand this, slowly driving past all of these people who needed their help, ignoring the pleas for help from frightened, hysterical by-standers who were trying to help the injured who were pouring with blood.

Despite Norman's overpowering instinct to get out of the slow-moving vehicle and start treating these people, this initial assessment was proving to be a sensible idea. From the information that the ambulance operators were receiving from their trusted crew members at the scene, they quickly escalated the major incident to neighbouring ambulance services and requested the support of Merseyside, Cheshire, Lancashire and West Yorkshire. Soon, a total of 81 ambulances were racing towards the scene, some from local stations a few miles away, some from as far away as Liverpool, Preston and Halifax.

Once this initial visual assessment was completed, Les and Norman were instructed to park their vehicle and begin assessing injuries. They were to manage the ambulance allocations as crews entered the city-centre, their primary objective was to get the most urgent cases prioritised for a vehicle, whilst calming the walking wounded who would require treatment, but not in the first wave.

Norman and Les looked at one another, wondering how the hell this had been sprung on them. It was utterly baffling to both of them, they'd never seen anything like this before and were stunned that the ambulance service hadn't been placed on standby for this, the biggest and most serious incident that either of them had ever attended.

After relaying the details to their control room, Norman finally won the argument and insisted that Les pull the vehicle over. A young girl was lying in a pile of glass and a woman, who the paramedics assumed was the girl's mother was standing beside her, screaming for help.

Les and Norman raced out of the vehicle and dashed to the girl who was bleeding from a number of nasty cuts and gashes all over her exposed areas, her face, her arms and legs had hundreds of cuts of various sizes and seriousness. The girl was awake, but she was extremely groggy and couldn't open one eye, which was pouring with blood. There was no time for any messing about, the young girl was quickly picked up by Norman and carried to the ambulance, her mother followed deliriously, in a state of deep shock. Les locked the doors and jumped in the driver's seat. As he pulled the ambulance into the middle of the road to perform a three-point-turn, the glass and wreckage was crunching and banging beneath the tyres as he informed the control room that they were mobile with a critically injured chid and would no longer be available to set up the triage point as they had been ordered.

The haunted looks on every face, as they watched the ambulance pull away was something that would stay with Les for a very long time. He knew that he'd never be able to forget the fearful expressions on those terrified, shocked and helpless faces as he hit the siren and tried to drive as quickly towards Manchester Royal Infirmary as he could.

11:21am

"Help!"

"Please! Help!"

As the smoke and the dust was gradually beginning to thin out, the dazed police officers who'd started walking from the exclusion zone towards the bomb-site heard several voices above them shouting for assistance. It took a while to figure out exactly where the voices were shouting from. There was a thick, putrid smoke and a dry, concrete dust filling the air, but it was getting thinner by the minute as the hot sun-rays penetrated the smog.

"Help! We're up here!"

A little time passed before the police officers could make out faces in the blown-out windows of Longridge House. This eight-story building, the offices of Royal Sun Alliance insurance had been completely devastated by the blast, which had taken place directly outside. Most of the building's distinctive green tiles had been ripped off the walls, every window was gone, along with its steel frame. Whole sections of the façade had concrete and metal-work dangling precariously from it, threatening to fall to the ground at any moment.

Miraculously, people were actually inside there and these people had survived the blast. This was an impossible scene for the police officers to comprehend as they began running towards the building. So many questions were suddenly raised. How had these people not been aware of the evacuation? How the hell had they survived that blast, being just metres from the epicentre? How many people were trapped inside this broken, partially demolished building?

The people were still shouting for help, despite the small group of police officers edging closer to the office-block. It soon became apparent that the smog was obscuring their view as they continued to shout.

"Please! Help us! We have a lot of casualties. Emergency!"

11:22am

A number of fire engines had been placed on standby on the outskirts of the exclusion zone, some of the crews had been in position for over an hour. Most of them had been called into the city centre long before the explosion, responding to the fire-alarm calls which had been generated by police officers and shop-staff smashing their fire-alarm panels in order to evacuate the shops.

The fire service control room had instructed the commanding officers that their appliances should stay on stand-by, local to the incident, just in case they might be required later. They'd been told that if a routine 999 call came in, they would be despatched from their current location. Several of the fire-fighters in attendance had volunteered to assist with the evacuation earlier and had been a great asset, particularly in clearing the Corn Exchange building and many other locations where people had been reluctant to leave.

But now that the bomb had exploded and the utter carnage of the city-centre was slowly being revealed by the dissipating smoke and dust, many more fire appliances were being instructed to get into town in order to assist this major incident, including the aerial ladder appliance.

Assistant Divisional Fire-Officer Dave Morris had been the most senior fire-fighter in the vicinity. He had been at his desk at his fire-station in Salford when the sudden demand for appliances in the city-centre had piqued his curiosity. He'd contacted the police and learnt about the bomb threat. As it was a nice, pleasant day, Dave had decided to drive the command car down the road to Manchester and try and establish exactly what was happening. After helping with the second evacuation of the Corn Exchange and ensuring that nobody else returned, he'd been standing relatively close-by when the bomb disposal team had failed to make the device safe. The Corn Exchange building's windows had blown out right in front of him, showering him with glass.

Now that the reality of what had just occurred was becoming clearer, Dave realised that he had a monumental task on his hands in managing this incredible scene. As he was assessing the best way to prioritise tasks and how to co-ordinate the response, his radio began beeping.

"Assistant Divisional Officer Dave Morris." He replied into his radio. He swiftly learned that the Greater Manchester Fire and Rescue Service's first task had already been allocated. They were required to rescue 40 office workers who were trapped inside Longridge House, the building which the Ford Cargo had been parked directly outside of when it unleashed the raw, unforgiving power of its one and a half-ton bomb.

11:23am

On John Dalton Street - just outside Habitat, a blonde-haired woman wearing sunglasses was in a heightened state of distress. The woman was screaming at a security guard, as she ran after him up the road. The harshness of her tone attracted lots of looks from the people who were dealing with casualties or checking their own injuries, all in a silent, stunned disbelief at what had just occurred on the streets of Manchester city-centre. The distressed woman kept shouting, attracting everybody's attention.

"Give me back my baby!" The woman pleaded, the raw emotion and panic was explicit in her voice, so much so that a couple of police officers had sprinted across the road towards her in order to find out what was happening.

A security guard from a neighbouring store had plucked her baby from his pram and had started running away from the area with the infant, who was covered in cuts from flying glass. The security guard had his hand clenched around the baby's wrist, and blood was dripping through his fingers.

"Give me back my baby!" Screamed the mother again, her face twisted with an expression of fear and anguish. The security guard stopped running as he realised that it was the baby's mother who was screaming after him. He looked shocked and confused as Lisa Hughes leaned forward and grabbed her 10-month-old son, Sam Hughes from his arms.

"I was... he needs a hospital." Said the security guard, Tony Gurrell, who was eager to explain that he had been trying to help as police officers rushed over to see what was happening. The baby's father, Perry, dashed across and thanked the security guard for trying to take his child to safety. His wife, Lisa didn't appear as grateful, as the sheer panic of seeing her child in a stranger's arms had raised her anxiety even further and had given her the shock of her life.

Tony Gurrell looked dazed and utterly lost as he began to realise that the woman thought that he was trying to abduct her child. It was an unbelievable situation, which demonstrated the sheer chaos and pandemonium which was all around.

People were shouting at others, whole families were walking around covered in blood and every shop alarm in the city was ringing out at full volume. These were scenes of madness, like something out of a blockbuster Hollywood movie.

It was all becoming too much and the security guard leaned up against the wall, his hand soaked in the baby's blood. "You need to get him to hospital," he repeated as Lisa Hughes walked away with Sam in her arms. Vanessa Thorpe, the WPC who had rushed across to see what was happening held her radio to her mouth and requested an ambulance for the injured baby.

Sam had several serious cuts on his exposed arms and legs, one in particular had caused the most concern, a deep laceration on his wrist, dangerously close to his main artery. It was this injury which had concerned Tony Gurrell, as he saw the blood spurting out and feared for the child's safety. He was so shaken up by the events which were unfolding all around him that he hadn't realised that the baby's parents were standing right there as he lifted Sam from his pram and dashed to find medical help.

Despite the drama and confusion, everybody was relieved that Tony had spotted the injury in amongst all of the ensuing panic and mayhem. The trauma of the bomb blast, and then moments later the sight of a perfect stranger picking up her baby and running off had frightened Lisa Hughes far greater than anything else ever had. She was in a state of absolute terror.

As all of this chaos and confusion was unfolding, a Manchester Evening News photographer called Carl Royle just happened to be there. He was taking pictures just a few feet away and as his camera clicked away furiously, he instinctively felt that he had managed to capture the sheer terror, panic and confusion on the streets of Manchester with these incredible shots. As the sudden fear began to die down on this street corner which was situated over 300 metres away from the bomb-site and littered with the glass of the Habitat windows, police officers began treating baby Sam's injuries.

Carl couldn't wait to get back to M.E.N offices and start developing the film. He felt pretty confident that he'd just managed to shoot the defining photograph of the terror attack.

11:24am

Karen Ellis was fast asleep in bed when the phone started ringing. She heard it, but after a couple of seconds of assessing the situation, she remembered that it was Saturday and Bob was at home, so he'd answer it. With this quick calculation done in her mind, Karen grabbed her husband's pillow from his side of the bed and put it over her head.

But the phone kept ringing.

"For God's sake!" Said Karen as she lifted the pillow off her face and sat up. The phone was still ringing and Karen realised that it must be an important call. If it wasn't, the caller would have hung up by now. She sat up in bed and reached across to the bed-side table and lifted the receiver.

"308 3569." She said, with a croaky voice.

"Hello. It's Greater Manchester Police, is that Karen?"

"Er, yeah. What's wrong."

"Oh, right, sorry to contact you, my name is Lisa, I work in HR at Chester House. I understand that you've been on the nightshift."

"Right?" This was weird. What were Human Resources doing phoning her on a Saturday morning? Karen's mind began racing.

"So firstly, apologies for disturbing you. We are contacting police officers to see if they can come in to work. We've currently got a major incident in the city-centre."

This news woke Karen Ellis up completely.

"What... what's the incident?"

"A bomb. It's very bad."

"Oh shit. Right, no problem, I'll come to work right away. I'll be about twenty-five minutes."

"Okay, thank you. Please make sure you have your ID on you as the city-centre is closed to civilians."

This was shocking news. Karen had never attended a major incident before, she'd only passed-out as a WPC the previous year.

"Right. On my way, thank you."

Karen jumped up out of bed and got dressed quickly.

She headed through to the bathroom for a wee and to wash her face and brush her teeth, her adrenaline was pumping.

Once she got downstairs, she saw Bob's parcel on the table in the hallway and realised that he'd gone off to get the shopping for the barbeque.

"Wouldn't bother now Bob!" She muttered under her breath, as she wrote a quick note for him.

"Hi love, been called into work. Speak later. Love you. K."

11:25am

"This is Piccadilly Key 103. Apologies for the loss of our service for a few moments earlier." Rick Houghton didn't sound like his usual fun, laid-back and charming self. The shock and fear that he was feeling was unmistakable in his voice.

"We have had a small power-cut at the radio station, but everything seems to be working again now." Rick pressed a button on the broadcast desk and pulled his microphone fader down as music began playing. His colleague and friend, Darren Stannage was standing behind him. They were both in shock. The way that the Piccadilly Plaza had shook so violently had given them both a major fright, they really had anticipated death, trapped inside this gigantic concrete box.

"Now what?" said Rick, completely unsure of what the next move was. Normally, managers and senior staff members would be on-hand to give official guidance. But there was nothing. The bosses were probably unaware of this situation in Manchester as they played around like big kids at Alton Towers.

As Darren and Rick tried to work out the best solution to this crisis, the XD number began flashing.

"Wait up, this might be the police. Hello, CR2."

"Rick, its Penky. What on earth is going on?" The voice on the telephone line was one of Manchester's most recognisable, the star of the station's hugely-popular breakfast show, Steve Penk.

"We don't know, Steve."

"I was just in my garden in Bramhall, I heard this almighty bang, and then the station went off air."

"Yes, the power supply dropped out for a few seconds. It's back on now. What, you heard it in Bramhall? That's miles away."

"Yes, fifteen miles."

"We didn't hear anything in here, nothing. But it felt like an earthquake, the whole place started bouncing. All the CDs and carts jumped off the shelves, they're all on the floor, smashed up."

"Holy shit. This must be bad, Rick. What's the strategy

for programming?"

"No idea Steve. Nobody's here, we can't get hold of anybody."

"Not even Danny?"

"No, they've all gone on a day-trip!"

"Oh, of course. Alton Towers. Shit. Well, listen. You can't stay silent about this. Go on air, open the lines, speak to eye-witnesses, ask them questions. Everybody will be tuning in to find out what's going on."

"Do you think?"

"Totally. Suspend all music, go into talk-station mode. And if it's the wrong decision, you can blame it on me, I'll carry the can. But trust me, our listeners won't appreciate us pretending that it's not happening. I'll make my way over there now, see if I can get in."

"Alright. Thanks Steve."

With that, the call ended. Rick and Darren started to feel a sense of relief. The biggest name on the station had just given them advice on how to manage this mind-blowing problem, as well as the authority of his name to back the decision up along with the offer of support if he could make it into town.

Rick Houghton wasted no time in taking Penky's advice. He opened the microphone and began talking.

"As I'm sure you've probably gathered, we're having a few problems this morning here at Piccadilly Key 103, if any eye witnesses to the events in Manchester are listening, can you please get in touch on 228 6262. Myself and my fellow Key 103 presenter Darren Stannage are the only people inside the radio station and we can't see what's happening outside. We just know that something very bad has happened in the past few moments."

It was a very raw and unapologetically honest appeal for information. But it worked like a charm. Rick cleared all of the phone lines which had been flashing non-stop since he'd first announced the city-centre closure. The first line that flashed up was connected on air.

"Key 103, hello?" Said Rick.

"Oh, alright. Yes, I know what's going on."

"Okay..."

"A bomb has gone off at the Arndale, but the place was evacuated about an hour before it so it shouldn't be as bad as what it looks."

"How do you know all this?"

"I'm a bus-driver. I had to dump my bus in the Arndale bus station when it was evacuated. This was like, roughly ten o'clock. I'm back at the depot now, Queens Road. We saw the bomb go off. It's bad, like. But they cleared the whole place an hour before it went up, like I say, so fingers crossed nobody's been involved."

"Okay, thanks for this update. Let's take another call. Key 103?"

"Oh, yeah, hiya, I've seen what's happened."

"Where are you?"

"I'm just above you actually, in Sunley House, the office-block over Piccadilly bus station."

"What's happening there, is everything okay?"

"Yes, well, quite a few windows have gone but it looks like most of them managed to survive. I was stood next to one when the bomb went off, they sort of bulged inwards, and then I heard the boom. Then this big mushroom cloud went up above Lewis's. It looks like every single window has been blown out of Arndale House. I just can't believe what I'm seeing."

Rick sounded shocked, hearing all of this information for the first time, but he was doing a great job as he dumped the regular music format and continued taking calls from the public. Rick had never handled a talk-show format before, and he had never presented the news, but this didn't show as he adapted his care-free broadcast style to that of a serious news journalist. One thing was certain, the twenty-three-year old had been on a real journey with his broadcasting experience so far today.

The down-side to the advice that Steve Penk had given was that this broadcast was creating a fresh wave of panic around the city, almost everybody who was listening knew somebody who would be in town today, either working or shopping or just changing buses or trains to get to their next destination.

The telephone lines for the local police stations all around Greater Manchester were engaged, as were the hospital enquiry lines. This major news story was sending a shock-wave of terror throughout Greater Manchester, everybody who was hearing about it found themselves suddenly gripped by a suffocating fear and the only thing they could think about was trying to find out if their loved-ones were safe.

The local hospitals had no information to release and in-light of the circumstances, they stopped answering calls. They'd reached this decision for several reasons. The main reason was that the anxious members of the public were becoming quite rude and aggressive down the phone when they learnt that the hospitals had no information to share. The city was in the grip of terror and its citizens felt lost and forgotten about in the vacuum of confusion and chaos.

11:26am

Longridge House had been crossed off the list of buildings which had been checked for evacuation. It was understandable that the police officers who had ticked the office-block off their paperwork had assumed that it was deserted. After-all, the building had appeared empty, it was all locked-up, and it was Saturday. Like all of the other city-centre office blocks, it stood to reason that there was nobody inside.

But astonishingly, there *were* people inside when the biggest peace-time bomb to ever explode on the British mainland had detonated right outside the building. Inexplicably, these people had somehow missed the continued, deafening announcements from India 99, for over an hour, right above the building. Seemingly, none of the staff had noticed that no traffic, or pedestrians, or anything at all had moved outside for over 90 minutes, and they'd missed the local radio announcements too.

This incredible, unbelievable information was the cause for great activity outside the insurance company's northern headquarters. As the dust continued to settle, and the surrounding area was slowly revealing the destruction and carnage which had been left in the bomb's wake, 12 fire-fighters were entering the building under the leadership of Assistant Divisional Fire Officer Dave Morris.

After smashing through the main doors with axes, the team of fire-fighters bravely entered the devastation, unsure of whether the building was stable, or not. Filing cabinets were lay on their sides, glass covered every surface, from desk-tops to window-sills, millions of tiny pieces of glass twinkled where they had come to rest. Ceiling tiles and lights were hanging down from overhead and the floor was hidden beneath a mountain of debris. Concrete panels, tiles from the exterior walls, paper, files and office chairs were strewn everywhere, photo-copier machines lay smashed-up on their sides or upside-down.

The ground-floor was quickly checked for casualties by the fire-fighters and was given the all-clear. They marched silently up the stairs to the first floor, stepping carefully on top of the rubble and debris that had come to rest on the stair-case.

The scene which greeted them on the first floor was even more chaotic and desolated than the destruction they'd encountered on the ground-floor. Moving quickly through the office-spaces, the fire and rescue officers were sure that they would encounter fatalities at any moment and the mood was low and tense amongst the crew members as they struggled to comprehend the scene of total devastation which lay before them. Entire walls had collapsed in between the offices, doors had been blown off their hinges.

"Look," said one of the officers as they searched under desks and behind fallen cupboards for casualties.

"What?" Asked his colleague.

The fire-fighter pointed at a red office-chair which had come to rest on top of a steel-cupboard. The blast had lifted it six-feet in the air and had deposited it unceremoniously on top of the cupboard. The clock on the wall had lost its glass, but had remained fixed in place. The hands had stopped at 11:17.

"All clear?" Shouted Dave Morris.

"Sir!" Came the response from his officers.

"Okay, all out, second-floor." The officers negotiated their way back across the debris, heading towards the stair-well where they fought past the carnage which was obscuring the path. The stairs were completely exposed to the outside of the building, the glass which had encased this section of the structure had been blown out, as had the frames and the supports which had held the windows in position. Every last piece of this wreckage had been smashed into an enormous pile of debris which covered the steps. This section didn't resemble a staircase at all now, just a huge pile of demolition rubble running up towards the next floor.

The further up the mountain of rubble they went, the greater the damage they witnessed. By the time they had reached the second-floor, it quickly became apparent that the destruction which had shocked them all on the lower-floors was nothing like as severe as the devastation further up the office block.

"Help!" Shouted a man as he met the fire-fighters at the top of the stairwell. He was covered in cuts and his hands were soaked in blood. His face was bleeding, but he gestured the rescue team to follow him, it quickly became clear that his own injuries were not the primary concern.

"Are there no paramedics with you?" He pleaded as the fire-officers managed to climb over the obstacles on the stairwell. "We have a lot of casualties!" The man was in shock as he began climbing over upturned furniture. "There are people upstairs as well. Some of you go to them!"

"Which floor?" asked Dave Morris as his officers fought through the rubble and headed towards the casualties on the second-floor.

"Just this floor and the third-floor. We were asked to do some over-time. It's only the renewals department. Second floor. Third floor. The other floors are new claims, nobody was working up there. Fourth floor, to sixth floor. We never get asked to do over-time. And then when we do it, this!" The profound shock that the man was experiencing was common and explained the waffle that was coming out of his mouth. The rescue officers recognised it immediately.

"Okay, let's get you out of here," said one of the firefighters.

"No, no, you need to help these people first. People are dying!"

11:27am

Ten minutes had now elapsed since the explosion and the gritty, dusty cloud was still hanging heavy. It still wasn't possible to make-out the true picture of the damage on Corporation Street as the menacing dust-cloud refused to settle and reveal a clear, defined view of the scene.

After reaching its maximum flying time, India 99 had now returned to its base at Barton airfield for refuelling and a routine mechanical check. With the chopper out of the area, the overwhelming sound in the city-centre was the high-pitched wail and squeal of hundreds of burglar, car and fire alarms coming from the shops, offices and car parks up to a mile away from the seat of the explosion.

The eerie silence and calmness which had immediately followed the blast was now long forgotten. People were shouting for police or ambulance staff, kids were screaming and throwing tantrums out of fear. Shocked, emotionally exhausted shoppers were trying to take in the destruction and the injuries all around them. People were dripping in blood, but seemingly not concerned about themselves as they walked around asking others if they were okay.

Ambulances were filling the streets all around the lower-half of the city centre, from Manchester town hall through to Deansgate, the vehicles were arriving at the scene, their crew members visibly confused about which patient they had been called here to treat. Hundreds of people were sat on the pavement, in puddles of glass and blood, holding hastily gathered appendages to their injuries. Dozens of men were shirt-less, they'd sacrificed their tops to be used as make-shift bandages. It was complete and total chaos all around.

The roads around the area where the most severely injured people were lay had become completely impassable due to the wreckage and the glass which covered the roads. It was impossible to see the tarmac beneath the devastation. Ambulance staff could be seen arguing amongst themselves, their tempers flaring up as the confusion of the scene ramped everybody's stress levels up to maximum.

As all of this madness was going on, bystanders were helping to clear a pathway, lifting up the newspaper stands, shop-signs, bikes and street furniture which had landed in the middle of the roads. Others were using their feet to sweep the rubble and debris away towards the pavement, desperately trying to clear a pathway for the emergency services vehicles to get through and get closer to the epicentre of the blast.

11:28am

Manchester Royal Infirmary is the closest hospital to Manchester City-Centre, located just a mile and a half away, on Oxford Road in the heart of the University district. This famous hospital had started life in Piccadilly Gardens, but work on the new, bigger hospital commenced on Oxford Road in 1904. It was officially opened by King Edward VII on the 6th July 1909.

Since that time, the MRI as it is affectionately known has seen a number of major incidents in the city. Not least the WW2 bombing in 1940 which destroyed 130 bedrooms in the nurses' home. Thankfully, nobody was hurt as the staff had been sent to the shelter in the hospital's basement as air-raid sirens warned of the imminent danger. Had the bomb hit any other part of the hospital, it would have been a very different story.

Today, MRI's Casualty department was full, as was common on a Saturday morning. It was quite normal for people with socialising injuries to sleep it off, or not notice how much pain they were in due to the excess of the alcohol or drug influences they'd been enjoying the previous night. But once Saturday morning came around, and they realised that they'd done themselves a mischief, it was quite normal to cadge a lift down to the MRI and get themselves looked at. Today was no exception. The waiting room in the Casualty department was filled with sad, hung-over people and their disappointed relatives. As well as the sprained ankles, broken noses and a variety of dancing injuries, the green, leather chairs were also providing comfortable waiting for dozens of people with a variety of health problems, from irregular heart-rhythms and asthma attacks, to injuries picked up on the football pitches in the Saturday morning leagues.

There was lots of discussion about what that almighty thunder sound had been. Everybody in here had heard it, some had said that they'd felt the vibrations through their chair. Nobody knew for sure what had happened, but the rumour-mill was in full flow as the injured and sick people took their minds off their ailments and passed some time discussing that terrifying sound and the subsequent, non-stop sound of emergency services vehicles blaring their sirens as they raced up Oxford Road in the direction of town.

The random suggestions of earth-quakes, fallen buildings and gas blasts were all about to be put into some perspective however. The most senior member of staff in the Casualty department was Dr Jonathan Alterman. He walked into the waiting room with his sleeves rolled up, his stethoscope was resting around his neck.

"Good morning ladies and gentlemen," he announced in a very loud and unmissable manner. "I'm afraid that we are closing the Casualty department to all people who are not currently experiencing life-threatening symptoms at this time. This means all of you."

This blunt announcement was met with fury from a number of the patients, some of whom had already been waiting hours to see somebody.

"Hee-yar! What are you going on about?"

"You can't close Casualty. What are you on about, you clown?"

Dr Alterman wasn't in the mood for listening to any bullshit so raised his voice an octave and spoke over the top of the loudest complainers.

"A gigantic bomb has exploded in Manchester city-centre, I'm sure that you all heard it about ten minutes ago. We have been placed on a major incident alert so we have to close the department to none life-threatening cases. There's no point arguing or sharing your thoughts about this, we will soon have hundreds of people in here with very profound, life-threatening injuries. Please make your way to another hospital and I would suggest that you avoid the ones which are closest to Manchester as it appears that this is a very serious incident. Thank you."

"Outrageous!" Said the mouthiest of the patients.

"Oh be quiet, you little dick!" Said an old lady, which received no reply from the young man who'd shouted out.

"Which hospitals should we avoid?" asked a young mum who was sitting with a little lad wearing his football kit.

"I would suggest that North Manchester General and Hope Hospital will be placed on major incident alert as well as us. So, the further away from central Manchester, the better really. Thank you."

And that was it. Dr Alterman stepped out of the waiting room as confidently as he had entered, heading off to make preparations for the first wave of casualties.

The people in the waiting room looked stunned, that had been a very scary announcement. One or two of them started a fresh wave of complaining, but the lack of authority in their voices confirmed that they didn't really feel confident that their complaints were valid. They were just letting off a bit of steam. An elderly man who looked as though he was in some discomfort stood slowly and several others followed suit. The Doctor had made it very clear what was happening, so the brightest people accepted it graciously and headed off to find treatment elsewhere.

"I hope everyone's alright," said one lady as she hobbled out of the waiting room in clear discomfort. "Sounds well bad, dunnit?"

11:29am

Like many of their fellow colleagues on duty, Miller and Cleggy had been called down to the posh shopping district of King Street to assist with first-aid. The scene that greeted them was shocking, pensioners and little kids were lay on the ground, concerned relatives trying to stop blood from spurting out of their injuries. This shocking scene of panic and fear was taking place all around Manchester's trendiest and most expensive designer shops and outlets.

"This is mental," said Cleggy as he left one injured person and was immediately faced with another. Miller was on his knees assisting a pregnant lady who was suffering from severe shock as well as minor cuts and bruising. Her thin white blouse was spattered with blood. Andy Miller's main priority was to try and calm her down as she was becoming increasingly agitated.

"Have you thought of a name for the baby?" He asked, trying his hardest to make this seem like a normal conversation and a normal situation. The lady didn't reply, she just sat there in amongst all of the glass, crying uncontrollably.

"Is nobody here with you?" Asked Miller, looking around for a partner or friend. There were plenty of people walking around, looking dazed and confused and Miller wondered if one of them belonged to this lady, but there was still no response from her, other than the tears and the frenzied crying.

"You're going to be alright, you've had a nasty shock. Just take a few deep breaths and we'll move you away from here in a couple of minutes, get you a nice cup of sweet tea, that will help to calm your nerves."

All around, police officers and security guards were tending to the people, the mind-bending shrill of thousands of alarm bells ringing incessantly was the only sound anybody could hear. The alarm bells were so loud that people were shouting at one another in an effort to be heard.

A GP who had been in town doing some shopping was treating a lady who had a very serious cut to her face, just above her eye. The lady's relatives were assisting him as he explained what they needed to do to reduce the blood-loss and avoid any further damage to the wound.

Police vans and cars were beginning to appear from every direction, as officers from across the Greater Manchester divisions had been sent to the city-centre to support the dedicated team of officers who usually looked after this patch.

As each new vehicle arrived, the officers were quickly sent to assist people as soon as they stepped out of them. The scene was surprisingly calm, considering. The people who were injured were glad of the assistance they were receiving and the police officers, security guards and firemen were all happy that they were dealing with cuts, bruises and shock and not something much worse.

But then a call came over the radio which changed this calm mood considerably. "All available units, there are reports of several casualties lay in the debris on Corporation Street, just outside Marks and Spencers, can all available units please attend urgently, over."

Miller looked across at Cleggy, who was trying to help an old man to his feet. Cleggy congratulated the man and made a gentle joke about him wasting a police officer's time before he looked across at Miller. The look of fear and dread that they exchanged confirmed that neither of them wanted to attend this job that had just come on the radio. But they both recognised that they had little alternative but to go.

11:30am

Amanda Hudson had tears in her eyes as she ran up Deansgate in her wedding dress, clutching it by her side to avoid tripping up. Her dad was trying to keep up with her, but she was surprisingly quick, despite the high heels. Her dad had no chance. There were lots of bemused looks from the shocked and scared looking people who were standing around in groups, they all looked at Amanda and her dad as though they were wondering if this day get any more mental.

But Amanda and her dad had no time to worry about what other people were thinking. They knew that the Register Office was around here somewhere and they were already late. The flights were booked for Florida, taking off from Ringway later on tonight, but it was going to be a pretty weird honeymoon if the bride and groom hadn't even managed to get married.

"Come on dad, it's just around the next corner!" Shouted Amanda breathlessly as she raced ahead without a care for her hair and make-up now.

A minute or so later, the bride was met on the steps of Manchester register office by her groom. The look of sheer relief on Franklyn Swanston's face was unforgettable, he broke down in tears as Amanda ran towards him and gave him the tightest cuddle ever.

"Aw God Mandy, I thought..."

"It's alright, I'm alright. My dad's not though, he's bloody knackered! We just had to run from the other end of town!"

Franklyn kissed Amanda on the lips as tears streamed down his face. "I thought... well, I didn't know..."

"It's fine, it's fine, are we too late?"

"I don't know... the next wedding's been cancelled so there's still a chance."

"You look really smart by the way! I said you'd scrub up well! Come on."

As Amanda's dad caught up with them, the small wedding party headed inside the famous building close to

Manchester Town Hall. The guests and Amanda's six-year old sister Lucy, who was chief bridesmaid, were all waiting patiently inside.

As the harassed looking couple entered the register office, the registrar appeared even more stressed-out than the bride and groom did. This was not a normal wedding day, by any stretch of the imagination. The photographer had been waiting outside with Franklyn but hadn't taken any pictures due to the bizarre and confused circumstances. He'd never encountered the spectacle of a bride sprinting to her wedding before and he'd certainly not seen one looking so dishevelled.

"Ah, Amanda, hi," said the registrar. She'd gotten to know Franklyn and his bride quite well when they'd come for the initial appointment and had been so lovely. But she didn't seem as happy and friendly today.

"Sorry I'm late!" Said the bride, "but I probably have the best excuse, ever!"

The registrar smiled politely before laying down her terms.

"Okay, listen, you've got two choices. We can press on and rush through the ceremony now, or we can book it for another day."

"Oh, well…" Amanda looked at Franklyn, who looked completely lost. "Shall we just…" She asked.

Franklyn nodded. "We're all here. Might as well just go for it."

"Okay, follow me. We're about to be evacuated, so we need to be quick."

"What?" Amanda looked shocked. It was clear from the expression on her face that she couldn't believe how badly this wedding was going.

"It's precautionary. The police are clearing everybody out, but they are a few streets away at the moment so we probably have enough time." The registrar was talking like a robot, it was obvious that she just wanted to get this done and then go home, no doubt for a large glass of something strong.

This information was too much for the photographer. He just said, "sorry, I'm going." And walked out of the building, breaking into a jog as he reached the doors. The bride and groom looked at one another in disbelief, this day had been many months in the planning, practically every detail had been poured over. And now, it was all turning to shit.

"Look, we can rearrange..." Said the registrar, but it sounded as though it was a plea, rather than a suggestion.

"No, balls to that. We're going on honeymoon tonight, it's all arranged. Let's just get it done." Amanda was demonstrating what kind of a wife she was going to make, as she took control of the situation and grabbed her dad's arm. "Come on dad, get your breath back, I need to get married," she said, before turning to Franklyn. "You look gorgeous, by the way!"

Franklyn smiled and realised that it would be wise if he returned the compliment, but before he had the chance, he was prompted to follow the registrar into the ceremony room.

11:31am

To the sound of hundreds of blaring alarms, Miller and Cleggy raced up Corporation Street, along with several other police officers as they headed to the location where the control room officer had stated that casualties were lying under rubble.

It made no sense, it was impossible to comprehend that people had been shopping here, outside Marks and Spencers, where the truck-bomb had been parked. The police officers who were racing down to the scene of the blast, where these casualties were reported to be, couldn't understand how it was possible that anybody could have managed to get anywhere near the location. The area immediately around the truck had been the first to be evacuated, and the rest of the evacuation process had moved outwards from this location, in every direction.

As they got a little closer, they saw a number of fire-fighters, police officers and paramedics looking silently at the scene before them. The utter devastation at this place was hard to take in. The famous corrugated canopy which covered the pavement outside Marks and Spencers had collapsed and was drooping down onto the ground. Most of the Arndale Centre's external walls were missing, exposing the crude concrete blocks which held the place up. Between each of the two-metre thick sections of concrete, the internal kitchens and restrooms at the back of the shops could be seen. The jackets on the backs of chairs, the kettles and lunchboxes on display in these normally hidden spaces added an extra layer of reality to what an unbelievable event had taken place here. The post box outside Marks and Spencers was still standing, in amongst all of this carnage and destruction. It was just yards away from where the Cargo truck had blown up, and it didn't appear to have a scratch on it. Everything else in sight had been destroyed and this post box looked brand-new, like it had just been installed in the minutes after the explosion. It was an utterly surreal scene.

Most of the caramel and mustard coloured tiles which had earned the Arndale the rather depressing tag-line of "the world's biggest public lavatory" were lay in millions of shattered pieces on the ground. Just beyond the bomb-site, a Metrolink tram was parked half-way across Corporation Street. The traffic lights just between this place and the tram were continuing to operate and had just changed to green. None of this seemed real. None.

"What's going on?" asked Miller as he reached the emergency services staff. "Where are the casualties?"

One of the fire-men turned to Miller and pointed in the direction of the road. It didn't seem authentic, seeing this place that he walked up and down several times a day on his beat, looking like this. It was like something out of a horrible dream.

Miller looked in the direction that the fireman was pointing. Sure enough, in amongst all of the debris and carnage lay several bodies, all covered with slabs of concrete, sections of walls and broken glass. There was no hope that any of these casualties had survived the blast. Miller looked on with an expression of shock and bewilderment.

"They're all dead." Said one of the fire-fighters, solemnly.

"Oh…" said Miller, looking away from the scene. He looked down at the floor, he felt an overpowering urge to be sick.

"But to be fair, they were all dead before the bomb went off. They're the fucking mannequins out of the shop windows."

Suddenly, the emergency services staff who'd already been aware of this false alarm burst into laughter, which made Miller and Cleggy, and the rest of the police officers who had just arrived, feel stupid.

"Oh, you rotten bastards!"

"It wasn't us," smiled the fire-man. "It was the CCTV operators who raised the alert. We knew as soon as we got here. I mean, look at him, there, still smiling. All he's wearing is a pair of swimming trunks!"

"Has somebody cancelled the job?" Asked Cleggy, failing to see the funny side.

"Yeah, you'll all be stood down in a minute. I bet it's absolute chaos in the control…"

Suddenly the sound of a lone voice disrupted the conversation. All of the emergency services staff looked up in the direction that the sound had come from. They saw the man who was shouting, he was at a window on the third floor of Arndale House, waving a white shirt above his head. From this distance of two hundred metres, they could all see that it was covered in blood. This desperate looking man's pleas for help put an immediate end to the light-heartedness which had been borne from relief that there were no bodies under the rubble. But the man screaming for help soon reminded everybody that there was still plenty of work to be done.

11:32am

The scene on the third-floor of Longridge House was hard to take in, it was impossible to recognise this place as an office building. The force from the blast had destroyed the internal walls which had separated a number of smaller, individual offices. The stud walls had fallen down, the three inch-thick wooden beams which had supported them had snapped like match-sticks, the plasterboard and glass partitions had been reduced to dust and crumbs. The air was heavy with dust, it stung the eyes of every member of the rescue team.

In amongst this devastation and chaos were several badly injured people with quite serious cuts and lacerations. But two people in particular were causing the most concern and were being cared for by their colleagues, some of whom were bleeding profusely. One lady was lay underneath a filing cabinet which had been thrown on top of her, the other person, another lady, was knelt-down on all fours with blood raining down from her face.

"We didn't know if we should move it!" Said one of the workers as the fire officers stepped over towards the filing cabinet, taking great care where they stepped as the floor beneath them was hidden under a foot or so of debris. The look that the lead fireman gave to his colleagues said it all, as they quickly hoisted the heavy metal object off the lady who looked as though she was drifting in and out of consciousness. She had a very severe cut to her head and a deep wound on her shoulder, she was losing a lot of blood. The fire and rescue officers quickly checked her for any broken bones before they pulled her up and hoisted her onto one of the fire-men's shoulders and was swiftly taken by him towards the former stair-case.

The other lady, who was knelt-down on her hands and knees was in a very bad way. Her head was absolutely enormous, it looked as though she was wearing an over-sized motor-bike helmet. Her hair was matted with blood and a strange layer of dust, glass and cement crumbs covered the drying blood. Her whole body was trembling so violently that it looked as though she could be kneeling on top of a washing machine during a spin-cycle.

"What's your name, love?" Asked Assistant Divisional Fire Officer Dave Marsh, as he knelt down beside her. It was only when he had got down to her level that Dave could see what a poorly state the woman was in. Her face was literally in pieces, blood was pouring down from a number of serious, deep lacerations which had shredded her face, her ears and her scalp.

It was hard to make out what she said, although she did try to answer him. The agonising, slurring sound which came out of her mouth when she spoke was genuinely upsetting for the experienced fire-fighter.

"She's called Barbara. Barbara Welch." Said one of the lady's colleagues, looking on, extremely concerned.

"Alright, Barbara love. You're going to be alright."

Barbara tried to reply, but it was impossible to make out what she was saying. Dave moved his head down towards the floor, as far as he could get above the rubble and debris. He looked up at the lady's face and it soon became apparent why she was having difficulty speaking. The lacerations were through her lips, her cheeks and her nose, her face looked double the size that it should be. Treble, even.

"Okay, Barbara, we're from the Fire and Rescue service... we're here to help you... just nod if you can understand me."

She nodded slowly.

"Great stuff. Now, I need to move you from here. I can see that you've got a lot of injuries to your face and your head. But before I move you, I just need to work out if you have any other injuries anywhere else on your body. Just shake your head for me if you don't have any other injuries. Okay?"

Barbara shook her head very slightly from side to side as the blood and tears continued to flow from her disturbingly swollen face.

"Okay Barbara, you're doing great. You're a lot braver than me, I'll tell you that."

Barbara nodded, and tried to respond with a gentle laugh. This simple gesture, with a slight movement of her head brought tears to Dave's eyes. He'd seen a lot of bad stuff in his time, he'd attended car-crashes, building collapses, RTA's and industrial accidents, but he'd never seen anybody suffering with injuries of such a horrendous nature before. The way that Barbara was conducting herself, whilst clearly in an unimaginable amount of pain, was extremely moving for Dave and several of his officers who were assisting.

"Barbara, if I give you my hands, can you try and stand up slowly for me please?"

Again, she nodded gently. Dave moved around so that he was facing her and offered her his hands. Two of his colleagues got into position at either side of her and the three fire-fighters slowly raised her to her feet. Dave was stunned for a moment as he realised that Barbara's watch had stopped working at 11:17. The force of the blast, which she had taken the brunt of, had also destroyed her watch.

As soon as she was stood, with her head still bowed down, Dave lifted her onto his shoulder and began the arduous task of getting out of there, stepping over and around the devastation inside the office-block, trying to make the journey as smooth as possible for this poor lady. As he made his way slowly but surely down the unrecognisable staircase, tears were streaming down Dave Marsh's face.

11:33am

Several of Mike Unger's staff had stayed on with him at the Manchester Evening News' offices. The very nature of the vocation of journalism was fed by a desire to report news, so the police officer who had come here earlier, asking these enthusiastic news people to abandon ship had grossly under-estimated the motivation and tenacity of the MEN's journalists.

Now that the bomb had gone off, Mike realised that he had made the right decision to stay in the office. His calculations had been proved correct. The buildings which stood between his building on Deansgate and the bomb's location, had shielded the MEN offices from any serious damage from the after-shock. Only a few windows had been cracked – but in the grand scheme of things, the newspaper's offices had got away with it where other buildings, much further away than this one, hadn't been so lucky.

Mike's team of photographers were out on the streets of Manchester right now, capturing the raw, honest images of a city in crisis. Half of his team of junior reporters were busy on the phones, trying to get the facts from the official sources. These sources included the police, the army, the fire brigade, the ambulance stations and hospitals. The other half of the reporting team were out on the streets of the city-centre, interviewing eye-witnesses and collecting first hand-reports on the event and building up a picture of those areas worst affected.

A number of Mike's staff had followed the police advice to evacuate and nobody had any problem with that, it was a decision which was respected completely. The staff that had opted to stay put had done so because in all honesty - they were quite excited by the prospect of covering a story of this nature. After all, the evacuation of Manchester on the busiest shopping day of the week was a major story in itself and the M.E.N. had a second edition to publish. What followed was turning out to be a much bigger story.

The copy for the first edition of the popular newspaper had almost been complete when the policeman had visited the famous black-brick offices at around 10am. The bulk of each day's first edition was usually written the previous afternoon and was headed to the printing presses by 11am. It was available for sale from 12 noon. The second edition was generally a revised version of the first edition which had some more up-to-date news. The second edition was usually printed by 1.30pm. It was at this time that the well-oiled job of distributing it to the region's newsagents and street vendors became the daily challenge that kept the MEN's journalists and printers adrenaline pumping.

Today's second edition was going to be late, there were no two ways about it, so Mike decided that they were going to cancel the second edition, and would be running a "Special Edition" which would need to have been printed by 4pm at the latest, and would have an additional 100,000 copies printed. A number of phone calls had to be made to various departments to let them know about this decision.

This was going to be a big job, which only gave Mike and his skeleton crew of reporters until 3pm to come up with a decent account of what had just taken place in Manchester, packed full with photographs, eye-witness accounts, factual reports on casualties and fatalities along with reaction from key spokespeople from the city, such as Richard Leese, the Leader of Manchester City Council and would also, hopefully, include a few words from John Major, the Prime Minister. There was a lot to achieve in little over three hours.

But the monumental task ahead didn't phase Mike Unger or any of his team members, they were feeling excited by the challenge which lay ahead. They also felt angry, shocked and apprehensive about what awful news was likely to be included. One thing was for certain though, the award-winning newspaper would be providing a first-class account of the events which were currently unfolding in the centre of Manchester, come what may.

11:34am

"And that concludes the fastest wedding ceremony that I have ever overseen, in a career spanning thirty-two years! Franklyn, you may kiss your wife, but very briefly." The registrar looked relieved that this was done, finally. It was time to get the hell out of here.

The audience applauded enthusiastically as Franklyn and Amanda shared their first kiss as husband and wife. This moment looked to have been in serious jeopardy for the past couple of hours and it came as a huge relief to everybody that the ceremony had gone ahead, especially as the honey-moon plane to Florida was leaving in a few hours.

The mood amongst the guests was tense, but vaguely excited too. It might have been a bit of a bodge-job of a wedding, but at least it was going to make an interesting wedding story that the couple would be able to talk about for years to come. The worst wedding stories are the ones where everything goes perfectly, as Amanda's dad had been saying all morning, since the Bride had been getting ready and the guy on the radio started saying that Manchester was closed.

"Normally we would now be writing out the marriage certificate, but I'm afraid that under the circumstances, we will not have the opportunity to do this today. So, may I now ask you all to leave as quickly as possible, and follow the directions of the police officers who are waiting outside the building. Franklyn, Amanda, I wish you both a long and happy life together. Congratulations."

Despite the sign which clearly stated that confetti was not permitted to be thrown inside the building, under any circumstances, one or two of the guests decided to flaunt the rule this time, and chucked a few handfuls at the beaming couple as they walked hand-in-hand past them towards the doors.

"Right, everyone," said Amanda's dad as the newly-weds left. "Safe travels back to the Working Men's Club, the party started half-an-hour ago and the DJ is charging by the hour so let's get a bloody shift on!"

In what was now being widely accepted as the weirdest wedding of all time, the guests just got on with it and raced out of the register office and headed in the direction that the police officers were pointing them in as they reached the bottom of the steps. It was odd not to stop outside and pose for wedding photos, but the photographer had already made a run for it before the couple had even gone in to take their vows, so it wasn't a major shock. Everybody just ran away from the Register Office as quickly as they could.

Amanda looked scared as she ran down the road, hand-in-hand with her little sister, six-year-old Lucy, who'd been so excited about this day for months, and her important job as the chief bridesmaid. Franklyn was running by the side of them, clutching the wedding bouquet, unsure of where they were headed or how to get back to their wedding cars, wherever they might be.

The three of them were running directly towards a photographer, who was standing in the middle of the road taking snaps. The sun was still beating down relentlessly and the streets were filled with people heading in the same direction. The photographer was still clicking on his camera, rooted to the spot as the wedding party got nearer. Amanda with her brilliant white wedding veil and dress with white tights and high-heel shoes, Lucy looking scared but adorable in her tiny bridesmaid dress with flowers in her hair and Franklyn, clutching the flowers, smartly dressed in a stunning grey suit. Dozens of people on all sides of the street were staring at them, wondering why there was a bride, a groom and a bridesmaid running around in the middle of all this chaos.

"Well, at least there's going to be one photo from my big day!" Said Amanda as she hurried past.

11:35am

Dave Marsh was standing outside Longridge House, covered in blood. His fire-fighter's uniform, his radio and his hands were completely covered in Barbara Welch's blood and he was becoming increasingly concerned about this poor lady's injuries.

"Control, come in over." He barked into his radio.

"Control receiving over."

"It's Dave Marsh, at Longridge House. I need to know where my ambulance is, I've got a lady with critical injuries here. She's dying right in front of us. Over."

"Received. The ambulance service are aware and you have a priority shout, over."

"I need them here now or we're going to have to take her in an appliance to the MRI."

Barbara Welch was several metres away from Dave, being looked after by two fire-fighters, but there was frustratingly little they could do to help her due to the complex nature of her facial injuries. She needed a blood transfusion and surgery, and she needed it urgently.

"Just checking on that now, standby. Over."

The radio static seemed to last forever, but eventually the radio beeped and the controller's voice came back on Dave's blood-spattered radio.

"Control to Dave, over."

"Receiving."

"There's an ambulance waiting to collect on Cannon Street, but it can't get through, the crew are reporting that half of the Arndale Centre facade is blocking the road. Can you get the patient to the vehicle? It is reserved for your job and the crew are expecting you. Over."

Dave looked up the road and saw the ambulance, about a hundred or so metres away, close to the Arndale Bus Station entrance. The walls and debris which had been blown off the Arndale Centre's structure were completely blocking the road, gigantic panels of the hated mustard and caramel wall-tiles had fallen from both sides of the centre, along with the steel cladding and other building materials such as breeze-blocks and drain-pipe systems. It wasn't ideal that Barbara would have to be carried that distance, beneath numerous vulnerable, hanging objects, but Dave considered the lack of alternative options.

"Right, lads, look behind all that rubble on Cannon Street - that's Barbara's ambulance. We need to take her to it."

As two of Dave's officers set off carrying Barbara Welch to her ambulance using the two-person arm-carry method, another team of fire-fighters were emerging out of Longridge House towards him, with another severely injured worker who was losing a lot of blood.

John Hogan had been working on the same floor as Barbara Welch and had also taken a direct hit from the flying debris. He was being carried out of the building by fire-officers Martin Sykes and Ian Ainsworth, he was semi-conscious with visibly-severe face and jaw injuries, as well as wounds to his upper torso. An ambulance had been called whilst the victim was still being tended to on the second-floor. Once again, the hunt for an ambulance to ferry this violently injured man was about to start.

The rescue teams were becoming increasingly frustrated by reports that ambulances were flying off to Casualty departments with walking-wounded cases, whilst there were no crews available for people like John, who had far greater and more concerning injuries such as his jaw hanging off the side of his face. But this was no time to get distracted about things like this, complaining or moaning wasn't going to change a thing. As Dave Marsh had done moments earlier, Martin Sykes just raised his radio to his mouth and asked what the position was.

11:36am

Michelle Hartshead had been standing in the garden of her new house in Hattersley, the huge council estate on the border of Tameside and Glossop, right on the eastern border of Greater Manchester, 10 miles away from the city-centre. She'd been enjoying the sunshine while she was planning on how to have the garden and where the baby's swing was going to go, when she'd felt a sudden, unannounced gush of heat and moisture between her legs.

"Aw shit!" She touched the crotch of her dungarees and almost fainted with shock as the realisation hit home. Her waters had just broken.

"Danny!" She shouted as she leant up against the wheelie-bin. "DANNY!"

Her boyfriend came to the back-door holding a paint-roller in his hand, he had a concerned look on his face. "What's up?"

Michelle pointed down at her bump.

"What?"

"My waters have popped you fucking spacker."

Danny's eyes widened as the reality of the situation caught up with him. "Shit! Wait there!"

Danny ran from the back door, raced through the house and slammed the front-door behind him as he dashed up the path and sprinted across the grass to the phone-box. His hands were trembling as he lifted the phone from its cradle, relieved to see that it looked as though it was in working order. The kids were always smashing this phone-box up and he'd been worried that when the day finally came, he'd find it was out-of-order. But everything was looking good. He pressed the nine button three-times and waited for the call to connect.

"Emergency service. Which service do you require?"

"Oh, erm... ambulance."

"Putting you through."

Another voice came on the line. "Greater Manchester Ambulance service."

"Hello, yes, what it is, my, my missus has... she's.. I think her waters have gone."

"Okay, thank you, how far gone is she?"

"Well, er, I'm not sure. But the baby's not due for about two week."

"Okay. And how far away are you from the nearest hospital?"

"Miles away."

"Can you make your way there?"

"Eh? What do you mean? Course I can't. That's why I'm phoning you!"

"It's just that we have no ambulances available at this time..."

"What do you mean? This is mad. My partner's waters have just popped."

"I know, but there's nothing I can do I'm afraid, all of our ambulances are engaged."

"Engaged... what are you on about? My missus is... her water's have gone..."

"You will need to get to hospital straight away, can you get a relative to drive you?"

"No..."

"You will have to get a taxi then."

"A taxi? That'll be at least seven quid! I haven't got that sort of money!"

"I'm really sorry. But we have no ambulances. I need you to find an alternative mode of transport and get her to your nearest hospital."

Danny just stared at the phone handset in his hand. What the hell was going on? He wondered as he placed the phone back on its cradle. He was gripped by a sudden panic as the seriousness of the situation caught up with him.

He threw the telephone box door open and sprinted back across the grass towards his house. He stopped as he reached the gate and turned on his heels, running to the house next door. He's seen the guy who lived there, he looked alright. Danny started pounding on the door.

A few seconds later, a middle-aged man answered the door.

"Hiya, alright? I'm Danny, I'm just moving in next door."

"Oh, nice to meet you, I'm Nigel..."

"Yeah, listen, sorry, I'm... I hate to ask, but my girlfriend's pregnant, her waters have just popped."

"Oh, right. Er. Bloody hell!"

"Yeah, I've just phoned for an ambulance but they said there aren't any!"

Nigel nodded, it looked as though he had a better idea of what was going on. "Yes, I've been listening to it on the radio. It's the bomb. In Manchester."

"What? No way? A bomb?"

"Yes, it was a bloody big one apparently, I'm pretty sure I heard it, it was about quarter of an hour ago. So, I'm guessing that's why there are no ambulances."

"Aw shit. I knew something like this was going to happen! They said I need to get a taxi but I've spent all my wages on decorating stuff for the new house. I've not got any money and my dad's in Birmingham, working."

"Oh, don't worry, I'll give you a lift, we'll soon have you down there." Nigel turned around and grabbed his car-keys off the hook.

"Aw, honestly, thanks a lot. That's really good of you! I'll go and get Michelle now."

Danny raced up Nigel's path and ran around into his own garden.

"Chelle! Chelle, come on, the guy next door is going to drive us. Where's your bag?"

11:37am

Tina Bradshaw was in a state of deep shock and was sitting in a passenger chair in the back of Les and Norman's ambulance, rocking back and forth.

"I've told you. She's going to be fine. Try not to worry." Norman was patting Tina's hand as Hayley lay on the stretcher-bed, looking sad and lost.

"I can't believe it. I just can't believe it!" Said Tina. She looked drained, all of the colour had gone from her face and she was a grey, pasty complexion. Her eyes were red from the tears. The emotions that she had encountered in the past twenty-minutes had ranged from utter shock, to heartbreak, with a large dose of relief and reassurance when Hayley had woken up and made a comment about missing Will Smith's segment on the TV.

"You okay, Hayley?" asked Norman as he checked the monitoring equipment which was keeping an eye on the young girl's blood-pressure and pulse-rate.

Hayley nodded silently.

"You've got a nasty bump on your head, but none of these cuts are very deep. You were lucky, if you'd been stood a few metres further away from the window, the cuts would be very serious. I bet your head's killing. But you're alright. You'll live."

"I can't believe it!" Repeated Tina. "I was literally stood a foot away from her when it happened. Why wasn't I knocked off my feet?"

Norman didn't reply, he just listened and nodded sympathetically. He was used to dealing with people who were suffering from shock. Tina Bradshaw was suffering quite badly, her mind was stuck in that awful, distressing moment that her whole world had come crashing down and Norman knew that she would be reliving it over-and-over again for a few hours more, if not days and weeks. But he was glad that it was just shock that she had to deal with right now, and not the grief of losing her child.

"Okay, nearly there. How are we all doing?" Shouted

Les from the front of the ambulance.

"All good back here, Hayley's a little superstar. She's more bothered about missing Swap Shop." Norman looked at the young girl and smiled affectionately.

"It's Live and Kicking." Said the youngster.

"Well, it used to be called Swap Shop when my ones watched it. Anyway, do you want the good news or the good news?"

"Good news!"

"Okay, well, the good news is, you're the first patient to arrive here, so you'll be the first to be treated. And then you can get on your way and watch Swap Shop."

"I can't believe it!" Said Tina.

"Mum, stop going on with yourself. I'm fine. Have you got dad's pressies?"

"Eh? No, erm... no. I don't know. We've left them." Tina looked confused, as though she had no recollection of the events before the bomb had gone off.

True to form, Hayley huffed and looked moodily at the ceiling of the vehicle. It was clear to Norman, and to Tina that she had absolutely no concept of how unimportant her dad's bag of Father's Day presents was in the moments leading to her coming round and being rushed into the back of this ambulance. She just looked annoyed.

"I can ask my bosses if we can go back and pick your shopping up!" Said Norman with a gentle smile. "But they'll definitely say no!"

"Alright, we're just pulling in." Said Les as the ambulance stopped and the hand-brake was pulled on. "Let's move it Norman, we've got another shout."

11:42am

From attending the scene of the lifeless mannequins, Miller and Cleggy had been sent to assist with the first-aid efforts which were taking place around the back of the Corn Exchange area. Several triage stations had been hastily set up by fire officers, paramedics and police officers at numerous points around the areas that the casualties had congregated. A number of ambulance staff were assessing people's injuries and deciding which person needed urgent care, and which of them would be able to wait a little longer for an ambulance.

On top of the familiar flying-glass wounds, there were a number of other injuries caused by the bomb, particularly around flying debris and the subsequent panic which ensued, causing hundreds of injuries which ranged dramatically in nature. From some really nasty eye injuries caused by the flying glass and debris objects, to sprains and twists and broken bones, suffered by people of all ages, from youngsters to pensioners.

Staff from nearby shops and restaurants had brought all of their chairs out onto the streets, offering them to the people who were waiting to be seen by the paramedics.

"So, what's the system here?" Asked Miller of the nearest paramedic.

"Sorry?" He asked as he cut a piece of bandage.

"You've got two rows of seats out. I can't help thinking that there's a system?"

"Oh, right, yes, well it's a system of sorts. The people on this side of the pavement are going to be alright waiting for an ambulance. The people on these seats are in need of one much sooner."

To Miller and Cleggy, it all seemed quite ruthless and pitiless. But that wasn't their concern, they'd been sent here to help.

"Is there anything we can do to help?" Asked Cleggy.

"Erm, well, I'm not sure really."

"We've been ordered here to help with first-aid," said Miller, abruptly. He was quite frustrated that the area he policed every day had just been blown apart and there didn't seem to be any requirement for his or his partner's assistance at the time-being.

"We're coping," the man Miller was talking to nodded at the people who were being treated. Fire-fighters, police officers, shop staff and members of the public were all gathered around each of the people who were seated on the chairs, talking to them, reassuring them and tending to their injuries. "Listen, if you really want to help, there are forty people here who need to get to hospital, but who can't really justify taking priority of an ambulance at the present time. There's a similar amount at the triage point outside Victoria station. Anything you might be able to do to hurry that process along will be a great help." The paramedic returned his attention to the bandages that he was cutting up, in an attempt to make the limited supplies which were available, go a little further.

"Like what?" Asked Cleggy.

The paramedic looked like he was becoming sick of these two young PCs now. "Well, I don't know. How many people can you fit in a police van? Anyway, I've got to get on." With that, the ambulance man set off walking along the long row of seats, handing out the bandages he'd been cutting.

Cleggy looked at Miller. "Looks like we're at a loose-end on the day that there's more to do than any other day. It's a shit storm, isn't it? People don't know their arse from their elbow!"

Miller nodded quietly.

"What's up with you?"

"I'm thinking."

"What about?"

"North Manchester general, that's on the tram route to Bury, isn't it?"

"Yeah. It's not far from Crumpsall tram stop. It's about, I dunno, a five-minute walk."

"Well, there's a bloody tram there, doing naff all."

Miller's colleague laughed loudly. "What? You don't even know how to drive a tram! The sun's going to your head Andrew!"

"Ian! Don't be a pillock all your life. I'm not on about driving it am I? That's going to be your job!"

Miller's daft answer completely confused his colleague. "Oh, forget it. Come on." The two police constables began jogging past Manchester Cathedral, and through the waste-ground towards the railway station. The Metrolink tram which had been abandoned halfway across Corporation Street had inspired an idea. Now, Andy Miller just wanted to find a tram driver to see if this great big vehicle could be used as a make-shift ambulance. It was a mad idea, but it could work.

As they approached the grand entrance of Manchester's oldest serving railway station, both officers were visibly shocked by the scene which greeted them. In the middle of the the road, where the buses were normally parked nose to tail, a similar first-aid triage point had been constructed, almost identical to the one which the two officers had left near the Corn Exchange just a moment ago. Scores of people were being treated by ambulance staff and fire and rescue officers, as well as staff from the railway station. Some of the people being treated were suffering from serious cuts, whilst others were showing symptoms of shock. There were children and grandparents, all waiting to be seen by the medical staff and hopefully, allocated an ambulance soon.

The ornate cast-iron built glass canopy which surrounded the front of the building had been smashed to pieces. This fine Victorian feature of the railway station had been built to cover the pavement for the well-to-do people waiting for their horse and cart to arrive and take them on to their next destination. Today, all of the glass-work was lay on the floor. The thick, solid looking panes had managed to survive two world wars, but they hadn't been able to withstand the unforgiving force of the blast this morning. Most of the railway office windows above the canopy had been broken too, some with large holes in the panes of glass, but most of them had been completely blown out.

As they stepped carefully over the glass, they realised that things were a lot worse inside the railway station. The entire concourse floor was covered in fragments of glass. Both officers looked up and saw that the glass roof which covered the station had been blown out.

Worse still, as the PCs looked back down at the concourse, they saw pools of blood dotted everywhere.

"Jesus Christ." Said Miller, quietly.

"Andy, what are we doing here?" Asked Cleggy, after several seconds of eerie silence in this devastated place which was normally bustling with thousands of commuters, shoppers and tourists. Miller was about to answer, but was distracted by the sound of a single pane of glass falling down from the steelwork above. It made a menacing, echoing sound as it landed and broke up into hundreds of pieces.

"Let's get out of here," said Miller, nonchalantly.

Seeing the devastation inside this place really saddened Andy Miller. This had been his favourite place in the world when he was a boy. He'd glare up at the gigantic Victorian tile map of England's rail network for ages, before standing with his parents on the platform, excitedly watching as the enormous train came in, thirteen or fourteen carriages long, then it would slowly come to a stop and the place would be filled with the echoing noise of all the doors opening, people shouting and greeting their loved ones and the guard's whistle tooting it's mysterious tones. Dozens of railway staff would appear, pulling huge trolleys and containers full of mail and goods to load into the guard's van. At the front of all this, the deafening rattle and hum of the diesel engine was vibrating away, waiting to pull off again.

And then, as the sudden chaos of everything seemed to settle down a little, looking through the legs of all of the people, little Andrew Miller would see his grandparents standing there on the platform and he'd race along as fast as his little legs would take him, and then he'd be greeted with the best cuddles he'd ever known. A tear filled Andy Miller's eye as he walked out of this special place from his childhood. He couldn't believe the state that it was now in.

"Are you alright?" Asked Cleggy.

"Yeah. Got summat in my eye, bit of glass I think, it's out now. Come on."

"What are we doing anyway?"

"I thought we'd find a Metrolink driver. There's normally one stood out here having a smoke."

"Yeah, well. Today's not normal, is it?"

"No. You can say that again. I had no idea how bad it was here, though. Did you?"

"I heard something on the radio. You were busy bandaging that little kid's arm up at the time."

"I imagine that he's gone to hospital now?"

"Hopefully. Anyway, look. I thought you said you wanted a tram driver? Well I've found you one." Cleggy pointed in the direction of the first aiders. Sure enough, further down the road, crouched down on one knee was a young woman wearing the familiar Metrolink uniform, talking to a very distressed looking teenage girl.

"Top man. Nice one Cleggy." The two police officers began jogging across the road, which was littered with glass, building debris and lots of random items that had been dumped including bags of shopping, blood-soaked clothing and various pieces of emergency services kit such as stretchers, first-aid bags and an oxygen bottle. The whole scene looked like something out of a corny film, it was hard to take in.

"Listen, you distract the girl and I'll talk to the driver," said Miller as they approached.

Cleggy launched straight into it, using his familiar greeting which he thought was funny. "Hello hello hello. What's happened to you?"

The girl looked up at Cleggy and fresh tears began pouring from her eyes.

"She can't find her mum and dad. She's getting really worked up." The tram driver was trying her best to calm the young lass down. "I've told you darling, they'll turn up in a minute."

"What's your name love?" Asked Miller.

"Natalie."

"Well listen Natalie, if you give your details to my colleague, your name and address and everything, we'll put a shout out on the police radio and we'll soon find your parents. Does that sound okay?"

Natalie nodded frantically, as more tears poured down her sun-burnt face.

Cleggy knelt down beside the teenager and took his note-book out of his pocket. As he did so, Miller tapped the tram driver on her shoulder.

"Have you got a minute?"

"Yeah, sure."

Miller gestured her to move away from Natalie and walked a few paces onto the pavement.

"What's up, are they okay?"

"What. Who?"

"Is this about her mum and dad?" Asked the driver, she had a deeply concerned look on her face.

"Oh, right. No. No, nothing like that. I wanted to ask you something about the tram that's been abandoned in the middle of Corporation Street?"

"Oh, I see. Shit, I thought it was..."

"Is it your tram?"

"No, it's one of my colleagues. He was pulling out of the station and was forced to stop and evacuate the tram by a policeman. Another tram had just pulled into the station behind, so he had nowhere to go."

"Oh, okay, that makes sense. See the thing is, I was wondering how hard it would be to organise using that tram as transport to North Manchester General? There are more injured people than ambulances you see."

The tram driver looked as though she thought it was a good idea.

"Well, yes, I suppose it can be done. It'd need authorising by control though."

"How hard would that be?"

"Well, technically, not hard at all. We'd just need all the signallers to allow us through and any trams blocking the track would need shifting. None of that's particularly difficult, but it'll probably be a head-ache trying to get the right person to authorise it!"

Miller nodded sympathetically. He knew all too well how much red-tape existed in these types of organisations. The police service was no different.

"Alright, well, if I get my superiors to sort it with your

superiors, what would be involved?"

"Well, nowt really at my end. Just load the tram up with the people and I'll drive it."

"Brilliant. Is there any step-ladders or anything, to get people up to the doors?"

"Yes, we have some on board, for emergencies like. But they're not ideal. They're pretty steep. We could do with something a bit better than that."

"I'm sure we can work something out. Right, give me a couple of minutes."

Miller raised his radio to his mouth and began relaying his idea to control. He asked them to get the Chief Inspector to authorise it with Metrolink as soon as possible and ended the conversation by announcing that he was about to start bringing the less severely injured people to the tram.

"Okay, standby. Over."

Miller returned his gaze to the tram driver. "Sorted. Just waiting for the big cheeses to agree to it. Nice one. I'm Andy by the way."

"Helen." She held her hand out for a shake. "I wish I could say it was nice to meet you."

"I know. I can't take it all in."

"You know what really pisses me off though?" Helen suddenly had an angry look on her face.

"What?"

"The fucking Irish."

Miller laughed. It seemed completely inappropriate under the circumstances, but the way that Helen had said it had really tickled him.

11:45am

WPC Karen Ellis was driving into Manchester, stunned by how quiet the roads were, whilst feeling anxious about what she was likely to be involved with once she reached the city-centre. She was listening to the radio, the local station Key 103 was taking calls from listeners who were describing what was going on. To Karen Ellis's ears, it sounded as though all hell had broken loose.

The roads were eerily quiet on the approach to the city, it felt as though she was going in for an early Sunday shift, there was literally nothing moving on the roads and there were no pedestrians around. She felt spooked by the strangeness of it all and noticed that her arms had goose-bumps. But as she got closer to town, she began to see the queues of cars, buses and vans which had all been abandoned on the outskirts of the city-centre, parked half on the road, half on the pavements. Buses were sitting there on the tarmac, their drivers all sitting on the grass verges chatting and sun-bathing.

Soon, she met with the first police road-block at the Mancunian Way. Luckily, she recognised the officer, he worked at Bootle Street station too. He waved her through as he realised who she was, but she slowed her Mini Metro down as she reached him and put the hand-brake on.

"Alright Mike, what's happening?"

"What, you mean you haven't heard?"

"Yeah. But, only what they're saying on Piccadilly. I'm on nights, just got phoned in by some woman at Chester House."

"Yeah, quite a few officers have been through already. It's pandemonium apparently, the whole of Corporation Street has gone. It wasn't an ordinary bomb, that's for sure. There's talk that the Arndale is ready for collapsing."

"Bloody hell! Seriously? Anybody killed?"

"Not yet, but it's still early doors. The building where the bomb went off had forty office workers inside at the time. The fire brigade are in there now trying to rescue survivors. But it's not looking good. They are expecting about ten fatalities so far, I'm told."

"Oh God." Karen suddenly felt sick as her adrenaline surged.

"Anyway, I won't keep you, I know they need more bodies for getting the rest of the punters out of town, they're all standing around gawping apparently."

"Right, okay Mike. Cheers."

Ellis put her foot down on the accelerator and set off for the last half-mile of her journey, gripped by an awful, panicking feeling. This did not sound like it was going to end well.

A couple of minutes later, Ellis found herself trapped by the emergency services vehicles ahead. They were all here, police cars and vans from every division, dozens of ambulances and fire engines, most of which were abandoned, their doors left wide-open as the emergency services personnel had dashed off to their jobs. Ellis pulled her car up onto the pavement and parked it up outside the entrance to a shop, she didn't want it to become an obstacle for any other emergency vehicles who would be trying to get in or out of this part of Manchester. After locking up the car, she started running towards Bootle Street.

Ellis was dazed by the scenes as she ran, there were so many people covered in blood, one old lady was being seen to by paramedics. She had a white blouse on, which was bright red on the back, blood was still pouring from a deep gash on the top of her head.

The blood was everywhere, on every pavement, up the walls. If it wasn't blood, it was millions of shards of broken glass, everywhere. The people were all really quiet though, they were comforting one another, or helping with first aid. Everybody looked shocked and out of it, even the police officers and the ambulance staff, they were all wearing looks of complete disbelief on their faces. The only sound that Ellis could hear was the ear-piecing shrill of burglar alarms coming from all the shops and offices, and then, bizarrely, loud music coming from some of the shops, their CD players still playing the feel-good music that's pumped out in a cynical attempt to encourage customers to part with a bit more money. The closer Ellis got to her destination, the more she noticed that the glass from the windows were all gone. It was hard to miss as the pavements were covered in the stuff, making it really difficult to run on.

"What the actual hell is this?" Said Ellis as she finally reached the steps of Bootle Street police station, the place she'd left just under six hours ago, when everything had been perfectly fine around here.

Miller was standing with Helen the tram driver, Cleggy and Natalie. Cleggy had done a great job of settling the teenager down and reassuring her. She was smiling and laughing at his stupid comments now, her fears for her parents safety had clearly been pacified.

"Control to 616."

"616 receiving, over."

"That request to the Chief Inspector has been agreed. The tram driver just needs to radio Metrolink control for official clearance and instructions. Over."

"Oh, that's brilliant. Thank you. Over."

"Received. Oh and Andy, the Chief Inspector said that you're a jolly good chap. Over."

Miller smiled widely. That was a good compliment to receive. "Received and understood. Over." He turned to Helen, still beaming at that rather vintage compliment from the main man at Bootle Street nick. "Right, we're in business. You just have to talk to your control room apparently."

"Okay, that's good news."

"How will you do that?"

"I'll use the radio in the cab." The tram driver seemed quite excited that she was getting the opportunity to help out in some way.

"Excellent. You go and do that and myself and my colleague will go and start gathering the patients."

Helen nodded and began jogging towards the abandoned tram which was just around the corner

"One sec Andy, I'm just waiting for control to tell me where the lost relatives meeting point is. For Natalie."

"Right. No problem, I'll just go and tell these what's happening."

Miller stepped past the dozens of injured people who were sitting on the kerb, or on chairs which had been provided by the railway station's buffet bar staff. The drops of blood all over the road and the pavement troubled him greatly. He'd seen so much spilled blood today, it wasn't something that he could get used to. He began explaining the situation regarding the tram to the paramedic who looked as though he was in charge of running this haphazard, impromptu first-aid operation.

"That sounds like a great idea. It'll take a lot of pressure off the ambulances. We're not coping at all."

"Okay, well, start sending the walking wounded to the tram, it's just around the corner. They'll have to board outside the station, there's no way we can let anybody inside the station, the glass is half a foot deep on the floor, and its still falling down every time there's a breeze."

"No problem."

"One last thing. The walk from the tram-stop at Crumpsall is about five hundred metres to the Casualty department. So, we can only take people who are able to walk that distance. Can you make sure that anybody who opts to come with us is fully aware?"

"Understood. Leave it with me. I'll start sending them round."

"Cheers." Miller turned and tapped the first fire-officer that he bumped into amongst the dozens of first-aid helpers.

"Alright, I need a favour."

"Go on," said the fireman, without moving his eyes from the man whose leg he was bandaging.

"We've got a tram leaving for the hospital, it'll take a bit of pressure off the ambulance staff."

"Okay?"

"Trouble is, it's not in the station, it's parked half-way across Corporation Street. The doors are about a metre off the floor. Do you think your guys could bodge some sort of a step together?"

"Yeah, can't see that being a problem. There's plenty of stuff lying about to knock something together." The fire-man hadn't taken his eyes off the dressing that he was applying. "Just let me finish this and I'll get a few of the lads together."

"Brilliant. Thanks very much."

"No problem at all."

Miller turned and headed back to Cleggy. He was using his hands to explain to Natalie where the meeting point for missing relatives was.

"And then if you just walk round the back of there you'll be back at Piccadilly. Everybody who has become separated from relatives are meeting just by the Kodak shop. I'm sure you'll find them there."

"Thank you," said Natalie as she headed off. Cleggy had done a great job of calming her down and she looked a lot more composed as she walked purposefully in the direction that she'd been sent.

11:47am

18 year-olds Dale Robson and Brent Casey had come into Manchester today to see if they could find a bit of work on one of the market stalls around Tib Street, or some casual work at the Arndale Market. There was usually plenty of cash-in-hand work to be found around the area on a Saturday, doing all the shitty jobs that the traders couldn't be bothered doing themselves, like loading or unloading vans or emptying bins or just watching the stall for a bit while the owners had a break.

It wasn't great money, but it was better than nothing, and well worth the trip into town to see if anything was going. A good day could be worth a tenner, maybe even fifteen quid. The best ever had been a full day on a fruit and veg stall which had paid the lads twenty-five quid each. But that had been a one-off as the usual staff had been off that day and Dale and Brent had just been in the right place at the right time. As the two lads were unemployed at the moment, it was always worth the bus fare to see if anything was going.

It had started out as a pretty miserable day for the pair who'd been best mates since primary school. Everybody had been evacuated from the main shops in the Arndale and the underground market, so there was absolutely no chance of any work going. After an hour or so of sun-bathing with all the other people in Piccadilly Gardens, the two lads gave up on the prospect of making a few quid and had set off for home, but soon realised that there were no buses running.

Wythenshawe, the district where they live is made up of the biggest council estate in Europe, right next to Manchester Airport. It is an area with very few jobs going, and any that are advertised are very rarely given to young lads off the estate. As a result these young men had to travel to find casual bits of work, which they tended to do in Manchester on a Saturday, at Stockport Market on a Thursday and sometimes they'd get some work at Ashton market on a Friday, but it was hit and miss there. The rest of the time, they just hung about on the estate, dreaming of better days and smashing up bus shelters.

Wythenshawe is ten miles away from Manchester, and

neither Dale nor Brent were prepared to even contemplate walking back there. They had little choice but to stay put in Manchester and see what happened, confident that the buses would soon be running again. But then the bomb had gone off and everything had become even more mental.

After walking around the permitted areas around the city centre for half an hour, being turned away at the police cordon lines, the two youths were becoming quite irritable. Here they were, stuck in town with no money and with no prospects of finding any work – and now there was no way out of the place. They were trapped.

After being sent back to wait at Piccadilly Gardens, the two friends had become restless and began arguing amongst themselves, mainly down to the circumstances of their wrecked day but also because they were both getting hungry and thirsty.

"Absolute fucking bobbins this! We should have gone Ashton, I'm telling you." Said Brent, despondently.

Dale decided it was time to change the subject from moaning about the situation or squabbling about how to get home.

"Did you notice how all the doors were all still open in the Arndale?"

"No." Brent was sitting on the floor, pulling at the grass. He was in a shitty mood and he didn't seem remotely interested in his friend's observations.

"I did, when we was walking past and that copper shouted at us and sent us back here."

Brent didn't say anything.

"So if the Arndale's still open, but everyone has been kicked out, I reckon we should go in Allsports and take any pair of trainers we wanted."

Brent glanced up from the grass that he'd been picking at and looked across at his mate.

"Nobody would ever know! We could put them on in the shop and leave ours in the box. Even if we got found in there, we could just say we were looking for our cat."

Brent laughed loudly at his friend's typically mental comment.

"What you laughing at? They wouldn't think we've robbed our trainers. Would they? Anyway, even if they did, they'd be too busy to fuck about trying to prove it."

This idea definitely interested Dale's friend, his face had really come to life. "Reckon?"

"Telling you! You heard that bomb go off, it's taken half of town with it. I don't think anybody is going to give a fuck if we got a new pair of trainers out of it!"

"And a new tracky?"

"Ten new trackies if we want, we could sell 'em when we get home. We could take anything we want out of there and no-one will ever know!"

"Fucking hell! We could, couldn't we?"

Suddenly, the low mood had switched dramatically to raw excitement.

"How are we going to get in though?"

"Dunno. Just need to sneak down the back of Debenhams, wait 'til a copper's looking the other way and then peg it across the road. It'll be a piece of piss. This is our day mate!"

"Hey, fucking hell! We could get a pair of twelve-tens as well!"

The pure excitement at the prospect of having the Arndale Centre to themselves, to be able to help themselves to literally anything they wanted in there was making their imaginations run away. The "twelve-tens" comment was in reference to the Technics turntables which they had always dreamed of owning a pair of some day. But they cost £330 each, so the likelihood of ever getting some, even second-hand ones, had always seemed very remote. But not today. Anything seemed possible.

Dale leapt to his feet. "Come on Brent. It's show-time!"

"Wait!"

"What? What's up?"

"What if we get caught?"

"Who fucking cares?"

"Well, we at least need to agree on the cat's name."

11:50am

Miller and Cleggy were walking slowly past Manchester Cathedral with twenty-seven "walking-wounded" victims of the bomb. These people covered all age-groups, from small toddlers with facial cuts from flying glass, to pensioners with concussion from falling masonry. As things currently stood, they all needed to be seen by the hospital staff, but the waiting times for an ambulance to transport them to a Casualty department was impossible to forecast as the people with life-threatening injuries had naturally taken priority.

It wasn't ideal, commandeering a tram as transport, but it would certainly take the heat off the Ambulance service whilst ensuring that these people were in the correct place for treatment.

The mood amongst the injured people was quite flat, most of them were still in a deep state of shock, the sense of mortality that an event such as this stirs up within people is always very sobering. These people had set off this morning with heads full of tasks to do, purchases to make and plans to carry-out and were now wandering in a dazed line of sad, emotionally drained and injured people towards the back-end of Manchester Victoria. It had been a stark reminder to everybody that you just don't know what life has in store for you.

As they reached the tram, it was already looking quite full. Firemen were standing at the doors, two inside and two on the ground, helping people on board using a make-shift platform that they had constructed from a couple of Manchester Evening News vender stands as well as various bits of debris from the blast. Most of the pieces of wood, plastic, shop signs and bricks had been lying on the ground just yards from the tram. It was quite an impressive construction, under the circumstances.

"Hey, the A Team would be happy with that!" Said Miller cheerfully as he inspected the handy-work.

"I ain't getting' on no plane, fool!" Said one of the fire-men.

"Come on."

"Up you come. Gently does it."

The fire-officers were being cheerful and welcoming to the injured people as they helped the frightened looking passengers make their way on board. Once the last person from Miller and Cleggy's group had boarded, the tram was almost full, as a similar amount of people who'd been receiving triage care at Victoria had already boarded whilst the two PCs were guiding the other group from Deansgate.

"Are we going with them?" Asked Cleggy.

"I don't know. Haven't thought about it."

"Well they might need someone with them. In case there's a problem."

Miller lifted his radio. "616 to control. Over."

"Control receiving, over."

"Yes, we've loaded the tram, it's full now and ready to depart. We're just wondering if we are going along with them? Over."

"Standby. Over."

Miller stepped up onto the tram and walked through the carriage to the cab, where Helen was sitting with the power on, waiting to take the vehicle on its unusual outing.

"Everything set?"

"Oh, hiya, yes, I'm pretty shocked that it's all gone to plan. I might ask your boss to ring up when they forget to pay me my over-time. I've never known Metrolink to respond to anything so quickly!"

"Ah, it's different when it's the Chief Inspector. He's a man who gets things done."

"You can say that again."

Miller's radio burst into life in his hand. "Control to 616. Permission granted to proceed to the hospital. Can you confirm that the tram is coming back to the city-centre or will you require transport from NMGH? Over."

Miller turned to Helen. "Is that okay?"

"What? You want a lift back?"

"Wouldn't mind. Unless you've got anything better to do?"

Helen rolled her eyes dramatically. "You're a bit cheeky."

"Please?"

"Go on then!"

Miller smiled and lifted the radio handset back to his mouth. "616 to control. The Metrolink driver can bring us back. Over."

Miller finished his radio conversation while Helen started her own, informing her control room that the special service was required for a return trip and that the signal people needed to authorise the extra journey. Miller laughed as the lady in the control room agreed to the request, the grumpiness in her voice really tickled him.

"Bloody hell. I bet she's a good laugh at parties!"

"Who, Beryl? You're joking aren't you? She's got a face like a smacked-arse."

"I know, I can tell. Right, well... oh, just wait a sec!" Miller bounded out of the tram's cab, ran through the carriage and across to the doors. He couldn't believe his eyes.

"What the hell are you doing here?"

Standing beside Cleggy and two fire-men, next to the make-shift platform was his colleague, WPC Karen Ellis.

"Alright? I was just telling Cleggy. Sergeant Harris told me to come and assist you two morons. He said you'll need some support!" Ellis smiled widely.

"How come you're here though?"

"Got called in! Most of the night-shift are back in now, and afternoons have been called in early."

"Right, well, we're taking these to Crumpsall hospital, so you'd better jump on board. You too Cleggy, come on."

Miller held out his hand and helped his colleagues onto the tram as the two fire and rescue officers stepped down and assisted the other two in dismantling the platform. Miller walked back along the carriage to the cab and tapped on the window to let Helen know that it was time to close the doors and get going.

Almost every seat inside the two carriages was occupied by somebody with a bandage on them. They were covering head injuries, backs, stomachs, arms and legs. Some of the bandages were weeping blood. The mood on the tram was extremely low, several of the passengers were crying. Ellis decided to try and pacify them as the tram began pulling away, heading into Victoria station.

Most of the passengers were distracted from their injuries as the tram crunched over the glass that was covering the tracks, they were mesmerised by this exclusive look at the damage inside the railway station, caused by hundreds of tons of glass that had been thrown from the gigantic roof and dispersed right across the station's concourse.

Helen wasn't happy with the glass popping and exploding under the wheels, but she could see that there was only ten more metres of the debris covered tracks and then the tram would be outside the previously covered section of the station. She used the slowest speed as the crunching and banging continued beneath the wheels. Within moments, the unnerving sound ceased and the vehicle started speeding up and began making some progress along the tracks towards Cheetham Hill.

Miller, Cleggy and Ellis were all spending the time talking to passengers, trying to reassure them that everything was going to be okay and trying their level best to be as positive as possible. But it wasn't easy, the people on board were feeling wretched, they were in shock, in pain, many of them were also suffering the discomfort of sun-burn and dehydration. It was a miserable experience for all concerned, including Helen who was worried that she might have caused some damage to the tram after proceeding over the obstructions on the tramway.

Cleggy was kneeling down, holding the hand of an old lady who couldn't stop crying. She never went into town, she'd explained, she always found it too busy. But for some reason, because of the nice weather, she'd decided to catch the bus and have a look around C&A.

"I'm 81. I'm too old for all this kerfuffle!" She announced, as though she imagined that this was just a normal day in the city.

"81? Is that all? I had you at fifty-six. Fifty-seven, tops!"

"Get away with you!" Said the lady, smiling for the first time, but with tears still streaming down her face.

11.59am

"972 to control, come in over."

"Control receiving, over."

"Yes, I'm just guarding the cordon at the top of Market Street, at the junction with High Street and I've just seen two young males running into The Arndale Centre. Have we got a dog unit in the area?"

"Received and understood. I'll check availability of a dog handler. Standby, over."

The policeman at the cordon line had been talking to another officer who'd been standing outside Debenhams when he saw two youths leg it across the road and into the shopping centre out of the corner of his eye. He had sprinted the twenty-five-metre distance to the High Street doors but there was no sign of them when he'd got there. His first instinct was to rush inside and find them and try and get to the bottom of what they were doing. But his orders had been to guard the top of Market Street which was now a crime scene and if he did go chasing two scallies into the Arndale, he'd be facing disciplinary action for a variety of offences, not least entering a dangerous building without permission or back-up.

"Control to 972, dog unit is en-route, ETA five minutes, over."

"Received. Thanks very much. Over and out."

*****

Inside the Arndale Centre, the damage was plain to see everywhere. At the eastern end of the shopping centre, on High Street, which was the furthest point away from the bomb, there were broken windows and stock items had been thrown all around the retail units. Each step towards the western end of the complex revealed much more serious damage, as the tiled floors slowly became impossible to walk on due to the amount of glass, debris and shop fixtures, fittings and items which had been thrown and strewn in every direction.

There were only two people inside the vast shopping

complex, and they were laughing to one another. This was without doubt the best day ever for these two eighteen-year-old lads from Wythenshawe.

"It's fucking mad in here, isn't it?"

"Yeah, but let's not piss about. We're in now, so lets just go and raid Allsports and get the fuck out of here before someone comes."

"Shut up Dale! Who's gonna come in here? Look at the state of the place, it's totally fucked. No-one's coming in here now, they'll be worried it'll fall down on them!"

"I know, but I'm just saying. The sooner we get our shit, and get back out, the better."

Brent wasn't listening. He was walking into a shop.

"Here, what are you doing? Don't fuck about!"

"Shut up will you, chill out! I thought we were saying that we were looking for a cat if anybody caught us."

"Yeah, but what are we doing in here? C and A? It's where me nan buys her underskirts from."

"Watch." Brent walked over to the shop's till and pressed the "no sale" button. The till drawer opened, almost hitting him in the balls.

Both lads laughed loudly as Brent lifted a wad of five-pound and ten-pound notes out of the till drawer and waved them in the air.

"Fuckkk!" Dale's face was frozen in a state of disbelief and ecstasy.

"Don't stand there like a spaz, go and empty that one!"

"What do you do?"

"Just press the button that says no sale on it."

Dale did as instructed and the till drawer flew open, receiving another hearty laugh from the two youths. This was unbelievable.

"Stick it in all your pocket and go to the next one, leave the coins or your pants will fall down!"

The lads continued doing this at each of the eight tills. Within no time, their pockets couldn't fit anymore money in. Five-pound, ten-pound and twenty-pound notes had been shoved in, screwed up in balls. There was no more space left in their pockets.

The mood began to change between them quite quickly. The sense of adventure of coming into this smashed up shopping centre for a pair of trainers had changed to wonder when Brent had opened the first till. Now that they had emptied every till in the C&A store and they had literally nowhere to put any more cash, the mood was changing to panic, particularly as far as Dale was concerned. His heart was thumping harder than he had ever known it.

"Come on. Let's go."

"Where?"

"To get the fuck out of here. We've got grands here."

"Yes, and there's about fifty more shops in here you mong."

"Nah Brent, fuck that. Let's just go. We can get a taxi back home and then count all this money."

"Don't be a dick. We're never gonna get this chance again!"

"We haven't even got anywhere to put the money."

"Well we'll have to steal a fucking suitcase from Argos then won't we? Come on, don't be such a chicken-shit."

"Seriously, Brent. It's on top. Let's just go."

"You're losing it you Dale. Shit-bag! You know that if you steal five quid or five grand, it's still the same crime. So we might as well take every fucking penny in this place. Come on, this is the best day of our lives and you want to shit out. Don't be a yellow-belly-custard."

The pep talk seemed to have worked as Dale followed Brent out of the C&A store and back towards the main shopping arcade concourse. They both stopped as they reached the doors and peeped around a pillar to check that the coast was clear. There was nobody around. All that they could see were the flickering lights and the wreckage on the floor. There was a strange silence which seemed louder than the echoey sound of the noise outside, the police and ambulance sirens, car alarms, burglar alarms and the occasional helicopter noise above the building. But it was certain that there was nobody in here, the place was completely deserted.

"Come on, let's go in Tandy."

The lads were so carried away, it hadn't occurred to them that they were inside the building with the most surveillance cameras in Manchester. Dozens of CCTV cameras covered every fifty metre stretch of the Arndale Centre. It hadn't struck them that the C&A store was also heavily covered with the cameras, and they were walking around emptying the tills in hundreds of CCTV stills, their faces completely visible in every frame.

Inside Tandy, they were dismayed to see that the no sale button wasn't opening the till.

"Must be locked or summat."

"Leave it. There's plenty more tills in plenty more shops."

"Do you reckon they've got any twelve-tens?"

"Nah, they only sell the shit ones in here. Come on."

Dale followed Brent as they headed into the next store along this never-ending row of fully stocked shops and retail units. "Tight bastards, look they've locked the jewellers up!"

The jewellery shop which Dale was talking about was Ratners, the store which had once been Britain's most successful, until the chairman of the chain had described their stuff as "total crap" in ear-shot of a journalist a few years earlier. The shop had never been more successful until that point, with profits growing year-on-year. Nowadays, they store which was one of 250 across the UK was selling its stuff at a third of the price it had previously, despite Gerald Ratner, the man behind the fiasco resigning shortly after he'd made the comments.

"Why, were you going to get your mam some earrings?"

"Nah, was thinking I could have got her a gold necklace and a matching watch!" The two lads laughed enthusiastically and the laughter reverberated loudly around the gigantic, abandoned shopping centre.

"Come on, there's a birds clothes shop there, their tills will be bursting with cash, that's what they spend all their money on!"

"And make-up!"

"Yeah, what's a good make-up shop?"

"You should know."

"Shut up you prannet."

Inside the Dorothy Perkins store, the tills were opening without any problem. It was a magical moment, the wonder of it all was written across both of the teenager's faces.

"Grab a carrier bag and shove it all in."

"Nice one!"

Lost in their own world of all this free money and the sheer excitement at the ease of taking it all, Dale and Brent were oblivious of the police-officer who was walking in their direction through the shopping centre with his German Shepherd police dog, five-year-old Buster who was pulling keenly on his lead.

12.00pm

"This is BBC One. A news report now, from Moira Stewart."

The normal BBC output from the Queen's 70th birthday celebrations in London was being interrupted with the unsettling, black "News-Flash" screen, which appeared on the BBC network very rarely. But when it did, it was always to report bad news.

The famous newscaster, a familiar face on TV screens across the United Kingdom came into shot. Moira had a very serious look on her face as she began her news-flash report.

"Within the last hour, there has been an explosion in Manchester city centre. It follows a security alert earlier this morning. Police say that bomb disposal experts were working on a vehicle, when a device of some sort detonated. They say a coded warning had been received, but its not clear from whom. A number of people have been seriously injured, but as far as they're aware, there have been no fatalities. A number of people have received injuries from flying glass. It's understood that police were cordoning off an area around the Arndale Centre, a busy shopping area after receiving reports of a suspect car parked near a branch of Marks and Spencer, when there was a large explosion. We've just received these pictures of central Manchester."

The screen changed from the head and shoulders shot of Moira Stewart, to be replaced with video footage of the huge black cloud which had been billowing above the city centre just after the explosion, a number of office blocks and buildings were also in shot, demonstrating the enormity of the mushroom cloud in scale with the area. As other shots and angles appeared on screen, Moira continued with her report.

"Police are concerned that there may be other devices in the area. And we're joined now on the phone by Brendan Pittaway, who is at the scene. Brendan, what can you tell us?"

The eye-witness sounded very shocked and nervous as he began replying, the sound of a number of alarms and sirens made it quite hard to hear exactly what he was saying. A photograph of Manchester city centre appeared on the screen as he gave his account of the situation.

"Well what I can tell you is that from about a quarter past ten this morning, police were cordoning off a large portion of Manchester city centre having received a coded warning and after also becoming concerned about shopper's reports of a suspect car parked near Marks and Spencers on Cannon Street, which is right in the heart of Manchester's shopping area. About an hour after police had begun cordoning off the area, and evacuating buildings of people into the main centre of the city, there was a loud explosion. It could be heard right across the city-centre, buildings shook, windows shattered, the centre of the city where all the main office buildings are is now a sea of glass. Certain people have been injured, I myself have seen two people injured by flying glass, there have been hordes of ambulances ferrying people out of the centre. Certain people in basements were ordered to stay put and not move from those buildings when the explosion happened. We don't yet know if any of the bomb disposal officers who were working on the car when they explosion happened, have been injured, or how seriously people have been hurt."

Moira Stewart's voice interrupted the stressed sounding commentator. "Brendan, I take it that you are okay?"

"Perfectly okay. I was sat having a cup of tea when it happened, but certainly there are a great deal of people who will have been shocked by what's happened, people in floods of tears, others trying to get back to their buildings to see if any of their colleagues were hurt and make sure that everybody is okay. There's still a great deal of confusion in the city-centre, of course there are a great number of football fans in the centre today, for the Germany Russia game and they are also adding to the confusion because a great deal of them don't speak English and they are walking around trying to get around and are being forced away."

"Brendan, thank you so much for your report."

Moira Stewart's face reappeared on the screen. "We'll bring you more details in our next scheduled news, at one o'clock."

12:02pm

Buster was pulling strongly on his lead, his nose was twitching and he looked extremely alert and focused as he made his way through the Arndale Centre. His handler could tell that he was eager to be freed and allowed on his way to overpower some criminals. This was when Buster was at his happiest. The five-year-old German Shepherd was a total softy when he wasn't working. But the moment he was given the command, he could turn into a very vicious and frightening dog, and could switch back to being a placid, well-behaved, cuddle-loving softy again in a heart-beat. His attack prompt was switched on and off just like any command, such as sit or shake-a-paw.

Buster is one of Greater Manchester Police's 45 working police dogs, all of which live with their handlers. It is the force's policy that even in retirement, the PDs stay with their handlers, swapping a life of chasing criminals for a life of relaxation with their handlers once they'd got a bit too old for biting burglars and over-powering aggressive people or calming down a hostile crowd. Nobody answers back to a police dog when it is ready for a confrontation. Well, some people do but they never talk about it.

Police dogs are one of the British police's most valued assets in the never-ending fight against crime. They can sniff out money, drugs and people. They can alert their handlers to bombs, fire-arms and knives and their most useful ability is to chase criminals after they have run away from the scene of a crime, be that a burglary, running away from a stolen vehicle or an assault. By just picking up a scent from a crime scene, a police dog can trace the way that the criminal went and in most cases, find the place where they have gone to hide. They are so successful that all of the UK's police forces are constantly expanding their dog units and welcoming new PDs into the force each year.

Police Dogs are still a relatively new addition to the police service's armoury. Their introduction in the 1960s has never been taken for granted and most forces in the UK now employ the services of numerous specialist dogs that can work on very specific jobs, whether that's searching buildings for people or houses for cash, or drugs or any number of illegal items, including counterfeit currency.

The first time that dogs were used to support the work of police officers was during the infamous Jack the Ripper investigation in London towards the end of the last century. The search for the notorious killer was national news and the police service's consistent failure to catch "The Ripper" was creating some extremely negative headlines.

The Home Office were desperate to assist the police as best they could and to get the man responsible for the brutal deaths of 5 women in the East End of London between August and November 1888, off the streets and sent to the hang-man. Senior staff at the Home Office had heard about a man in Scarborough who trained Bloodhounds, and who had claimed that his dogs would be able to pick up the scent of the killer by examining the victim and the crime scene, and that they could then follow the direction that the killer had gone in and potentially take the police straight to the perpetrator of the shocking crimes.

This rather extraordinary claim was met with a great deal of cynicism from many people at the time. But none-the-less, the government were desperate to show that they were open-minded and determined to try anything to catch The Ripper and so, the man from Scarborough was instructed to board a train south with his Bloodhound dogs.

The newspapers made a great deal of the story, there was a mixture of fascination and downright pessimism about the fact that the police were relying on "dumb animals" as their best hope in catching a killer who stalked the streets of London in the dead of night. But Sir Charles Warren, who was the Commissioner of the Metropolitan Police, was leading the investigation into the Whitechapel Murders as they were known at the time, was extremely open-minded about the experiment. Sir Charles was full of hope that the Yorkshireman's dogs would live up to the incredible claims which had been made about them.

This may have been one of the first recorded examples

of dogs assisting the police with their work, but it was by no means the most successful. The experiment ended in total farce. One of the dogs bit Sir Charles, before both of them ran off and were lost in the fog on the streets of London. Police officers were sent out to try and find the animals, as journalists filed their newspaper reports, making as much of a mockery of the sorry tale as they possibly could.

Luckily, that early example of dogs assisting police wasn't the end of the story, and they have gone on to become the most valuable assets to the British police forces, responsible for detaining thousands of criminals every year, detecting millions of pounds of concealed drugs and cash as well as protecting the police officers at the scenes of serious crimes.

Today, in the heart of Manchester city-centre, Buster was becoming more and more eager with each step forward. The two lads that he and his handler had been sent here to locate weren't exactly trying to keep their presence quiet. Loud laughter was echoing all around the deserted, smashed up shopping centre and Buster was absolutely desperate to go and meet the people who were making such a din, his breathing was becoming extremely loud as the scent of his target filled his nostrils as strongly as fresh bread baking would tantalise a human's nostrils.

Buster's handler wasn't too keen to let him off his lead just yet. The glass and the debris which became more dense the further they walked looked like it could be a real hazard for Buster's delicate paws. The last thing the handler wanted was an injured dog. And judging by the sound of the two offenders, they appeared to be a couple of dickheads rather than a serious risk. Despite Buster's excitement to be free, the dog-handler decided that the best tactic would be to sneak up on them and simply use Buster's bark as the weapon today.

Each step on the glass was crunching loudly beneath the handler's boots and he was becoming increasingly concerned about the noise that he was making underfoot could quite easily give the game away. But he needn't have worried, as the two youths appeared right in front of him, laughing and joking as they looked triumphantly inside their carrier bag full of cash.

"Shit! Dibble!" Shouted Dale and he dropped the bag full of cash on the ground as he attempted to run, but his feet couldn't get a grip on the floor as the millions of pieces of shattered glass acted like a bag of marbles beneath his feet. Instead of getting the forward traction that he'd hoped for, Dale Robson just slipped spectacularly on the floor and collapsed in a heap on top of the particles of glass.

His partner in crime, Brent had managed to get a bit more purchase on the unsteady ground and had somehow succeeded in sprinting off, heading across the mall towards the Warner Brothers store and the Market Street exit. Buster was thrilled to be released from his handler's grasp and make chase.

As the dog barked his warning to Brent and raced behind him at three times the speed that the youth was travelling, the handler walked over towards Dale who was lay in a heap on the floor, covered in the fragments of glass which had led to his graceless downfall.

"Are you alright?" Asked the dog-handler. Dale didn't reply, he just stayed still and held his wrists up for the cuffs which were being held out in front of the police-officer.

The barking stopped suddenly, and the terrifying sound of Buster's aggressive woof was replaced by an ear-piercing scream. The blood-curdling shriek was coming from the lips of Brent Casey as the dog's teeth sunk in deep and clamped the teenager's calf, applying the required amount of pressure to ensure that the criminal stayed put and waited for rescue.

"Good lad Buster!" Shouted the dog-handler and the dog let go and stood guard over the screaming youth, with his tail wagging excitedly. He knew he was going to get a treat now.

"Can I have an ambulance and a custody van at the High Street entrance to The Arndale please? Two looters apprehended, one's been chewed up a bit by Buster. Over."

12:05pm

The Metrolink journey felt very bumpy today, people were moaning and grimacing as the tram swayed and clunked along the tracks on the Bury line. Considering that the tram system was only four years old, it all felt rather old and rickety.

"So, what's happened to you?" Asked Ellis as she sat down next to an elderly man who looked as though he was starting to get a bit worked up. His arm was in a sling and there were a number of cuts on his shoulder and his face.

"Something whacked me as I was trying to run away. They don't think its broken, but they want it x-rayed."

"Can you move your fingers?" Asked Ellis. She was no medic, but she did want to distract this old-boy from his misery, if only for a few minutes. She knew that he'd be facing a hell of a wait once they reached the hospital.

"Yes, I can move my fingers. I'll be alright."

"Well, we're nearly there now. Have you been in touch with your relatives to let them know that you're okay?"

"No, not yet. Do you think they'll let me use the phone at the hospital?"

"Yes, I'm sure they will. God, it's like an oven in here, isn't it?"

Ellis continued with her distraction tactics, as Miller and Cleggy passed the time with similar conversations with the sad looking people on board. There wasn't much smiling as the tram continued to judder and clank along the rails.

Gladly for all on board, it only took ten minutes to reach the tram stop at Crumpsall, the journey was speeded up today as it hadn't needed to stop at Queens Road or Abraham Moss on its way. Everybody, including the three police constables on board, were glad to hear the familiar squeak of the wheels as the vehicle pulled up at the platform at the former Lancashire and Yorkshire railway station. As modern as the new tram network was, it relied heavily on the Victorian infrastructure.

"Okay, ladies and gentlemen, can I have your attention please?" Miller was standing at the front of the tram. "We've got a five-minute walk ahead of us, myself and my colleagues will be walking with you all, so... well, let's go."

Hayley opened the doors and the passengers began limping off the tram and followed Cleggy who started making the climb up the ramp to Station Road, encouraging the walking-wounded to follow his lead.

It was something of a surreal spectacle for passers-by in Crumpsall, a suburban district which is four miles north of the city-centre. The sight of sixty people emerging from the Metrolink station, limping along towards the hospital covered in bandages and wearing slings and neck-braces was quite an extraordinary thing for the passing car drivers and pedestrians to witness.

It took ten minutes for Miller, Ellis and Cleggy to escort the walking-wounded to the Casualty department, a number of the group were elderly and were slow on their feet. As the enormous line of people got closer to North Manchester General, they saw that a number of the hospital staff had walked up the road to meet them. Some of them were pushing wheelchairs for anybody who might need one. It was a simple gesture, but it was one which gave the three police officers an enormous amount of pride in their NHS partners.

All three were already feeling extremely proud of the way that all of the public service organisations had reacted today, including their own. Ellis wasn't the only member of staff who'd been called in after a couple of hours sleep. Police stations right across Manchester were sending officers down to assist with the logistical requirements of closing one of Europe's major cities, and officers from neighbouring forces were on their way from Yorkshire, North Wales, Merseyside, Lancashire and Cheshire constabularies. All of the services staff had conducted themselves brilliantly today and it felt good to be part of the team who were providing such a superb response to an event that was on such a scale that it exceeded everything that they all routinely planned and rehearsed for.

As soon as Miller, Cleggy and Ellis saw the last person enter the building, they turned and began jogging back towards the tram stop and their lift back to town. A very concerning message had been received on their radios as they'd been walking down, informing them that they were required back in the city-centre as a matter of urgency.

12:08pm

"So, do you think it'll be back open in a bit or should we just sack it and go home?"

"Don't know. But someone down there was saying that there's no buses or trains running so we can't get home anyway. Looks like we're stuck here."

A group of employees from the Focus Points Store facing Piccadilly Gardens were getting bored now. They'd been standing out here since the bomb had gone off and the shop had been locked up. There was a long queue of emotional and stressed-out people waiting in line for the phone boxes on the corner outside their store. The queue must have had a hundred people in it, at least, it went all the way past Piccadilly 21's nightclub and Spud-U-Like and around the corner onto Lever Street. Nearer the front of the queue, the mood was becoming increasingly hostile and tempers were beginning to fray, people were shouting things like "hurry up" and "get on with it" whenever somebody seemed to be spending too much time on the phone.

"How long does it take to say I'm alright?" Was the most common complaint as the long line moved painfully slowly towards the four phone-boxes, one of which was Phonecard only and another was out-of-order.

Faced with the prospect of this long queue of annoying and grumpy people standing right in front of them, the Focus Points staff had decided to move across to Piccadilly Gardens and were sitting on the sloped grass, soaking up the glorious sunshine and gossiping about what was going on all around them.

"There'll be a lot of dead people from this though. Someone was saying that there was an office-block full of people right next to the bomb. You're not walking out of that."

"I know. Did you feel it though. It went right through you that bang, didn't it? Mad as ten."

"I swear down, I felt my bones shake inside me. I've never felt anything like that before."

"My ears are still buzzing from it. Are yours?"

"Yeah, mine are ringing like mad. Someone down there was saying that it was so loud, you could hear it in the Lake District!"

"Shut up!"

"You could!"

"Hey, Michael," said one of the staff, breaking off the conversation. "I'm not being funny, but… what's that in the bush, behind you?"

Michael, the store manager turned around quickly and saw that there was a large rucksack hidden in the foliage, just half a metre or so away from his back.

"What the hell?" Said Michael as he leapt to his feet. The rest of the group also scrambled up off the floor and began running away from the area. Some of them were shouting "bomb!" as they went.

A police officer was quickly alerted to this commotion and began jogging down to the area, just behind the Queen Victoria statue at the corner of Piccadilly Gardens.

"What's going on?"

"There's another bomb!" Shouted one of them, pointing at the suspect package which was concealed in the bushes.

The policeman ran towards the area and after a couple of seconds of very basic investigating work, he ran away again.

"Everybody – move away right now! GET BACK!"

The look on the policeman's face confirmed that he was concerned and suddenly people began screaming and shouting, running away from Piccadilly Gardens as quickly as possible.

"809 to control over."

"Control receiving, over."

"Suspect package found in Piccadilly Gardens, behind the Queen Victoria statue close to the Piccadilly Approach junction. We need to evacuate this area and we need the bomb disposal team here ASAP. Over."

"Received and understood. Standby. Over."

12.12pm

There was a great deal of screaming and panicking in Piccadilly Gardens as the helicopter reappeared in the skies overhead. The officers on board had been sent back to town after re-fuelling to carry out some aerial inspection work at the scene of the blast. They hadn't anticipated overseeing another evacuation.

The officer on board began repeating the same, chilling message that he had been broadcasting through the aircraft's powerful Tannoy system an hour or so earlier.

"EMERGENCY! Leave the city-centre now!"

"WARNING! Everybody get out of Manchester. NOW!"

The crowds of people who'd been gathered in the area were suddenly terrified as police officers and soldiers began running towards the area.

Dozens of police officers were barking orders at the public as they ran.

"Get out!"

"Move it! Go that way!"

The look of terror and panic on the police officer's faces confirmed that this was a very real threat. Bearing in mind what had already been witnessed less than an hour earlier by all of these people, the sense of fear and alarm was far greater than it had been earlier in the day, during the first evacuation. This time, the lackadaisical sense of "oh, it'll be reet" was non-existent.

Hundreds, if not thousands of people began running up Oldham Street, away from the Piccadilly area, many of them were screaming as they ran. Pensioners were knocked around as younger people sprinted past them. The sense of imminent danger and terror was everywhere as people of all ages and physical abilities ran in every direction to get as far away from the second bomb as possible.

Portland Street was over-run with people, as was London Road. Oldham Street and Portland Street had been the nearest exits from the Gardens and both streets which headed off in opposite directions were seeing the most people streaming past with scared expressions, rushing past Afflecks Palace in the direction of Ancoats and the edge of the city-centre on Oldham Street and down between China Town and the Gay Village on Portland Street in the opposite direction.

High above, the thunderous roar of the police helicopter continued to broadcast the scary, threatening message at full volume.

*****

Rick Houghton was still on-air on Piccadilly Key 103, fielding calls from eye-witnesses and survivors of the explosion. Some callers were watching the developments from office blocks or hotel rooms, offering running commentaries on what the emergency services teams were currently doing, whilst others were describing the nature of the damage to the city-centre as they understood it.

Rick was in the middle of taking a call from a member of staff at Manchester Town Hall who was advising that the public were welcome to come in for a cup of tea and to make telephone calls home, when he noticed some activity on the CCTV monitor in the studio. The screen showed the camera in reception, so that presenters could see if any visitors had arrived at the station outside normal office hours. Rick was stunned to see two soldiers standing in view of the camera, fully dressed in combat uniform and with weapons across their chests. He blinked a few times to see if he was imagining things.

"Okay, well, I'll have to end this call now. Thanks for the update." Rick closed his microphone and pressed play on a CD. This was the first song he'd played since Steve Penk had advised him to open the lines forty minutes earlier. With music playing out on the air, Rick left the studio and ran down the maze of corridors to the reception area.

There were no pleasantries exchanged as he opened the door. The two soldiers began speaking loudly in Rick's face.

"How many people are in this building?"

"Two."

"You need to get out of this location, right now. The

building is being evacuated." Rick saw other soldiers further along the Plaza floor, and then others who were also shouting at staff in the Air Iraq travel agency, another unit which faced the radio studios.

"What, well…"

"We need to move. Now."

"I need to go and put the emergency tape on. Or the radio station will go off air!" Rick had a pleading look in his eyes. There was no way he could abandon this place and willingly allow Manchester's biggest radio station to go off the air.

"Go and put your tape on and get the other staff member out. Thirty seconds!" The soldier was shouting at Rick as though he was just some naughty schoolboy.

"Right!" Rick ran back inside the radio station and sprinted up the corridors. Upon reaching his studio, he flicked the talk-back button on his broadcast desk, so that Darren Stannage could hear what he was saying in the other studio.

"Daz, I don't know what's going on, but we've got to get out of here now. Stick your emergency tape on now, there's soldiers outside waiting for us."

As Rick was shouting his instructions, he was feeding the big reel-to-reel tape spool onto the machine. As soon as he'd twisted the tape around the empty spool, he pressed play and pushed the fader up, abruptly ending the track which had been playing out on CD. To anybody listening at home, or around the city, waiting for more information, the harshness of the segue didn't go unnoticed.

The same thing happened in the studio opposite, Darren Stannage quickly set-up the emergency play-out tape and set it going. Both radio stations now had a three-hour back-up, a selection of music and jingles on a non-stop mix. This would keep both stations on air whilst the building was left completely unattended. As both young men raced out of their studios and sprinted towards reception, they were both worrying about what would happen if nobody was allowed back inside before the tapes ended, rather than worrying about whatever danger they may be in personally.

"Okay, come on, come on, we've got to evacuate the

hotel upstairs now," barked one of the soldiers.

"Thanks for that," said Rick as he reached them.

The army officers had no time for polite chit-chat. They shouted at the two young DJs as though they were the enemy. "Straight out, up onto the roof and down the car park ramp and out the city. Move it!"

*****

The scene on Portland Street, heading down past China Town was total chaos. A single police-man was walking behind hundreds of frightened people who were fleeing Piccadilly Gardens, a police van was driving very slowly just behind him. The policeman's voice was becoming hoarse from the constant shouting.

"Everybody keep moving, head down towards the police van at the bottom of the road and take a left onto Oxford Road." He was pointing his arm in the direction that everybody was walking, many of them extremely slowly. The crowd included pensioners, people with walking difficulties and a number of wheelchair users as well as people who were dawdling, caught up in the excitement and the drama of it all. Some were stopping dead and looking back up Portland Street, in the direction of Piccadilly. It was unclear whether they were looking for friends, or just having a nosey.

"Keep moving. Everybody. Get out of the city-centre!"

An ambulance's siren blared behind the officer, and he now had the extra complication of trying to get the public to step out of the road and onto the pavement. The sun was still blazing and one lady had stopped for a rest by Yates Wine Lodge, at the foot of Portland Tower.

"Come on, you need to keep moving!" Barked the officer as the ambulance driver kept his siren blaring as he inched forwards behind the crowd of shocked, frightened and disorientated evacuees.

"I can't go any further. I'm going to faint!" Pleaded the lady. She was a little overweight and was gesturing towards her feet. "Look at my blisters!" She added.

"I'd rather you had some blisters than missing limbs. There's another bomb, so you have to keep moving!"

Just a few yards further down Portland Street, a long queue of people were waiting by the phone boxes, desperate to phone home and let loved ones know that they were safe.

"Guys, you need to move now. There are plenty of phone boxes on Oxford Road. The BBC are letting people make calls from their building. MOVE! NOW!"

It was a nightmare. A large group of football fans were standing on the street corner opposite, holding pints of lager that they'd bought at nearby pubs. Their football shirts suggested that most of the fans were English, Scottish, Dutch, German and Croatian.

"Come on chaps, you can take your beers with you. We need to keep moving!"

How this single police officer and the trailing van were managing to herd all of these people single-handedly was a mystery. Nobody was answering back or challenging him, everybody just followed the orders without much fuss. This surprised the officer, particularly the football fans who had obediently joined the crowd and began following the rest of the people, their pints still in their hands. Behind the trailing police van, the road up to Piccadilly Gardens was deserted. Apart from another police van and an officer stood by it, there was nobody in sight and it looked very strange to see one of Manchester's busiest roads looking so abandoned.

Half a kilometre above, India 99 was continuing to perform the same manoeuvres as it had done earlier in the day, only this time, the flight path was centred exclusively around the Piccadilly area, as opposed to the entire western section of the city-centre. The helicopter was circling the gardens, all the way up to Ancoats in the north, and down to the Midland Hotel to the south, repeating the same, chilling message.

"EMERGENCY! Get out of Manchester! You are in danger!" pleaded the officer on board, the unapologetic harshness of the amplified message was not losing any of its assertiveness through the constant repetition.

As the policeman who was herding hundreds of people

down Portland Street reached the studios of Kiss 102, he was surprised to see the place was filled with people. He popped his head in the door and saw that there were at least a dozen pensioners sitting in the reception area on the sofas, many of whom were holding cups of tea and the coffee table was proudly displaying a plate of biscuits. A few office chairs had been wheeled out as well. It was the most bizarre scene, Manchester's hippest youth radio station was filled with exhausted, emotional pensioners.

"Who's in charge here?"

All of the pensioners looked around at one another. It seemed quite clear that there was nobody in charge, these people had just ended up here in the reception of the radio station and were being treated quite splendidly by all accounts. The police officer was just as confused as everybody else in the place and it was written all across his face.

"Everybody needs to leave this building right now!" He shouted. "This area is being evacuated and you are all in danger if you remain here."

He didn't have time to stay around and check that anybody followed his orders as he had to get back to his main task of guiding hundreds of people down Portland Street and away from this part of town.

12:14pm

The Bomb Disposal Unit truck was still in Manchester and gladly, the officers were unharmed. But the unit was now lacking a vital part of its kit. The robot which had been in the process of disarming the bomb was now nothing more than debris, just like the Ford Cargo and most of the buildings that had been close to them.

This new alert in Piccadilly Gardens presented a logistical headache, as the bomb doctors had no equipment to investigate this suspect package which had been found. The RLC officers had radioed their base and another bomb disposal unit had been despatched from Merseyside on blue lights, but it wasn't going to reach Manchester until 1pm at the very earliest. There was every chance that this second device could go off at any moment and tensions were running high.

With the area all around Piccadilly currently in the process of being evacuated, and dozens of injured people still being treated on the streets on the opposite side of the city-centre, this was an extremely anxious and difficult time for the members of the uniformed services, the police and fire and rescue officers in particular.

The description of the rucksack in Piccadilly was worrying enough to justify all of this activity, but to the senior officers, it was in no way as troubling as the first alert that had come in earlier. This rucksack was a fraction of the size of the Ford Cargo truck. None the less, if it had of exploded whilst hundreds of people were stranded in the official evacuation zone, it could have killed dozens of innocent bystanders. With this in mind, there was a sense of relief that the package had been discovered, but there was still a very real concern that there may be more packages, hidden in bins, inside vehicles or abandoned in evacuated buildings. There was absolutely no time to relax, even if it was going to be another forty-six minutes before the second bomb unit could attend.

*****

"Can I ask you all to move back please?" A very frustrated looking WPC was trying to keep a group of angry business owners quiet at the cordon line at the bottom of Mosley Street at the junction with Princess Street, just a stone's throw from the magnificence of Manchester Central Library. The grand, roman inspired architecture of the much-loved rotund shaped building made it look much older than its sixty-two years.

"Look, we were promised that we'd be able to return to our buildings and make the necessary arrangements for locking up properly. And now we are being evacuated again. This really is getting beyond a joke. In all seriousness."

"Can I ask you to move back please?" Repeated the WPC, who was not interested in any of these trivial problems at this time. She was aware of some horrific injuries that people had suffered just around the corner and the efforts that her colleagues from all of the emergency services were currently putting in to help hundreds of injured people. The bleats and moans from all these people about not having access to their businesses to lock up, or pick up a file, or car-keys, or to check the windows weren't broken was very low on her list of concerns at the present time. It was written all over her face.

"Are you ignoring me?" Asked the man.

"No Sir, I'm not ignoring you, I'm asking you to move back please."

"And I'm asking you if I can please just go and lock my shop up?"

The WPC could hear that India 99 was getting closer overhead, doing another sweep of the area with its loudhailer.

"Sir, can I ask you to listen to this?" She pointed upwards and as she did so, the officer on board began speaking into the powerful PA system, bang on cue.

"WARNING! Get out of Manchester now. You are in danger! You have to leave NOW."

As the chopper roared overhead and continued further on its journey, heading towards the G-Mex centre, the WPC smiled politely and said, "I can only repeat what he just said."

12.20pm

Greenfield is one of Greater Manchester's prettiest little town. It is situated to the north of Mossley and sits right on the fringe of the Greater Manchester county-line where it meets with Yorkshire. The quiet little town is situated next to Dovestones Reservoir, a very popular walking spot for people from all across the region at all times of the year. Greenfield is the last place you can get petrol before the steep climb up to the peaks of the moors which rise and fall for ten miles before the next town comes into view. Holmfirth is the filming location for the popular Sunday evening sit-com Last of the Summer Wine, famed for its idyllic rolling countryside and fine, stone-built houses. It looks identical Greenfield in many ways, although on the Manchester side of the Pennines, old men generally find their pleasure in betting shops and pubs rather than bob-sleighing down hills in abandoned bath tubs.

The staff and customers at Greenfield's most popular cafes, "Betties" had been listening to Piccadilly Radio's reports on the bomb in Manchester with interest. But now, it had just been music for the past ten minutes and the DJ hadn't said anything.

"It's definitely gone off air." Said the owner, Bettie.

"But if its still playing music, there must be somebody there pushing buttons or whatever it is they do. I think they've been given a black-out message from the authorities!" Albert - one of the busy café's regular customers, was a World War II veteran and he knew a thing or two about the way the media worked in times like this.

"What do you mean, Albert?" Asked Shelley, the young Saturday girl who was standing behind the till with Bettie.

"Well, it's simple. What we used to do in the war, we would broadcast completely false information across our entire radio network. The BBC would also broadcast this incorrect information as well because we all knew that the enemy were spying on us by listening in to our broadcasts. So, what we did, we told fibs." Albert laughed loudly at his statement, and the customers joined in. He was a very cute old man.

"By my reckoning, the police will be concerned about the things that the radio is transmitting and will have told them to stop broadcasting information. I'm surprised they were allowed to say as much as they did in all honesty."

"But how would not talking help?" Asked Shelley, who was confused by Albert's statement and was also experiencing a peculiar range of emotions from all of this. She had countless schoolfriends who had Saturday jobs in Manchester, and dozens more who would be in the city-centre shopping today. She was scared and frightened, but also weirdly excited that something so big was happening in town. She'd never known anything like this before.

"Well, they will be concerned that the IRA are listening to the transmission, and planning where to place another bomb. You heard everybody saying that the public are all standing in Piccadilly Gardens, didn't you?"

"Yes."

"Well, that is enough information to tell the IRA that it's a good target." Albert lifted his cup-of-tea and took a big slurp. The people in Betties Café weren't convinced by his theory, but as another song ended, and another one began without so much as a word from the DJ, they were all forced to accept that it was a possibility. Something definitely wasn't right.

*****

Piccadilly had been dealt a serious blow in having to evacuate the building. Piccadilly Radio was well regarded as the premier local media provider that the city's residents turned to for the very latest news. The Strangeways riots in 1990 had seen listening figures reach an all-time high as the local population who didn't normally listen to local radio ditched Radios 1 and 2 and retuned their trannies to Piccadilly.

It was also widely acknowledged that Piccadilly's coverage of the Ringway Disaster a decade earlier had been tuned into by "everybody in Greater Manchester" on that fateful morning.

At 7.13am on the 22nd August 1985, a British Airtours

Boeing 737 bound for Corfu burst into flames as the plane was preparing for take-off, killing 53 passengers and 2 crew members. It had happened during Andy Crane's breakfast show, and the radio station had immediately switched from its usual music output to a talk format as eye-witnesses and airport staff phoned the station to report on the horrific incident, interspersed with reports from Piccadilly's news journalists. The station's chief football reporter Brian Clarke had been covering Manchester City's game against Leicester City at Maine Road the previous evening and as a result, he still had the radio car. He was sent to Manchester Airport to cover the story, and despite being a sports reporter, Brian did an excellent job of covering the tragedy in a very sensitive and respectful way.

It had been a very challenging news story to cover because everybody at Piccadilly was fully aware that the concerned family members of those caught up in the incident would be listening in, desperate to hear that their loved-ones were safe. The disaster had been a traumatic event to report on for all concerned - not least for Andy Crane, who was only 20 years old.

It was becoming more and more obvious that Piccadilly had switched its output to a "muzak tape" and the station was ditched quickly as people cottoned on. The local listeners were determined to find out the latest news and retuned to other services. GMR were the main beneficiary of Piccadilly's evacuation. The BBC local station still had Phil Trow's NEC broadcast from Birmingham on the air, but as the events had unfolded over the past hour or so, listeners were hearing less and less from the popular presenter as the BBC journalists reported on the events with outside broadcasts from various locations around the city-centre. GMR were first to announce the second evacuation and were doing a great job, under the most difficult of circumstances. Phil Trow, who was based in Manchester for his programme 99% of the time could hardly believe that he was trying to hold this extraordinary broadcast together 100 miles away from the scene.

Fortune 1458, the oldies station based at Salford Quays were also providing up-to-the-minute updates on the eventualities. Paul Fairclough, the DJ on air was doing a sterling job of finding out the latest information in-between records and then relaying it to the listeners from his 4th floor studio at Quay West, the only radio studio in the region which had a birds-eye view of Manchester city-centre. Paul Fairclough had heard the bomb go off, but at the time, he thought that a bird had flown into the window. As he looked up from his radio equipment expecting to see an injured pigeon, he saw the mushroom cloud lifting high above the Arndale.

Live broadcasting was also continuing at Kiss 102, despite the fact that the radio station had been over-run with pensioners who were "taking a weight off." Behind the walls of the luxurious reception area with its leather couches and posh coffee machines, the Kiss 102 presenters and senior staff were working hard to provide up-to-the-minute news and reaction to the situation which was unfolding in Manchester.

One of their news presenters, 22 year-old Mark Ovenden had volunteered to go out on the streets of the city-centre with the station's mobile phone, offering listeners a live commentary of the situation from the ground.

David Dunne, a well-known former Piccadilly Radio presenter who was now at Kiss 102 following a stint at Atlantic 252 in Ireland, had managed to get through the police road blocks at the Mancunian Way, after telling the police officer that he was from Kiss 102. Luckily for David, the policeman was a regular listener and allowed him through, after making him abandon his car at the roundabout. Twenty minutes later, David arrived at the studios and went on air, delighted to hear that Mark had gone out on the streets with the mobile phone. David had realised that Key 103 had ceased live broadcasting on his way into the city and saw this as the station's best opportunity to show Manchester's radio listeners that Kiss 102 was a very serious and professional broadcaster.

"It's Kiss 102, and we are broadcasting live from the scene of an almighty explosion this morning in Manchester. We are keeping an eye on all of the reports coming in from the police, the hospitals, the ambulance and fire service as well as the bus and train companies and we will soon be releasing the information regarding an emergency telephone line for concerned relatives. Those details are still being finalised by GMP and we'll bring you the details as soon as we have them. In the mean-time, lets cross live to Kiss 102's Mark Ovenden, who is close to the scene of this explosion. Mark, what can you see?"

Mark had ducked and dived his way around the back alleys and ginnels of Manchester, dodging the cordon points as he slipped between all of the police vans and officers between the Kiss studios on Portland Street and the scene of the devastation half a mile away on the opposite side of town. After ten minutes of this heart-thumping exercise, Mark had finally arrived at the bottom of Shudehill, and was stunned by the sight which greeted him. The shock was clear in his voice as he gave his report to the Kiss 102 listeners.

"Oh, well, I'm just... this is quite... this is actually impossible to take in. I'm standing just fifty metres away from the scene where the bomb went off, I'm at the bottom of Shudehill, outside Maxwell House, facing the Corn Exchange. The devastation I can see before me is, I just can't put it into words. As I look up, I see that every single window has been blown out of the Arndale House office block. Across the road, the Corn Exchange has no glass left in any of its windows, the dome appears to have been completely destroyed. All around me are lumps of concrete, huge pieces of steel and debris. The wall at the back of the Arndale Centre building has completely collapsed and I can see right into many of the shops, their stock has been thrown in every direction. Although there are numerous fire engines obscuring my view, I can see that there is a deep crater in the ground near Marks and Spencers. This is impossible to comprehend. The whole place has been destroyed. It's heart-breaking David."

"Tell us about the emergency services, Mark. What are they doing?"

"Well, there's not a lot happening here at the moment, it's eerily quiet but for the alarm bells that I'm sure you can hear down the line. There are two firemen working close to the entrance to Marks and Spencers, but that is the only activity that I can see here right now, but I have passed dozens upon dozens of fire officers and police officers who are tending to people's injuries as I made my way down here. It's not good."

"Describe the damage that you're seeing."

"I can try, David, but what I must say is that this place is unrecognisable right now. Corporation Street is completely impassable by vehicle, in fact it looks like it would be a challenge to walk across this area. There is at least two feet of debris covering the ground for as far as the eye can see. Thousands upon thousands of random items from shops are scattered everywhere, and as I say, I can't see a single window which still has any glass attached to it, including the twenty floors of the Arndale House complex. Across the road, the insurance building has been partially demolished, as has the front of Marks and Spencers, the familiar canopy which was set in that peculiar wavy style has collapsed and the bridge between Marks and Spencers has been reduced to a concrete shell. Looking over to my right is Victoria railway station and I can see that the windows have all been destroyed there as well. This is quite honestly a very shocking scene, I'm completely stunned that a bomb could have caused this much devastation, it looks more like Kosovo right now. I'm not exaggerating when I say this... this part of Manchester has been completely destroyed and it is utterly heart-breaking to see."

12:44pm

On their return to Manchester on board their special Metrolink service from Crumpsall, Miller, Cleggy and Ellis had thanked the driver profusely for her assistance, before being sent to assist with the second evacuation of the city-centre. The three young officers were stationed at a cordon line close to the Midland Hotel. Their purpose was to restrict any people from heading towards the city-centre and point them in any available direction which led out of town.

The public were being quite good about everything, considering. Many of them had cars parked in the areas which were either affected by the bomb or were now within the new exclusion zone. The major car parks at Chorlton Street, Tib Street and Piccadilly railway station had all been cordoned off in the face of the new threat. These locations, added to the car parks already affected, such as the Arndale multi-story and Deansgate multi-story – meant that thousands of vehicles were stranded in the city-centre. Their owners were also stranded as there was no public transport running. It was a nightmare for the thousands of people who just wanted to get out of the blazing sunshine and get home. But they couldn't.

This was the main complaint that police officers were hearing at all of the cordon lines. Miller, Cleggy and Ellis were standing five metres apart along the cordon tape which prohibited anybody from walking towards Piccadilly. All three of the constables had a group of frustrated shoppers surrounding them. All they wanted was access to their vehicles so they could make the journey home and put this awful day behind them.

"I'm really sorry, but we cannot allow anybody past this area." Explained Ellis to her group, sounding sympathetic to their perfectly reasonable complaints.

"We'll know more in an hour." Said Miller to his group. "There's a good chance that the cars will be staying put for the next few days though as structural engineers will have to do safety checks, so you're best advised to try and find alternative transport. I'm really sorry, but it's the best I can offer." This comment was met with frustration and anger. The people surrounding Andy Miller had really had enough now. It was almost as if this young copper was responsible for all of this chaos, judging by the reaction he was receiving. But he took it in good humour, he'd learnt early on in his police training that people see the uniform first and the person wearing it second. These people were just kicking off with his uniform and what it represented, not him. He had to keep reminding himself of that as the comments and questions continued.

Cleggy was also inundated with frustrated, sun-burned people asking the same questions. His response was slightly different to Ellis and Miller's. He just kept repeating things like, "I haven't got a clue," "no idea," "you're asking the wrong man, they don't tell me nowt." Whilst Cleggy's responses weren't very helpful to the concerned citizens who were asking him questions – they were certainly helpful in the sense that they all left him alone quite quickly and joined the other groups surrounding his colleagues who were trying their best to respond constructively to the barrage of questions and pleas.

Ellis was arguably the best of the three coppers, her crowd was the biggest and she was constantly relaying her group's questions to control through her radio. But despite the excellent attempts at pacifying everybody, she knew in her heart of hearts that these people were completely frustrated, and they were hot and bothered too. Ellis continued to offer sympathy and constructive information as best she could – but she was acutely aware that this could all boil over at any moment. The people before her were thoroughly pissed off and she sensed that tempers could start to flare at any moment.

12:55pm

Much of Manchester city-centre was completely deserted now. There were absolutely no civilians on the ground around the Arndale, Market Street and the Piccadilly Gardens sections of the city-centre. The only places where India 99 could still see groups of people was around the cordon lines, and significant crowds of people were gathered at the Town Hall, Oxford Road and the top end of Deansgate.

The staff on board the aircraft had been swooping all around the area and were pleased to see great lines of people walking out of the area in huge numbers. Others were assembling right on the fringe of the city-centre, in large groups, presumably waiting for lifts home. That's certainly what it looked like from 400 metres above.

The crucial thing was that the area was cleared of people, particularly Piccadilly Gardens, which was completely deserted but for the police vans blocking the junctions of all surrounding roads. The only other vehicles in the area were the two-dozen double-decker and Little Gem buses which had been trapped inside Piccadilly bus station for the past three hours. Their drivers had long since abandoned any hope of driving them away at any time in the foreseeable future and had made their ways back to their respective bus depots on the outskirts of the city-centre at Hyde Road, Queens Road and Princess Road. The bus drivers had all been eager to get as far away from any potential danger as possible. All of them knew that bus and rail services were not completely suspended unless there was a significant threat to the transport system.

It had only been four months since he IRA bus-bomb in London on the 18th February, involving a would-be IRA bomber who was transporting a device which had detonated, accidentally blowing the man up and seriously injuring 10 passengers on board the bus, which was completely destroyed. This shocking event, which came just days after the IRA had announced that the 17-month cease-fire was over, was still very fresh in all of the bus driver's minds. After all, this kind of terrorism was the very worst nightmare for any public service vehicle driver.

The crew on board India 99 informed their control-room that the only notable assembly of people which remained in the city-centre itself now was at Manchester town hall, where a large crowd of people were staying put beneath the grand neo-gothic building, which those in-the-know consider the jewel in Manchester's crown. Built at a time when Manchester was one of the richest places on earth thanks to the industrial revolution, no expense was spared on this building project, the construction of one of the UK's most extravagant town halls. Indeed, it is well documented that this building is considered a far superior government building than the palace of Westminster. This fine compliment is well deserved as any visitor who has seen the sheer splendour inside the grand building at Albert Square can testify.

Manchester town hall is noted for its black appearance, but that black finish to the Yorkshire stone-work was added later, by decades of smog and air-pollution from the thousands of mills, of which their success had made such an elegant and opulent structure possible. Building such a fine piece of architecture took a long time, starting in 1868 and completed in 1877, when the gigantic clock tower became the number-one focal point from every corner of the city for almost 100 years, before the skyscrapers began appearing and obscured the majestic view.

The first of the skyscrapers constructed in Manchester was the Co-op's CIS tower, across the road from Victoria railway station, which was opened in 1962 and was the tallest building in the UK at that time, standing 118 metres tall. It was considered as a glimpse into the future by the younger generation, and hated for its vulgar appearance by older members of the community, who felt that it was guilty of spoiling the city's attractive skyline, which up until that time had been made up of the Palace Theatre clock-tower, St Mary's church spire, Strangeways prison tower along with the old mills and their chimneys, the city-centre tenement buildings and of course, the jewel in the crown, Manchester town hall with its resplendent clock tower which stands almost ninety-metres tall.

The next skyscraper which came along and transformed the sky-line further came three years later, in 1965. Sunley House, part of the Piccadilly Plaza complex was even taller than the CIS building, which seemed an incredible feat of engineering at the time. Today, a number of Sunley Tower's windows had fallen victim to the almighty blast a couple of hours earlier.

Ten years after Sunley Tower was constructed, another gigantic building appeared on Manchester's horizon, helping to block out the view of the town hall even further. Arndale House, the huge 20 storey office-block which had seen every window blown out today stands just three metres taller than the top of the town hall clock tower.

Beneath that giant clock tower which had stood so prominently on the Manchester skyline for the past century, almost three-hundred people were gathered on the cobble-stones outside the town hall. Some of them were the last of the nosey-parkers, eager to see what would happen next, but this was a tiny minority of the large crowd of people. Most of the spectators had gone now, the heat and the drama of the past few hours had been plenty for the vast majority and they had now headed off for home, hopefully in time for the big match kicking off at 3pm.

Most of the people who remained at Manchester town hall were the business owners who were desperate to hear the latest news from council officials. They were eager to learn which streets had been worst affected, which buildings had been destroyed, and most crucially of all - whether their business had survived. The mood was extremely sombre as these distressed and frustrated members of the business community waited to hear from the new leader of the council, Richard Leese, what today's terrorist attack meant for them.

At 45 years old, Richard Leese was a very young man for his position as the Leader of the city council. Today's attack comes only 26 days after Richard succeeded Graham Stringer in the most powerful role in Manchester's politics.

A large number of journalists and TV reporters were also present, keen to report the first official statement from the people who would be in charge of putting right the seemingly incalculable amount of damage which had occurred today. There was a sense of impatience and panic amongst the reporters as well as the business owners, they had stories to write for their newspapers, TV news bulletins and radio stations. It was incredibly frustrating that no sound-bites or announcements were currently forthcoming. It felt as though there was a wall of silence regarding the most significant event that had happened in the city in modern history and the silence was stirring up a growing sense of exasperation and anger.

As India 99 completed another lap above the city-centre, the officers on board were satisfied enough to advise the control-room that "the city-centre is 95% clear of civilians. The only people still inside the central zone are assembled at the town hall. Piccadilly and all surrounding areas are completely clear. Over."

"Received India 99. Permission to proceed with your original mission. Over."

13:06pm

The second bomb squad had finally arrived from Liverpool. The RLC truck which was identical to the one which had arrived a little over two and a half hours earlier drove into the city-centre up London Road. This area coming past Piccadilly railway station appeared completely fine, but for the peculiar lack of people. The RLC officers on board had heard numerous radio reports that Manchester had been flattened by the bomb, which had also destroyed one of their robots. But as the truck pulled up close to the old fire station, there was no sign of any damage around this district.

"This side of the city looks like it has got away undamaged. Let's make sure it stays that way, eh?" The commanding officer was speaking to his two officers who were eager to get the job done. As they jumped down from the cab and began opening the truck's back doors to drive out their robot, Chief Inspector Ian Seabridge was waiting to greet them and inform them of the scene they were about to send their remote-controlled bomb disposal robot to. The briefing only took a minute, much of the information regarding the suspect package had already been relayed to the bomb squad officers via radio as they'd made their way up the motorway from Merseyside. This final briefing from the Chief Inspector was simply about the physical location of the package, and the most accessible route to it.

"So, what is the plan?" Asked the Chief Inspector of the BDU officer, as the exhausted looking policeman wrapped up his briefing.

"We'll send the droid in, investigate the package remotely on our AV equipment and probably carry out a controlled explosion. That's if it doesn't blow up first." As with the bomb doctors that he had encountered earlier that day, Ian Seabridge was stunned by how relaxed the soldier appeared.

"You think it's due to go off?"

"Night do. Might not. We can't rule anything out, or in at this stage. If it is a bomb, and it has been planted in this location to injure, maim or kill civilians, then it's difficult to understand why it hasn't gone off yet. Whichever way it goes, any device we can recover before it is detonated is a major triumph as it allows us a good look at the level of sophistication that the bombers are working at. So, there's a good chance it will blow before the robot gets too close, no terrorist is comfortable with the idea of us taking their bombs away to examine."

Ian Seabridge nodded sombrely, it all made sense. But there was one thing that didn't quite stack up.

"How would it be detonated now?"

"Oh, there are a number of ways. The most common is a tamper-trigger which will detonate the device if it is touched. But these bombs are getting a lot more sophisticated as technology advances. Mobile phones are becoming quite easy to get hold of now. That's a concern because any mobile phone could detonate a bomb. Somebody could be standing in any one of these office blocks now, watching what we're doing and planning to set it off. All it would take is for somebody to ring it while it was wired up to a tamper-trigger and then boom!"

The Chief Inspector stepped back slightly as the bomb doctor animated his boom comment with two hands. "Anyway, let's set the droid off and we'll have a see what we're playing with."

Once again, the senior policeman was shocked by how relaxed the munitions expert was talking. It wasn't just the way he was speaking, but the manner in which he was discussing such a dangerous and worrying situation as though the two men were just passing comment about a football match. He'd often thought that soldiers were a bit bonkers and this one was doing nothing to change that view.

Chief Inspector Seabridge stepped away from the BDU vehicle and back to his cordon line close to Piccadilly railway station approach. He watched on as the soldiers set their expensive piece of technology on its way up the road and in the direction of the Queen Victoria statue, behind which was the suspicious package, hidden away in the bushes.

13:12pm

Roy George had not had any luck in trying to find out what was going on in Manchester once he'd returned home from the top hill. But once he'd heard the radio announcements on Piccadilly and had learnt that a bomb had gone off right next to where his daughter Caroline was working, he felt that he had no other choice but to get to Manchester and start looking for her.

Roy had knocked next door to ask for a lift to town, but Morris, his neighbour was out playing golf and his wife had no idea what time he'd be back.

"You can borrow his bike if you want?" She'd offered, concerned by how anxious Roy looked.

Roy was grateful for the offer. He knew that he couldn't just sit in his house waiting for news. He needed to get down to Manchester and start looking for Caroline himself.

"I'll look after it!" He said.

"I know you will Roy. Come round to the side gate and I'll get it out for you."

A couple of minutes later, Roy was flying down the hills out of Dukinfield, peddling like mad. The tears running down his cheeks were a combination of sadness and fear as well as the force of the wind as he raced down Chapel Hill by the side of the town hall. He kept peddling, within minutes he was climbing the steep hill into Audenshaw, and a few minutes after that, he reached Ashton Old Road which was a nice steady ride, slightly down-hill for the next five miles.

Upon reaching the first cordon line beneath Piccadilly Railway station, he was met by a police officer who told him in no uncertain terms that he wasn't getting through.

"I need to find my daughter," Roy pleaded breathlessly.

"What's her name mate?"

"Caroline George."

"Age?"

"Seventeen."

"Just give me a sec, I'll ask control if she's on any of our lists."

Roy felt fresh tears filling his eyes. "Lists. What lists?"

"Oh, you name it. We've got lists of people who've become separated from their family and friends, lists of all those who have been taken to hospital. Then there's lists of people who have registered for transport home, we're trying to arrange some coaches but it's a nightmare – everybody's geared up for the football and nobody is answering the phone. So, we're not having much luck in getting the basics done."

"Could she have been taken to hospital?"

The policeman could see that George was in a state and he desperately wanted to give him some comforting news. "Well, there's a possibility. But I know the names of those who have sustained serious injuries and there isn't a Caroline. And there's nobody that young, either. So that's positive."

"Have there been any..." Roy couldn't say it, but the officer knew exactly what this sad looking man was getting at.

"Where was your daughter working?"

"Er, Arndale Centre. Mark One, it's a clothes shop. It's her first day as a Saturday girl."

"Yes, I know it well. My wife drags me round there all the time. Listen..."

Roy's tears were flowing at full force.

"Listen to me," said the policeman, quite assertively. Roy looked up at him and saw that he was wearing a very reassuring smile. "The Arndale was the first place to be cleared of people, there was nobody anywhere near there for over an hour before the explosion. So I can guarantee you that she's fine."

"Really?"

"Really. We've just got a lot of people stranded in town because all the buses and trains have stopped running. I'll bet you a fiver she's stood with everybody else, wondering how the hell to get home. Let me radio through now and see what I can find out for you. Okay?"

"Thank you." Roy began wiping away his tears with his shirt sleeve. As he stood there, beneath the huge railway bridges which made up a large part of Piccadilly train station above, he saw a figure walking slowly towards him. He rubbed his eyes and stared hard at the figure in the darkened viaduct.

"What..." He rubbed his eyes again. It looked like Caroline, but he couldn't be sure. Whoever it was, 200 metres away under the dark bridge had an identical walk to his daughter's.

"CAROLINE?" He shouted at the top of his lungs, making the policeman jump with fright. Roy's booming voice echoed all the way down the darkened underpass. A second or two passed before he heard his daughter's reply. "DAD?" She shouted, and began running towards Roy and the policeman.

"Oh my God, it's... it's her..." Said Roy as a fresh wave of emotion washed over him.

"Cancel that call. Got a happy ending here. Over."

Caroline was sprinting towards her dad, as fast as her legs would carry her.

"Oh thank you God! Thank you God!" Said Roy as his daughter approached him. She ducked under the cordon tape and gave her dad the strongest cuddle he'd ever felt.

"Are you alright?"

"Yes, course. I was phoning the house. It took me forty minutes to queue up – and then there was no blummin' answer!"

Roy laughed loudly, as did the police officer.

"Anyway, what the hell are you doing with that thing?" asked Caroline, pointing at the bike.

"I borrowed it off Morris."

"What, Morris next door? You mean you rode it all the way here?"

"Yes. I couldn't find anything out. I wanted to come and find you."

"Well if you'd just stayed at home you'd have got my phone call! What are you like dad?"

The police officer was smiling, it was nice to see the scared bloke looking so happy and relaxed now.

"Come on, we've got a long walk. We'll stop at a pub and get some dinner eh? You can tell me all about it." Roy climbed off the bike and turned it around. "Thanks for all your help officer."

"My pleasure."

Roy began pushing the bike along the pavement as he walked back up the long hill towards Dukinfield with his beloved daughter by his side.

"So... how's the new job going?"

Caroline laughed sarcastically and gave her dad a toy-punch in the arm.

13:11pm

Carl Royle, the Manchester Evening News photographer who had spent the past couple of hours walking around the city-centre capturing the reaction and the devastation to the terror attack was returning to the MEN offices to develop his films. But there was a problem. The police officer at the cordon line on Deansgate wouldn't let him through.

"Seriously, you've got to let me through. I need to develop these pictures for this afternoon's paper." Carl was pleading with the policeman, but he could see that the officer wasn't interested in hearing about his problems.

"As I have explained to you already Sir, nobody is permitted to pass this line."

"But it's fifteen yards away. Come on mate, please."

"Sir, I don't care if its two inches away. I've been ordered to guard this cordon line, and I am not permitted to allow anybody through. It's for your own safety."

Carl could see that this copper was nothing more than a jumped-up jobsworth. He could see loads of people walking around inside his cordon line. Shop workers were sweeping up glass right next to the MEN office building. "Look at them there, why aren't you getting them away from the danger?"

"Sir, I have been told to ensure that nobody passes this line. If those people were already there before I was posted here, then there's nothing I can do about it."

"And what would you do if I just ignore you and go underneath your tape?"

"I wouldn't advise that, Sir."

"Why not?"

"Because you'll be arrested."

"Well I don't care! I'll be bloody sacked if I don't get these pictures to my boss in the next five minutes."

"We're going round in circles here, Sir."

"And what about him there?" Carl pointed beyond the policeman's shoulder and as soon as he turned around to see what Carl was pointing at, the photographer ducked under the tape and launched into a sprint down Deansgate, towards the newspaper building. He looked over his shoulder as he ran. The police officer had stayed put, but he didn't look too happy with the photographer's stunt.

Carl raced into the MEN building and ran straight through to Mike Unger's office.

"Alright Mike?"

"Hiya Carl, what have you got?"

"Loads of great shots. The best one was a picture of a bride and groom running away from their wedding!"

"Seriously? Can't wait to see that."

"Got tons of cracking stuff. Some security guard was trying to move a baby out of harms way and the mother went nuts at him. I think she thought he was snatching the kid. Honestly, it's absolutely crackers out there."

"Good grief! Did you get any good shots of the damage?"

"Not as many as I'd have liked. It's impossible to get near the scene, it's been locked down from every angle. But I've got a few long-distance frames which might work out."

"Good stuff. Well, off you go to the dark-room."

"Sure. But before I go..."

Mike looked hard at his photographer. "What?"

"Well, I might have a police officer looking for me. I had to run through his cordon to get back in."

Mike laughed loudly. The thought of Carl legging it past a police officer really tickled him. "Don't worry. If anything comes of it, I'll handle it."

"Cheers boss."

"Go on, off you go. I want to see these snaps."

13:15pm

The bomb disposal robot had encountered a number of obstacles in reaching the suspect package behind Queen Victoria's statue on the eastern corner of Piccadilly Gardens. The hindrances were due to the obstructive terrain of the ornamental layout of the location. The site is built into a basin and is surrounded by a decorative two-foot wall around much of the area on the street level, and another identical wall down at the ground-level. The remote-control operator, who was around the corner on London Road, had struggled to find an entry-point which allowed access to the embankment section of the Gardens where the package was situated. It had been a surprisingly challenging job, using the robot's on-board cameras to try and negotiate a route between the walls and then find a way past the trees and shrubs and into the foliage where the package was reportedly hidden.

But after several frustrating minutes, the robot had finally arrived and its operator was running a number of routine checks on the rucksack. The first test was to check for any sounds coming from the package. Most IRA bombs are routinely built with a simple alarm-clock detonator, the clock set to a specific time. Once the alarm goes off, the vibrations within the clock trigger the bomb to explode.

The robot's boom arm was extended to a distance of five centimetres from the big red rucksack and the operator turned the microphone gain to maximum and listened intently through his head-phones. With the microphone turned up to full-power, this would normally detect the ticking of an alarm-clock very clearly, even the quietest ones. In normal circumstances, the sound from a clock can reveal its exact location within the concealed package using a very simple procedure. The microphone would slowly be moved up and then down, and the bomb doctor would be able to determine exactly where the clock was situated based on the simplicity of where the sound was loudest. But there was no sound coming from this package at all.

The next test involved the thermometer which was

attached to the same boom arm which held the microphone and the video-camera. The resting temperature of an unexploded bomb is normally much warmer than that of an innocent package due to its chemical composition. The bomb doctor began moving the boom arm up and down again, in exactly the same way that he had with the microphone. After a thorough sweep of the front and sides of the rucksack, the BDO spoke calmly and clearly into his head-set.

"Audio detection negative. Thermal impression negative. I'm happy to retreat the droid and carry out a controlled explosion. Please advise. Over."

"Permission to retreat and engage in controlled explosion granted. Over."

The BDO wasted no time in reversing the robot away from the package and began the arduous task of driving the million-pound piece of equipment back around the trees, bushes, walls and steps which had made its destination so difficult to reach. It turned out to be a much easier task to retreat from the location, than it had been in negotiating the heavy machine towards it. After a minute or so of skilful manoeuvre, the bomb doctor had his robot situated twenty-metres away from the suspect package and was in the process of lining up the on-board gun towards its target.

The method of carrying out a controlled explosion was relatively simple in theory. BDU officers would shoot the suspect package in the area they had determined the detonator was situated. The hope was that the shot would disable the detonator, by blowing it up, before it had the chance to blow the explosives up. It was a risky procedure and it had a fifty-fifty success rate in these circumstances. Had the bomb doctor managed to identify a detonator, the task of opening the package and trying to reveal the inner-workings would have been a much simpler method. Had that happened, the robot could have disabled the device by shooting a powerful jet of compressed air at the wires, breaking them off and disengaging the circuit.

But today, with a complete lack of clues as to where the detonator might be located within the package, the riskier method of disarming would be required. The robot is fitted with a shotgun which can fire a shell which is filled with water rather than the lead-shot which is usually contained in a shotgun cartridge. The sheer power of the shot can, and usually does, break the connections between the detonator, the trigger and the explosive.

Now, it was time to see if this method would safely disarm this device, or if Manchester was about to see its second terrorist explosion of the day.

"Target is locked, the shell is aimed and ready to fire. Over."

"Copy that. Permission to proceed. Over."

"Understood. Over."

The BDO took another look at his communications devices, he wanted to be 100% confident that the shot he was about to take via the robot was perfectly aimed at the top third of the rucksack. Visibility was hindered greatly by the poor line-of-sight of the device due to the foliage. But after several seconds of focused deliberation, the BDO zoomed the robot's camera in as far as possible, before checking again that all of his calculations were accurate.

"Standby. Over." He said into his headset radio. "Weapon engaged. I'm about to fire."

The sound of gun-fire echoed around the deserted site at Piccadilly Gardens. The sudden, piercing sound reverberated against all of the buildings which surround the location. Thankfully for the bomb doctors and the police and fire officers situated all around the area, there was no further sound. The bomb had been disarmed.

The BDO looked on his TV link to the robot's cameras and examined the visual-feed. It came as a huge relief to see a pair of underpants hanging from a bush, and a Manchester United shirt falling out of the rucksack.

"Threat neutralised. It looks innocent, it appears to be a tramp's overnight bag. It's not all positive news though. We've ruined his underpants. Over."

13.25pm

More than two hours had now passed since that almighty explosion on Corporation Street. Manchester Royal Infirmary's Senior Consultant, Professor Mackway-Jones had raced into the hospital as soon as he'd heard about the incident. He was now fully-armed with the latest information and walked out of the MRI to speak to the growing crowd of media reporters who were desperate for the first official announcement about the casualties, and to see if there was any truth in the growing rumours about fatalities.

All kinds of numbers were being banded around, from one person dying on the way to hospital, to a dozen bodies being found under rubble. In any major incident such as this one, the rumours and embellishments that the public tended to create made life very hard for the people who were responsible for fact-based reporting. Greater Manchester Police had been very quiet about the situation since the first announcement which had come soon before noon. GMP's press officers had since been fielding calls from journalists across the world, but had revealed very little information, advising that "all of their senior officials are still engaged in the ongoing incident."

As such, the press were desperate to hear something solid from a reliable source which they could then take back to their newspapers, radio stations and TV networks. The information from the chief at the MRI would be the first official announcement on the situation as it was currently known.

"Good afternoon," said the hospital chief. He looked nervous and agitated as he stood before the cameras and microphones, his voice was shaking with nerves, as were his hands, the shaking was exaggerated by the piece of paper he was holding before him. "Over the course of the afternoon, I aim to deliver updates on the response of the city's local hospitals to this morning's explosion in Manchester. As I'm sure you will all appreciate, this is very much a live and ongoing incident, but I am able to let you all know the facts as we currently understand them. Firstly, may I take this opportunity to praise the NHS staff, as well as my police and fire service colleagues who have worked incredibly hard today in the face of much adversity." The professor's hands were trembling noticeably as he looked down at the piece of paper which he was holding in front of himself as he stood nervously outside the main entrance to the hospital.

"Between the Casualty departments at this hospital and North Manchester General, we are currently treating over one-hundred and sixty-five casualties as a result of the bombing. Of those people, I'm very relieved to announce, the vast majority of injuries are superficial cuts which were sustained from flying glass in areas of the city-centre which were outside the police cordon zone and we expect these people to make a complete recovery from their injuries. However, at this moment in time, we currently have six people who have sustained life-threatening injuries and our surgeons are working on those individuals now and will be doing so for a number of hours, possibly into the early hours of tomorrow morning. We are not aware of any fatalities at this moment in time, but I must remind you all that a full search of the area around the scene of the explosion has not yet been completed. Police dog handlers and fire and rescue officers are currently in the process of carrying out intensive searches in these areas and more information will be made available on the outcome of that as soon as we have it. Hospitals in other parts of Greater Manchester are reporting walking-wounded patients presenting themselves at their casualty departments, these hospitals include Tameside General, Stepping Hill and Park Hospital, totalling the number of injured parties at over two-hundred people at this moment in time. We are anticipating seeing more patients as the day progresses, we are currently on standby for more information on reports that sixty, that's six-zero people are trapped inside the Arndale shopping centre. That's all of the information that I have in my possession at this point in time. I must get back inside."   With this abrupt conclusion, Professor Mackway-Jones turned quickly and walked briskly back into the building. The press members turned just as quickly and headed back to their OB vans, radio-cars and to nearby phone-boxes to ring their reports through to their bosses.

The revelation that sixty people were trapped inside

the Arndale cancelled out the good news that nobody had died. It was a gentle reminder to all of the media representatives that the day was still very young as far as statistics were concerned.

13:58pm

On the outskirts of Manchester city-centre, taxis and cabs were waiting in long queues by the police cordon-lines which surrounded the area, preventing any traffic which wasn't here on official emergency services business from entering the city.

The cabs in all of these queues weren't waiting long for a fare. As soon as they pulled up, they had customers climbing into their vehicles as there were no other transport options available. Hundreds of people from all across the north-west had given up on the idea of waiting around to catch a bus or train, or to collect their vehicles which were parked inside the exclusion zone. The idea of getting home and far away from the madness and terror in Manchester was the overwhelming desire for almost everybody in the long queues as they waited for a vehicle to take them home.

This unprecedented demand for trade had brought drivers from right across the Greater Manchester region. Private hire vehicles from as far away as Rochdale, Bury, Wigan and Bolton were lined up alongside a number of more centrally located carriages from Tameside, Salford and Stockport. Business was certainly booming, the drivers were thrilled by this unprecedented demand for their services.

These ad-hock taxi ranks were springing up everywhere, at Ancoats, Chapel Street, Hyde Road, Trafford Road and at practically at every major road junction which led into Manchester from the city-centre's dozen or so main-roads.

45 year-old Greg Harris from Bolton was one of the people who'd been waiting patiently for a cab. He'd stood in the queue for over twenty-minutes with his wife Chris and their two daughters, 10 year-old Nicola and 12 year-old Lyndsey. It was a great feeling for them all to realise they finally had the means of getting home. Today had been such a traumatic event, all four members of the Harris family had been scared out of their wits by the explosion, and then seeing all the people with injuries sitting in piles of glass on the pavement and the looks of sheer panic on everybody's faces. Then the second bomb warning had

terrified the life out of them. Finally, it was all coming to an end now as they got into the Ford Sierra which had Dolphin Taxis written all over it.

"Alright mate," said Greg as he got into the passenger seat.

"Alright mate. Where you going?"

"Little Lever. Near Farnworth. Is that alright?"

"Yes, no problem at all. It's going to be fifty quid."

Greg looked at the cab driver and laughed. "Fifty quid? Are you having a laugh? It's a fifteen quid fare that, tops."

"Not today mate. Fifty quid." The cab driver looked as though he couldn't give a shit whether the guy took him up on his offer or not, there was literally hundreds of other customers standing in the line just metres away, all of them were waiting to take his place in the Sierra.

Greg turned around and looked at his wife. She gave him the look that said, *yes, he's taking the piss but what other option have we got?*

Greg turned to face the driver. "Right. Go on then. But it's a bit of a fucking piss-take."

"Greg!" Said Chris from the back-seat. Nicola and Lyndsey were looking out of the windows, quite oblivious to the conversation which was taking place up front.

"It's supply and demand mate. I'll need paying up front."

"For fuck's sake!"

"Greg!"

Greg lifted his bum off the seat slightly as he wriggled his wallet out of his pocket. He opened it and pulled two twenties and a ten pound note out and handed them to the driver.

Not another word was uttered all the way to Little Lever, the small town on the outskirts of Bolton. As the Dolphin's Taxis car pulled into the town-centre, Greg told the driver to pull up outside Cellar-5 and the family got out of the vehicle.

"I hope your fucking timing belt snaps on the way back you horrible little wank-stain." Said Greg, making sure he was out of ear-shot of his wife and girls.

"Nah, had it done a few months back. See ya."

"Yeah, well I hope someone shits on your back-seat. And… and all your locks break so you're trapped inside with the turd." Said Greg as he got out and slammed the car door as hard as he could.

The taxi-driver just pulled off and did a u-turn in the middle of the road, pip-pipping the Harris family as he went.

"What a tosser!"

"Greg!"

The same thing was happening with most of the mini-cab drivers. The only way around this stealth tax on the journey home was if a customer was lucky enough to encounter a black-cab driver who hadn't turned his meter off. But those drivers were very few and far between today. As a result, most of the people who were stranded in Manchester had little choice but to stump up the price of a return train fare to London for a ten or fifteen-mile journey.

But not everybody in Manchester was being an arse-hole. At many of the impromptu taxi-ranks, people were pulling up and shouting "we've got two spare seats and we're heading for Stalybridge if anybody wants a lift?"

"Does anybody need a lift to Wilmslow? We've got three seats!"

Each time this happened, a huge cheer went up in the queue. It may have been easy-pickings for the cab-drivers of Manchester, but the ordinary people were keen to lend a hand in a small way, and all of the available seats were taken up within seconds.

A man and wife had been in Manchester when the bomb went off, but luckily for them, they'd parked outside the central area and would be able to collect their car without any hassle. As Carole and Eddie Keenan made their way down towards Salford Central train station to collect their car and make their way back home on the short journey to Eccles, they'd encountered a couple of young girls who were in floods of tears.

"Hey, hey, what's wrong?" asked Carole, sitting down beside them on the wall.

"We can't get home. And we can't get hold of mum and

dad, they've gone out."

"Well, don't worry. We can give you a lift home, can't we Eddie?"

Eddie nodded at his wife. It wasn't so much a question but an assertion of what was happening.

Carole's comment seemed to do the trick and the two teenage girls stopped crying.

"Honestly?" Asked the older of the two, wiping her tears away with her wrist.

"Course, no problem." Said Carole. "Whereabouts do you live?"

"Stoke."

Eddie didn't show it, but he wanted to smash the train station doors in. His last chance of getting home and catching the match in time had just been dealt the bitterest of blows. Stoke was 40 miles and a good hour and half away. A three-hour round trip.

"Stoke. Oh, well it doesn't matter. We can take you there. Can't we love?" Asked Carole as she looked across at her husband, once again, it wasn't a question.

"Yes. Yes, of course. No problem at all."

The four of them headed off to towards the car-park. Three of them looked absolutely delighted.

"So, Stoke eh? That's where Robbie Williams is from isn't he? What are you doing in Manchester?" asked Carole as they walked.

14:05pm

Miller, Cleggy and Ellis were enjoying a few moments of peace and quiet. For the two male officers, this had been the first time they'd managed to grab a breather since they'd enjoyed a sneaky fag around the back of Afflecks Palace, half an hour before the bomb had gone off. It was also the first time since then that they'd had the chance to take their heavy helmets off. Both of their heads were dripping with sweat. Cleggy sniffed inside his helmet and make a gagging noise, which was met with a good laugh. His head was soaking wet and he tried to flick the sweat off against the wall.

Ellis was ready for a break herself, despite not having as many hours of dealing with this chaos under her belt. She'd been fast asleep in bed when the biggest peace-time bomb that had ever been detonated on the British mainland had wreaked havoc on the city.

"Knickers, knackers, knockers!" Said Cleggy as he lit his cigarette. His colleagues laughed loudly at this completely random outburst.

"What are you laughing at?" Asked the confused looking PC as he exhaled the much craved-after smoke.

"You!" Said Ellis. "What the hell was that you just said?" She was beaming, despite her well-known disapproval of the smoking.

"What, knickers, knackers, knockers? It's something my grandad says when he's getting stressed out."

Cleggy's explanation received another hearty laugh from Miller and Ellis. Neither of them had heard that one before, and it sounded so strange coming out of a twenty-three-year-old's mouth.

"I'm going to start saying that."

"He says chuffing hell a lot as well. If he says anything stronger than that, he knows my gran will have his guts for garters."

Another hearty laugh reverberated around the back ginnel where the three coppers were having a sneaky, but well-earned break.

"Anyway Cleggy, stop changing the subject."

"You what? What subject am I changing?"

"When are you going to tell us about your date last night?" Ellis couldn't wait a moment longer to hear every detail about her colleague's rare date.

"Nothing to tell."

"Is that it, then?"

"Is what what?"

"Oh, don't play hard to get! Tell me about your bird or I'm going to kill myself!"

"She's not my bird!"

"What's she called?"

"Nothing for noses!"

"Aw, for God's sake Cleggy. Tell me about it her. I'm begging!"

Cleggy shrugged and took a long drag on his cigarette. It was written all over his face that he was enjoying the attention, but he seemed determined to continue with his coyness act.

"He's not saying anything because it was a disaster! The girl in question has moved house so he can't ever find her. As soon as she got back from the date she did a midnight flit." Miller smiled widely at Ellis. The twinkle in his eye told her that he was attempting a different route to the information.

"Aw, well... don't worry about it mate. There's plenty more fish in the sea." Ellis looked sympathetically at her colleague. She thought the world of Cleggy, she thought of him as a little brother.

"Have you heard yourselves?" Said the young copper as he blew another plume of smoke out. "For your information, I'm seeing her again."

"When?" Asked Ellis, her excitement was plain to see. Cleggy just shrugged again. "So, what's she like?"

"No comment."

"How old is she?"

"No comment."

"Where's she from?"

"No comment."

"I know where she's from!" Said Miller as he threw his cigarette dimp on the ground. "She's from the imagination of police constable Ian Clegg! That's why he won't say anything about her. Because she doesn't even exist!"

"Bollocks!"

"Aw please Cleggy! Don't be tight. I've been praying for this for ages and now my prayers are answered and you're being a shit-head about it."

"Alright, alright, Jesus H Christ! If you must know..."

"I must!"

"She's called Mandy, she twenty-three."

"What does she do?"

"She works on the bins. There's only one problem, she's got kids..."

"Aw, that's not a problem! You're ace with kids. How many has she got?"

"Eight. With six different blokes. They all help out with the kids like, so it's not too bad. She lives in a flat in Harpurhey."

"Oh..." Ellis could feel her cheeks reddening. She didn't quite know what to say to any of this.

"But she was telling me that she's a shit-hot wrestler and she reckons she's going to make it to the top in the women's Sumo. She's pretty well known on the circuit already. Big Mandy."

Miller was glaring at Ellis, urging her to laugh, she could feel his eyes drilling at her but she kept her cool and locked her gaze firmly on Cleggy.

"Sumo?" She asked.

"Yeah, well, hopefully. That's the plan. But she's not quite ready yet, got a bit of weight to lose before she can compete at that level."

Ellis kept her eyes trained on Cleggy. She knew that one look in Miller's direction would end badly.

"So, you're seeing her again?"

"Yes, well, I hope so. She borrowed two-hundred and fifty quid off me, so I better had. She's lost her two front teeth wrestling so I said I'd lend her the money to get some false ones put in."

A heavy silence suddenly hung in the air. Ellis didn't know what to say to any of this. Her mouth was open but she just couldn't think of any words.

"Anyway, we get on really well. She laughs at everything I say so that's a good start. I must admit though, she laughs a bit too loud! Everyone in the wine bar was staring at her last night. They stopped when she confronted one of them though, she put this poor bloke in a head-lock and started rubbing her knuckles on his head, he was screaming. I bet it was her Sovereigns."

"Oh, that's..."

The look on Ellis's face was priceless as Cleggy and Miller suddenly began pointing at her and laughing loudly.

"Oh, you set of dicks!" The WPC's face heated up noticeably as the two young PCs laughed mockingly at her embarrassed, speechless reaction to Cleggy's story.

"Absolute wankers!"

"Your face Kaz! Classic!"

The laughter continued for a few seconds more and Ellis joined in as she realised how she'd fallen for Cleggy's incredible love story a little too easily.

The police officers were interrupted from their merriment as they heard a gang of jeering males around the corner. Then a lady's voice could be heard shouting "just leave me alone."

The constables ran as quickly as they could out of the back alley that they'd been using for cover. As they reached Lower Mosley Street, they found the source of the noise. Seven or eight German football fans were following a young woman, shouting something at her. It was unclear what they were shouting as they were speaking in their native language.

"Hey, isn't that the girl from Market Street this morning? The one Tricky Micky was working on?"

"It is," said Miller as he set off running straight towards the group of men, all of whom were laughing and shouting, carrying cans of lager in their hands. The girl looked scared and stressed out and extremely vulnerable.

"HOI! STOP NOW!" Miller stood in front of the group

and they stopped walking. The young girl looked relieved to see the police, and visibly pleased that this scary situation was now being taken care of. The jolly looks on the football fans faces suddenly turned to panic. Cleggy was right behind Miller and the German fans didn't know where to look. They all knew that they'd been caught out.

"Kaz, go and check she's alright mate," said Miller.

Ellis caught up with the young woman and began walking beside her.

"Right, what the hell was that all about?" Asked Miller of the nine men standing before him. None of them answered, they all looked sheepish and embarrassed.

"Answer me. Or you'll all be locked up until Monday morning. You'll miss the match tomorrow." Miller had no idea if these blokes spoke English or not, but he knew that they all recognised that they were in trouble.

"Sorry." Said one of the football supporters after a few seconds.

"What were you doing?"

"Just fun. The girl."

"What, you think that a big gang of men shouting after a girl on her own is fun?"

"No, not fun. Just jokes."

Miller turned around and saw that Ellis and the young lady were out of sight now.

"Sit down on the floor and put your hands on your head. Now! Move it!"

The man who had volunteered as spokesperson repeated Miller's order in German and his friends all followed the instruction without question. It was clear that they didn't want any hassle at all. They all sat there in the middle of the road with their hands on their heads, their cans of lager by their sides.

Miller looked up and found a CCTV camera on the side of a building. He then turned to the unofficial spokesperson for the group and pointed at the camera, which looked as though it was pointing straight at the group.

"See that camera up there?"

"Yes."

"That's going to be keeping an eye on you. So, stay here and don't move. Do you understand?"

"Yes. Stay. Don't not stay."

"If you move from here, you'll be locked up until Monday morning. Do you understand?"

"Yes." The fear of this threat was unmistakable. The men were obviously excited about the following day's fixture against Russia at Old Trafford. It was the fear of missing the match which had made these yobs so easy to manage.

"Come on. Let's find Karen and check the girl's alright." Miller pointed to the CCTV camera again, and then pointed two fingers at his eyes before pointing back down at the tarmac. "Stay there."

Miller and Cleggy began jogging in the direction that Ellis and the young woman had gone.

"What are you planning to do with them?" asked Cleggy as they ran.

"Nowt. Just thought I'd shit them up a bit. I imagine another patrol will come across them and wonder what the fuck they are doing sitting in the middle of the street with their hands on their heads."

"I like it."

"There they are. God, I'm so in love with her!"

"Who, Karen? She's married now. I'll tell Bob!"

"No, you big lob-on. The person Karen's with."

"Do you want me to ask her out for you?"

"Don't be a dick Cleggy. I mean it."

"Ah, the cavalry have arrived!" Said Ellis. The girl smiled warmly at Miller as the two PCs caught up outside the Midland Hotel.

"We meet again!" Said Miller.

"Yes, thanks. That's the second time you've saved my bacon today! Thank you. I'm Clare, by the way." Clare held her hand out for a shake. Miller wasted no time in accepting it.

"I'm Andy."

"And I'm Ian. Nice to see you again, isn't it Andy?"

Miller blushed slightly. Ellis saw that it was becoming

awkward and stepped in to move the conversation on, Miller was blushing a little too obviously.

"Clare was just telling me that she's in the process of moving to town. She's starting Uni in September."

"Yes. I've picked a pretty awful day to look for a part-time job."

"You can say that again." Said Miller.

"There'll be plenty of work going if you're good at scaffolding or mending windows!" Said Cleggy.

"So what have you done with the men who were harassing Clare?" Asked Ellis.

"Oh, they're sitting on the floor with their hands on their heads like infants. Serves them right. They didn't do anything did they?" Asked Miller.

"No, no, they just all started shouting at me. It was pretty intimidating, but you guys came around the corner just in the nick of time."

"Well, we need to try and figure out how you're going to get back to your digs. Where are they?" Asked Ellis.

"Fallowfield."

"Well, you might have to walk it. There are no buses running. It's not that far though, couple of miles down that road." Ellis pointed towards Oxford Road.

The pleasant chat was interrupted by the police radio and an urgent call for Miller and Cleggy.

"Right, well nice to see you. We've got a shout now, so... well, bye."

"Oh, right. Well thanks again for all your help."

Miller and Cleggy began jogging towards Manchester Town Hall as Ellis explained the route back to Fallowfield to Clare. She picked up on the electricity between Miller and Clare, and was surprised to see how sad she looked now that he had dashed off. "He's single. And I can tell he really fancies you as well."

Clare laughed loudly. Ellis' brutal honesty had shocked her slightly, but the shock quickly turned to relief.

"Give me your phone number and I'll pass it on to him, if you want?"

"Yes please!" Said Clare without a moment's hesitation.

14.15pm

The events which were unfolding in Manchester were being discussed between the regulars in The Penny Farthing pub in Denton, five miles away from the city-centre and a million miles away from the noise, terror, confusion and chaos which had been taking place at the other end of Hyde Road. The popular boozer, famed locally for its cast-iron Penny Farthing model which was attached to the wall by the entrance, as well as its regular "A.T. lock ins" was widely regarded as the friendliest pub in the former hat making town.

The friendliness of the pub was thanks mainly to its location in the middle of the St Anne's development. The huge estate of well-to-do detached houses was built in the late 70s and early 80s, and the drinkers were all neighbours. It brought a great community spirit to the pub, and the area. The Penny Farthing had become the community hub over the years, its landlords and landladies had organised a number of charity events and collections for local people when they'd found themselves in hard times.

But today, there was no laughter and the mood was much flatter than usual. The news coming out of Manchester was getting worse with each new update. Much of the news was coming to the pub from second-hand sources as each regular arrived with something they'd heard from their brother-in-law or next-door neighbour. Things that had been heard elsewhere were being re-told as verbatim and subsequently, the latest information wasn't 100% accurate.

"There's at least fifty dead." Was one of the most troubling announcements, and it was made all the more serious by the next sentence. "Our Dave's next-door neighbour's mate is a copper and he phoned his wife up and told her, apparently. But it's not been officially announced yet."

The mood was becoming quite angry, understandably under the circumstances. As each extra pint went down, and the landlord flicked between the four TV channels trying to get the latest update, the mood gradually became even darker.

"Stick the radio on. Piccadilly will have all the latest

news." Said one of the regulars who was sitting at the bar.

"There's nobody on, it's just none stop music. They must have been evacuated." The landlord, Stan had already tried that.

"They were talking about it this morning, after it went off. I was listening before I came here."

"I know, I was listening myself," said Stan. "But then it just went to music."

"What about GMR?"

"I can't pick it up."

"Tell you what! You know who's missing here today, don't you?" Asked Billy Fraser, one of the younger regulars who was leaning up against the end of the bar.

"Go on?" asked Stan, the landlord.

"Irish Mick!"

The comment received a few grunts and mumbles.

"Well it's not got nowt to do with Irish Mick! What a dense thing to say!" Said one of the pubs most grounded regulars, Terry the plumber.

"No, I'm not saying he's done it. All I'm saying is, well... where is he? He's in here every Saturday lunch-time. Isn't he Stan?"

The landlord nodded as he dried a glass. "Well, he's in every lunch-time, to be fair. A very loyal customer."

"I rest my case!" Shouted Billy. "So where is he today?" The twenty-four-year-old began looking around the pub theatrically for a few seconds, before turning back to his audience at the bar. "Nope, no sign of Irish Mick today. I wonder why!" Billy picked up his pint of lager and took a greedy swig from it.

"He's probably not come in, because he's worried that people like you will start giving him shit for no good reason!" Said Terry the plumber, who had a lot of time for Irish Mick, one of his favourite drinking pals in the Penny Farthing. Billy Fraser, the gob-shite doing all the talking was one of his least favourites, but he managed to tolerate him most of the time. Just about.

"Bollocks! He's probably not come in because he won't be able to look any of us in the eye! Knowing that his mates have blown town up and killed fifty fucking people!"

"Hey, hold your horses Billy!" Stan used the correct tone of voice with his regular punter, asserting some authority whilst not making it sound like a bollocking. "I listened to the last news report, and they said there haven't been any fatalities. So, I think we should all calm down a bit and wait to see what's gone on before Irish Mick starts taking any of the blame for this." Stan tried to add a laugh onto the end of his remark, but it sounded flat. Nobody was in the mood for humour today, no matter how gentle.

"All I'm saying is… well, listen, there's more Irish living in Manchester than there are living in fucking Ireland! You know I'm right. So why are they bombing Manchester? It's stupid!"

"And this is exactly why Irish Mick has taken the day off coming in here!" Said Terry the plumber under his breath as he took a cigarette from his packet and lit it.

"There's no need for bombing Manchester!"

"Well where would you prefer they bomb?" asked Stan.

"I don't know. What's the point in them bombing anywhere?" asked the younger man.

"Well Billy, it's a conflict that's been going on for a long time mate, since about the twelfth century." Stan knew a bit more about the political problems regarding Ireland than this young bloke who worked as a pallet loader at Oldham Batteries up the road.

"So what's the point of bombing Manchester now, then? Eight hundred years later. I know they're famous for being thick, but what's the fucking point?"

Terry the plumber muttered something under his breath again, but nobody could make out exactly what he'd said.

"The IRA have been trying to get Britain to leave Ireland. They don't want Northern Ireland to be part of the UK, they want one Ireland, how it used to be. So, they leave these bombs to cause as much trouble as they can so Britain will just give in and withdraw."

"It's stupid."

"Well, they probably think its stupid that the Norman invaders went over there and claimed their country! They probably think it's stupid that the Irish were moved from their land and forced to live in areas that couldn't produce crops, and that most of them died from starvation. There's always two sides to a story Billy, I've tried telling you that before."

"I'm not being funny but you sound like you're on their side, Stan!"

"I'm not on their side at all. You just asked me what it was about so I'm telling you. It's a historic argument going back hundreds of years."

"Okay, but answer me this. What's that got to do with those kids they killed a couple of years ago in Warrington?"

"That was an outrage!" Said Pam, another regular who was sitting at the bar. She'd stayed quiet on the matter up until now, but a sudden anger was unmistakable in her normally relaxed, gentle voice. "Killing kids! What sort of a sick bastard gets involved in blowing up bombs in town centres? It makes me so bloody angry!"

Pam was talking about the atrocity that had taken place 20 miles away from Manchester, in Warrington town centre on the 20th March 1993. The IRA had planted two bombs in litter bins in the busy shopping area. One of the bombs was hidden in a litter bin outside Boots and McDonalds. The other bomb was in the bin outside Argos, about ninety metres away. There had been a coded warning, phoned through to the Liverpool branch of The Samaritans, and the caller had said that there's a bomb in the bin outside Boots and it will go off in half-an-hour. No location for the Boots store in question was given to the Samaritan who took the call, and Merseyside police had automatically assumed that it must be Liverpool, simply because the call had gone to the Liverpool office of the Samaritans. Liverpool city-centre was immediately evacuated.

No mention was ever made about Warrington during the coded warning, and as a result, there had been no evacuation of the area. The horror which followed resulted in the deaths of two children. Three-year-old Johnathan Ball died at the scene and 12-year-old Tim Parry was gravely wounded. He died 5 days later in hospital as a result of his injuries. A total of 54 people were hurt by the two blasts, which had taken place one minute apart. Most of those injured were running away from the first blast, straight into the path of the second bomb. Those injured included a young mother of two, 32-year-old Bronwen Vickers who had to have a leg amputated.

"You're not wrong Pam," said Stan. "The IRA have been responsible for some terrible, nasty things around this part of the world. I remember when they blew that coach up as well. On the M62, God, it must have been twenty years ago now. Longer."

"What was that, Stan?"

"Oh, God, it was terrible. There was a coach full of soldiers and their families, they were on leave and coming back home to Manchester from their base in Yorkshire. The IRA had planted a bomb in the overhead luggage thing in the coach, and it went off without warning in the middle of the night while they were all sleeping. Kids, wives, soldiers."

"Jesus!"

"It was terrible. 1974 I think, yes it was because our Brian was a baby in arms at the time. It killed twelve people if I remember right. It happened up on the tops heading towards Rochdale from Leeds. They are bloody ruthless these terrorists, make no mistake about it."

"I can't believe I've never heard about this!" Said Pam. "Have you Terry?"

Terry nodded solemnly, before speaking. "Yes. I remember it well. The bus driver was hailed a hero, he somehow managed to carry on driving the coach and brought it to a safe stop on the hard-shoulder, before being treated for his injuries. If I remember rightly, it was nine soldiers that were killed, and three family members. But when you saw the film of the coach on the news, it was a miracle that only twelve people died. It was bloody horrific."

Billy hadn't had anything to say about any of this for the past few minutes, mainly because he didn't really know enough about "the troubles" as he was a little too young to recall the horrors which had gone before, particularly in the 70s and 80s, when the IRA had carried out a campaign of terror which had contributed to over 10,000 bombs being planted, and over 3,000 lives being lost throughout the dark period.

"And what about the IRA bombs in Manchester a few years ago? It was coming up to Christmas and they let two bombs go off in the middle of the rush-hour, injuring loads of people. It's lucky nobody was killed then." Pam still sounded angry as she took a cigarette from her own packet and lit it, blowing a huge plume of thick blue smoke behind the bar.

"Nobody was killed but plenty were injured, the hospitals were all full, they had to close them."

The mood was rarely this low in the pub, people came in here for a laugh and a good chat with friendly locals. But the troubling news from Manchester was all they could think about today.

"This is exactly why Irish Mick hasn't come in this aft. He won't want to get trapped in a conversation about all this." Said Terry the plumber. "In fact, Stan, sort us out a carry-out mate, I think I'll go round to his house and watch the match with him. He'd prefer to talk about the football than the IRA, I know that for a fact."

"Yeah, no worries. What are you having?"

"Four cans of Stones I think. And a do us a couple of bags of peanuts."

"Make that six cans Stan, I'm going as well." Said Pam. "And I promise not to mention the IR bloody A!"

14:29pm

All of the police officers within the inner cordon zone were busy with tasks that had been allocated to them by control. There were hundreds of officers in the city-centre now, many GMP officers who had been called in by HR, as well as officers who had been seconded to Manchester from neighbouring forces. It was strange to see so many officers wearing Merseyside, Cumbria, Lancashire and even North Wales uniforms.

Like the majority of the relief officers who had been sent on blue lights to assist the Manchester force, Miller, Cleggy and Ellis had been tasked with cleaning up the streets. The city was hosting a major Euro 96 match tomorrow. Russia were taking on Germany at Old Trafford in little over 24 hours and most of the spectators were already here, a huge number of whom were in a pub in Ardwick right now, waiting to watch England and Scotland battle it out.

Whilst it was widely acknowledged that it would be impossible to return the city-centre to the condition it had been in prior to 11:17 this morning – it was still felt that some level of order could be restored. The Manchester police and the authorities would love to stick a middle finger up at the cowards who had committed this appalling act of mindless terrorism against a city that welcomes the Irish community more than any other in Britain.

Manchester was once known as "Little Ireland" due to the sheer numbers of Irish people who moved here 200 years earlier during the industrial revolution. Most of them came to Manchester to find work as the city became the world's workshop. Many more Irish immigrants followed, spurred on by the potato famine. In the 1850's it was said that 10% of the Manchester population was Irish, and the city was so over-run with Irish people that those who couldn't find work or accommodation were sent towards Liverpool or Nottingham to settle. Most of these Irish immigrants found work in construction or nursing, whilst many went to work as "Navvies" the hardy men who built the reservoirs, canals, viaducts, aquaducts, sewers and railways which empowered the north of England and made this place the powerhouse of the world. The Manc-Irish links have remained strong ever-since, the most popular football team in Ireland is Manchester United. Two of the team's biggest stars are Roy Keane and Denis Irwin, who both come from Cork. United's most famous player of all time and arguably the greatest footballer ever, George Best comes from Belfast.

This bomb, planted by a handful of extremists, would not be allowed to damage the historical and affectionate connection that the people of Manchester and those from the island of Ireland share.

Ensuring that a major football fixture went ahead without disruption was a great way of holding up a middle finger to the fanatics behind this attack and showing them that blowing up Manchester is no excuse to cancel the football. This is Manchester, we take football very seriously here.

The first task in succeeding to deliver a middle-finger salute was to tidy the place up. The damage to the area around Corporation Street would take many months, if not years. That was blatantly clear. Longridge House would probably need demolishing, as would the back end of the Arndale Centre. Marks and Spencers and the Corn Exchange would both need an extensive re-build and hundreds of surrounding buildings would require thorough structural examinations.

But the damage beyond the immediate bomb-site mainly consisted of broken windows. Lots and lots of broken windows. The glass needed cleaning up, the remaining glass that was hanging on within the window frames needed removing, and somebody at Chester House, the police HQ was currently in the process of phoning every skip-hire company in Manchester, to request as many skips as they could provide. Another member of HQ's team was charged with the task of phoning every glaziers in the Yellow Pages to ask them to make emergency repairs or board up the thousands of windows.

These would be a pretty weird requests, if any of the skip firms or glaziers answered their phones. This was, without any question, the worst possible time to ask for anything, when the biggest football match in decades was about to get under-way. The phones were ringing out and it was becoming increasingly obvious that glaziers and skip-hire staff were not available today, no matter how desperately their services were required.

The police officials weren't giving up though. With so many officers at their disposal, they planned to utilise this extraordinary man-power to its full potential. The cold-callers at Chester House were told to abandon the glazing and skip requests, and start talking to every B&Q, Wickes and Do-It-All store, requesting as many shovels, buckets and wheelbarrows that they could gather together. The DIY stores staff were told that officers in police vans and tactical aid vans would be along shortly to pick them up and that GMP would settle the costs next week.

14:32pm

Manchester Royal Infirmary's Senior Consultant, Professor Mackway-Jones was standing outside the hospital, preparing to present his second press briefing. The weather was still bright and sunny and the hospital chief's eyes struggled to adapt to the flood of bright light as he tried to focus on the media staff. His sudden appearance without notice had caught a number of reporters off guard and they had asked him to wait a few seconds so they could set up their recording equipment. The Professor kindly obliged and stood on the steps silently, using the time to adapt his vision from the dimly lit hospital to the glorious June sunshine.

"Okay?" He asked once it looked as though the media people had stopped fussing with their gear. The reporters and TV news presenters nodded appreciatively and the Professor began his update.

"Good afternoon. I have a further update on the hospital's response to this morning's terrorist attack in Manchester city-centre. I'd like to start by pointing out that the events of today have been extremely confusing and chaotic. With this in mind, I am pleased that I can confirm that the previous update that I gave you all was incorrect regarding the reports of sixty-people trapped inside the Arndale Centre. As the day has progressed, we have been given a number of inaccurate reports, and this one was no different. It is of course a huge relief to report that no people have been trapped in the Arndale Centre."

It was a relief, it was written all over the reporters faces. The idea that sixty people were inside the building had been a very concerning development an hour earlier. It was a huge comfort to hear that this detail was wholly inaccurate, quite frankly because it had sounded very ominous indeed. Sixty people being trapped inside a building following an enormous explosion was usually coded talk which meant that there were sixty dead people. This announcement was welcomed by all of the press representatives.

"I am very pleased to inform you all that we are

confident that we are now caring for all injured parties who were caught up in the attack. The number of people that we are currently treating for their injuries stands at two-hundred and twelve people. Police and Fire and Rescue teams are confident that the areas immediately surrounding the scene of this attack have been checked thoroughly and all injured parties have now been transported to hospitals around the city. As I reported to you a little earlier, we do have six seriously injured people, and our staff are working hard to help those people. I'm afraid I can't answer any specific questions at this time, but I will come out again a little later with a further update. Thank you."

14:46pm

Rick Houghton and Darren Stannage had been in a pub near the BBC headquarters for the past two hours. The landlady had allowed them to take over the pub's phone at the end of the bar as they tried desperately to make arrangements for Piccadilly Radio's output. The emergency tapes on both radio stations were due to run out at around quarter past three. If that happened, both the AM and FM stations would fall silent for the first time in the proud broadcasting company's history.

Rick and Darren had phoned as many people as they could in an attempt to salvage the situation. Starting with a pen and a piece of paper at the end of the bar, they'd phoned fellow presenters whose numbers they knew off by heart and subsequently gathered as many phone numbers as they could. The presenters passed on details for the senior engineers, managers at other radio stations, and the pair just continued ringing the numbers, explaining the situation and asking for ideas on who to ring next. This exercise was generating an impressive directory of "who's who" in north-west radio, written on the back of a brewery poster.

The stressful, often frustrating task eventually paid off when Darren got through to the boss at Red Rose Radio in Preston. Red Rose was owned by the same company which owned Piccadilly and the set-up in Preston very similar to Piccadilly's in that it ran two stations, albeit to a much smaller city. None-the-less, the call to Red Rose had finally got the wheels in motion for salvaging the situation. The boss there had been incredibly helpful and through the wonders of modern technology, had arranged for his engineers to switch Piccadilly's emergency tapes in Piccadilly Plaza to a live broadcast from the Red Rose studios. They continued with a "non-stop music" service on both Piccadilly Gold and Key 103's channels, whilst Rick and Darren were tasked with arranging for Piccadilly presenters to get up the M6 to Preston, and take-over the broadcast.

It was almost 3pm by the time that Rick and Darren were informed that everything was sorted. The two young lads had managed to save the day, and Piccadilly Radio's blushes. The most famous station in the region was not going off the air. Darren placed the phone down, looked across at the landlady and said "two pints of lager, please."

"Sorted?" asked Rick.

"Sorted!" Confirmed Darren.

Their nerve-wracking day was finally over, and just in time for the football too. Things were looking up, finally.

14.57pm

Wembley Stadium was packed out with a full capacity attendance as the teams lined up for one of the most eagerly-anticipated football matches in years. 76,864 fans were smiling, waving at TV cameras and singing as loudly as they could, overwhelmed with excitement for what the next two hours held in store. The sun was shining, the skies were blue and the noise inside Wembley stadium was deafening.

It was extremely rare that the rivalries between England and Scotland were pitched against one another in competitive football matches. But today, this game was going to be extremely competitive. The possibility of either team advancing to the knock-out stages of the UEFA Euro 96 tournament depended on it.

As expected, it was incredibly loud and boisterous at Wembley, the voices of the England supporters united in their chorus of "it's coming home!" was certainly loud, but the away supporters, the Tartan Army were making their own voices heard with a passionate rendition of "Flower of Scotland." The atmosphere was incredible in the stadium, and passions were equally as high inside the houses, pubs and clubs up and down the land. This football match had been a long time in coming, their last meeting had been seven years earlier, at Scotland's Hampden Park, when the English had won by two goals to nil.

Most England supporters were shocked to see that Paul Gascoigne had come out with the rest of the England squad and was lining up for kick-off. The 30 year old Glasgow Rangers star had been on the front pages of most of the papers every day throughout the past week, with headlines such as "Disgrace Fool!" These damning headlines followed the England superstar's involvement in a boozy night out, which had involved drinking neat spirits in a "Dentists Chair" with many of the other England players taking part in the ritual. The papers were encouraging their readers to be furious that Gazza was more interested in getting hammered, than focusing on his and the team's training for the Euro 96 tournament. The torrent of negative publicity about Gazza had been sustained all week, and many commentators had expected Terry Venables, the England manager, to rest the controversial player.

However, as the supporters raised their voices in support of their teams beneath the famous twin-towers of Wembley Stadium, Gazza stood with the rest of his team-mates and he looked relaxed and focused about the upcoming game. It had been a reasonable suggestion that Gazza would be on the bench today, as it was inevitable that he would be getting a hard-time from all sides. Not only had he been painted as a rogue and a fool by the English press, he was also the most popular and best-known player in the Scottish football league. His adoring fans from Scotland would today be forgetting their allegiances and Gazza was destined to be booed and heckled by the Scots every time he touched the ball.

As three o'clock arrived, and the referee blew his whistle, the game got under way and forty-million TV viewers cheered loudly as the fans with the oldest and bitterest football rivalry screamed encouragingly in support of their teams. England and Scotland are the oldest national football teams in the world and had played in the very first international football match in Partick in 1872 which ended nil-nil. The rivalry has remained passionate ever since.

For those people who had been caught up in the incident in Manchester just a few hours earlier, it was hard for them to believe that everything was just carrying on as normal. Most of the people who'd been in town when the bomb had gone off were still reeling from a deep sense of shock from the event, replaying the terrifying moment over and over in their heads, reliving that incredible blast that shook the ground beneath them, followed by the glass flying out of shop windows with great force, from every direction. The scenes of people lying injured, the look of terror and shock on their faces was still very raw. It seemed very odd that life was carrying on as normal while people were lying in hospital beds, others were in the middle of surgery, and there was no doubt about it, many people would be dead. It seemed weird, that a football match could have this much interest when one of the UK's biggest cities had just been destroyed by terrorists and hundreds of its citizens had been so seriously hurt.

Whether it was seen as weird or not, the football really was the main focus of the nation's attention, even here, in the city that had been reduced to rubble. Manchester had a number of city-centre pubs with the huge "big-screen" TV systems which were becoming more and more popular these days. But as the city-centre was closed today, the football fans who had planned to watch the game in town on one of the giant screens had to change their plans and visit pubs nearer to their homes. It was disappointing for many of them, having to watch the game the old-fashioned way, squinting at a 30-inch TV screen in the corner of a crowded bar.

But that's what people were doing, all of the pubs in the region were crammed full of fans with their England shirts on, singing and shouting, filled with the Three Lions passion, absolutely desperate to see an England victory today following the disappointing draw in the first game against Switzerland. If England didn't win today, there was every chance that they would be kicked out of the competition and since the tournament was taking place in England, this was an unthinkable outcome. This was the tournament where "football was coming home!" England *had* to win, there was no other option.

"COME ON ENGLAND!" Shouted the nation's men, women and children at their TV screens as Alan Shearer received an early cross from Paul Ince.

"Oh you donkey!" Shouted many of them as Colin Hendrie ran in and cleared the cross from danger. After many months of excitement and anticipation, the biggest game in football was finally here, and both England and Scotland looked like they were 100% up for it.

15.05pm

The big football match had finally cleared Manchester city-centre of the last of its loiterers. Those people who had stayed rooted to their spots in various locations around the area, watching the drama unfolding throughout the day had finally given up and retreated out of the area in the hope of finding a lift home. Most of them had been well aware of the fact that they could leave at any time, but had opted to stay around and see what happened next. For these people, a morbid fascination into the work of the emergency services staff had kept them all captivated.

As the police vans, ambulances and fire-engines had continued to drive as quickly as they could all around the area with their sirens wailing and blue-lights flashing, the spectators had continued to watch on.

But at 3pm, if all changed and for the first time since the bomb had exploded almost four hours earlier, Manchester was finally settling down and with the exception of the business-owners at the town hall, the only people in the city-centre area were the hundreds of emergency services and military workers who were still busy carrying out thousands of tasks that needed to be done.

Greater Manchester fire and rescue had most of the county's fire officers in town. Their primary objectives were to carry out safety checks on the buildings and structures worst affected by the blast, as well as to search all surrounding buildings for injured parties. The search operation was a gargantuan task, and one which was loaded with problems, most notably was the difficulty of gaining access to properties but there were plenty of other challenges facing the fire and rescue team staff. The alarms which were ringing all around, from every shop and office complex were all merging into one, almighty high-pitched tone which required ear defenders to stifle. The firemen and women had been ordered to search all basements and cellars in the inner cordon zone, which was every building within 500 metres of the blast. The most challenging part of this task came from the sprinkler systems which had been activated by the bomb blast and had continued to spray a steady stream of water into all of the offices and units for the past four hours. The result in most properties was a flood of several feet in each basement.

The police officers were finding that they had been handed every task imaginable, from sweeping roads to clear them of glass, to manning cordon lines and prevent members of the public from entering the vulnerable areas which contained hundreds of unlocked and unguarded business premises. The officers guarding the cordons looked on pitifully at their colleagues who were in charge of the sweeping up and moving debris from the carriageways. Their pity extended as far as making wanker gestures and laughing into their hands, which attracted a strong verbal reaction from those clearing up. Despite everything, the mood was jovial and the police staff just got on with it, eager to put the place back together as best they could.

Police vans were pulling up at the cordon lines, filled with spades, shovels and wheelbarrows which officers had been sent to DIY stores to collect. They also had dozens of pairs of rigger gloves and protective goggles to assist the officers who were clearing up thousands of tons of broken glass from every flat surface between Deansgate and the top of Market Street.

The ambulance staff had completed their operational work in the city-centre and all of the 212 injured parties had now been transported to hospital, many in ambulances, some in police cars, one in a fire-engine and sixty travelled by tram. There was still a number of ambulances dotted around the city centre, they'd had to be abandoned due to punctures and other technical issues caused by the state of the roads when they had arrived in the area. One or two of the ambulance crews had been tasked with walking around and collecting the various pieces of kit and apparatus which had been left lying around each triage point. These ambulance workers were being escorted by police officers who were collecting up lost property. There was literally tons of shopping bags, hand-bags and bunches of keys and personal belongings which had been dropped in the chaos and these officers were surprised how quickly their huge bin-liners filled with the items before they had to take the full bag back to the police's tactical aid van parked at the cordon line.

At the site of the blast, twenty-two fire and rescue officers were working on structural examinations. The results weren't positive, and every single member of the crew was stunned by the damage which had been done. Their tests confirmed that Longridge House was unstable and was at risk of collapsing due to the weakening of the gable end wall, which had taken the full brunt of the blast. They were also shocked to see that the concrete bridge which served as a walkway between the Arndale and Marks and Spencers had been lifted up off its foundations and dropped half a metre away. It was literally dangling from the two structures on either side.

"That could fall down at any moment so make sure nobody is working beneath it! Tape the whole area off!" Shouted the commanding officer at his men. Beneath his aerial ladder, on the ground where the Ford Cargo had been parked for almost two hours earlier that morning was a two-metre deep crater which could easily fit a police van inside. The blast had ripped up the tarmac, the hardcore, plus two layers of Victorian era cobbles and tons of earth, scattering it hundreds of metres in all directions. There was no sign of the truck, or the army's robot. It seemed that they had been blown into billions of tiny pieces, which wasn't going to make welcome news for the Forensics people who would have to try and gather some evidence from this shocking crime-scene.

At quarter past three, all of the fire-men were asked to assemble at the Deansgate cordon point. They climbed down their ladders, jumped off their appliances or climbed out of the flooded basements. A few minutes later, thirty-eight fire-men were assembled at the place they'd been instructed to meet. On the other side of the cordon tape was a young man standing beside an Austin Maestro.

"Alright fellas, we just wanted you to know, everybody really appreciates what you're doing for our city. So, my boss sent me down here to give you some lunch!"

The fire-officers smiled and laughed as the young lad

opened the hatch-back door and began handing huge pizza boxes over the cordon tape into the crowd of fire-fighters and placed crates of Coca Cola and Sunkist cans on the floor beside their feet.

"Wait, there's chips and some bottles of sauce on the back-seat."

"Aw thank you mate!" Shouted one of the firemen, not realising until now how hungry he was, as he'd been so wrapped up in his work.

"I've got to get back, my boss is getting another lot ready for the police."

The fire and rescue staff all gave the young lad a round of applause as he got back into his battered old car and headed off towards Salford. This gesture had brought about the first smile of the day for the men and women who were grabbing slices of steaming hot pizza and shoving it into their mouths as though they'd not eaten for days.

"Nice one!"

15:12pm

Mike Unger was pouring with sweat as he typed furiously into his computer. He was running late with the special edition and he was completely aware that the printing lads and delivery drivers would be far from happy, their dreams of catching the second-half of the match were slipping away fast. The deadline had been 3pm, at the very latest, for the printers to start producing the newspaper, then pack them and load them onto the vast fleet of bright yellow vans which would then distribute the 500,000 copies to the region's newsagents.

There would be no time for proof-reading today. If there were spelling or grammatical errors in the publication, then readers would just have to accept that today's edition had been put together in a very haphazard fashion. Mike normally prided himself on the high standard of his newspaper. But he wasn't quite so obsessed with layout today. He knew that they had a pretty strong excuse if they did receive any complaints or criticisms. The largest bomb that has ever been planted anywhere on the British mainland, detonating just a few hundred yards away from your newspaper offices, followed by a three-hour window to produce a paper from scratch, with a skeleton crew of staff, many of whom had been denied access to the area after trying to return to type up their stories, felt like a pretty water-tight excuse.

Fortunately, there wasn't quite so much writing to do as usual. The sensational photographs that his team of photographers had brought back filled many pages, and were increased in size to create cover for the lack of reports. Mike wasn't worried about it, this edition was being put together before the dust had properly settled. He knew that Monday's edition would benefit from all of the facts and figures being released, when everybody would know exactly what the outcome of this devastating terror attack really meant for the city. He was just glad that he and his team had managed to produce this edition, against all of the odds. It may not have every fact and detail included, but it certainly told Manchester's people what had happened, with some jaw-dropping photographs of the terror, the chaos and the mind-blowing damage that the city had suffered in this attack.

Finally, at twelve minutes past three, Mike finished writing his final piece. He saved the word-processor document he'd been finalising, and lifted his phone.

"Hi, it's Mike. I know, sorry. It's ready to roll." He announced to his production manager, before placing his phone down and finally, taking a moment to relax and reflect on the most challenging day of his career, confident that the newspaper which would be in the hands of its loyal readers with the next ninety minutes was as good as it could be, under the most extraordinary of circumstances.

16:08pm

As anticipated, the football match was turning out to be a great game, just as everybody had hoped. The first half had ended nil-nil and as both teams walked down the famous tunnel for half-time, they both looked confident and happy with their performance. Scotland had certainly shown the England team that they were determined and focused, and that they were giving this game everything they had. If England had been hoping for any favours from the under-dogs, the first-half had demonstrated that there weren't going to be any.

But soon after the second half began, England were on the attack. Gary Neville the Manchester United and England defender had found himself in the role of right-winger deep into Scotland's half and supplied a stunning cross into the goal-mouth which found the head of England's number one goal-scorer, Alan Shearer. This was only going to end one way, and there was nothing that Scotland's goalkeeper Andy Goram could do to deny the powerful six-yard header from smashing into the back of his net.

It was one-nil. The crowd at Wembley went crazy. The crowds in every pub in England did the same, beer was flying in all directions as a deafening roar echoed throughout the land.

In Scotland, the supporters were disappointed, but none of them lost heart. There was still 37 minutes of this game to play and every single one of them believed that the Scotland squad had what was required to get a goal back. And another one after that.

"Come oan Scotland!" Was the cry in every pub, house and club north of Carlisle.

16:17pm

WPC Karen Ellis was quite enjoying this shift, which surprised her greatly. It was so good to be back with Andy and Cleggy, she hadn't realised quite how much she'd missed working with them. No matter what was going on, she knew she'd always have a laugh with them. Today, of all days, with the tension as high as it had been, she'd still really enjoyed it.

Ellis had broken off from her tidying up duties for a few minutes after spotting an empty phone-box. She wanted to ring Bob and let him know what was going on.

"Hi, It's Karen."

"Hiya love, you alright?"

"Yes, yes, fine. It's all settled down now, we're just cleaning up. If I see another piece of broken glass, I'll bloody scream!"

"I've been watching Sky News, they've put some photos on, looks really bad."

"Yes, it's proper bad, Miller and Cleggy said the whole floor shook at Piccadilly Gardens."

"Bloody hell fire."

"The Arndale's going to be shut for months, and the Corn Exchange will probably end up being demolished. but no fatalities, that's the main thing."

"Is that official? They're saying there might be some bad news to come on TV."

"Nah, there's one woman who's critical, but she's in surgery now and all the best surgeons in the north of England have gone down to help so... fingers crossed, it'll be a happy ending. But that's privileged GMP information so don't be ringing Sky News and repeating it."

"Received and understood, over."

"Anyway, what are you doing watching the news? Thought you'd be watching the match?"

"Are you being stupid? My wife's been called in to deal with the biggest explosion ever seen, and you think I'd be watching football?"

"Yes, well, I'd be properly pissed off with you if you'd

said you were watching the match! So you've answered correctly."

"I'm taping it. Thought I'd wait for you to finish and we could pretend it was live and go ahead with the barbeque anyway."

"Yes, that's a top idea. I'd like that. Who's arrived?"

"No-one. I rang them all and explained that we're delaying, said you've been called in. I told them to have some dinner and come later, we can have the barbeque for tea. Everyone understands."

"Nice one Bob! That's ace."

"So, what time do you think they'll let you go?"

"Not sure, but every copper in Greater Manchester is here, as well as officers from all the neighbouring forces so there's plenty on hand. I don't think we'll be that long. Six o'clock is the time that everybody's talking about."

"Cool, well, see you in a bit. Love you."

"Love you too Bob. Oh, did your phone arrive?"

"Yes, it's mint. It's got this game on it called Snake, it's well good - so I'll just play that 'til you get home."

"Don't forget to walk up and down the street with it. Make sure the whole neighbourhood sees you!"

"Already been. Twice. Nosey Norah's curtains were twitching like mad!"

16:21pm

Barbara Welch, the lady who had been rescued from Longridge House by Dave Marsh and his Fire Service colleagues was in the operating theatre at North Manchester General Hospital. The stakes couldn't be any higher as a team of top surgeons battled to save this lady's face, and her life. Barbara was in a medically-induced coma and her monitoring equipment was showing healthy signs, her heart-rate and blood-pressure was stabilised and normal which was very positive news.

None of these well experienced medical experts had ever seen injuries as complicated as these ones before. Whilst the nature of the injuries was complex enough, the sheer number of them beggared belief. There were literally hundreds if not thousands of fragments of dirty glass particles embedded in Barbara's face, her neck, her scalp, her ears, her upper body and her arms. Most of the injuries were disturbingly complicated to work on, not only because of the sheer number of shards of glass of varying sizes that had entered Barbara's skin, but also because they had all penetrated her from different angles and at different speeds and velocities. What this crucially meant was that some shards of glass had been embedded so deeply into her skin that the surgeons couldn't see where they had entered, or where they had come to rest.

Barbara had taken the full force of the bomb-blast, at the same time as the flying glass that came with it. This was the reason that her head was three times the size of a normal human head when Dave Marsh had found her, knelt down in the wreckage. Glass which had been stationary in the windows that surrounded her desk had suddenly accelerated in Barbara's direction, flying faster than the speed of light from every direction. The result was this utterly heart-breaking and seemingly impossible task of trying to work out where the pieces had now ended up. One thing which was abundantly clear to every single member of the twelve-strong team in surgery – it was a miracle that this woman hadn't been killed outright. And it was this fact alone that drove them all on, determined to fix her, no matter how long it might take.

The sheer complexity of her injuries meant that she would be staying here for many more hours, whilst the most senior surgeons in the north-west region embarked on the seemingly impossible task of removing the glass at the same time as saving Barbara's nose, her ears, her face and ultimately her life.

There was no doubt in anybody's mind in this operating theatre that this was going to be a long and massively complex operation, one which would most likely involve several teams of surgeons working around the clock to save this poor lady. A poor lady who was only here because she had agreed to working some over-time on a sunny, Saturday morning. To see the state of her now was heart-breaking for everybody who had come into contact with her. The sheer randomness and pointlessness of it all made no sense at all, but it was this senselessness that drove the surgeons on as they pulled another deeply embedded dart of broken glass from Barbara Welch's face. And then another. And then another. And then another. Each one feeling like a major victory.

16:33pm

Scotland's goalkeeper, Andy Goram was having a great game, denying several England attempts on goal. His finest save had come from a Paul Gascoigne free-kick which was met by a solid Teddy Sheringham header. Wembley gasped for a second as it looked like a sure-fire second goal for England, but the heroic Scottish goalkeeper was playing a blinder and denied the team in white from doubling their advantage.

It was end-to-end stuff and the Scotland team were growing in confidence. It had looked as if they were about to level the score as Gordon Durie smashed a header at the England goal which was denied by a superb David Seaman save off the line. One thing was certain, this much anticipated match was a thriller.

In the 78th minute, Scotland were on the attack with an incredible halfway-line pass from Gary McAllister into the England penalty area. It was inch perfect and found the feet of Stuart McCall and Scotland looked sure to find the equalizer at any moment, when England defender Tony Adams brought down Gordon Durie right under the referee's nose.

"Penalty!" Shouted the ref as he pointed to the spot. It was the Scotland fans turn to roar, and they took the opportunity. But the celebrations were to be short-lived as Gary McAllister stepped up to take the penalty kick. Wembley fell silent.

McAllister took a long run-up and smashed the ball down the middle. The silence of Wembley was soon replaced with the sound of ecstasy as England's goalie David Seaman saved the penalty. But that wasn't the end of the drama. Seaman quickly took his goal-kick and the ball was back in the Scotland half, being passed to the left flank and Paul Gascoigne who was unmarked.

What happened next will still be talked about in twenty, thirty, perhaps even fifty years-time. Gascoigne was sprinting forward as the ball was passed to him at speed. The Scotland defender Colin Hendry was running towards the ball at equal pace and it looked like a fifty-fifty challenge. But Gazza had an incredible trick up his sleeve, he stuck a toe gently underneath the ball, lobbing it high over the Scotsman's head, then ran straight around the player that he had completely baffled with this extraordinary move, and volleyed the ball into the back of the net. It was a truly incredible goal, a moment of pure class and raw genius. As Gazza lobbed the ball up over Hendry's head, it seemed to lose all of its momentum and slowed-down in mid-air, before landing perfectly on Gascoigne's laces and being launched like a rocket into the back of the goal.

Gazza ran to the corner-post and lay on the floor as the euphoric roar of England's supporters deafened the Scots. The England squad came running towards Gazza and began squirting their water bottles in his mouth in a celebration which was the ultimate dismissal of the English press who'd been determined to make Gazza's life a misery for the past week. In his own, unique style, Paul Gascoigne recreated the Dentist's chair which had caused him so much criticism, after scoring one of the greatest goals ever scored by any football player.

Even the commentators on the TV had a hard time explaining that astonishing goal, it looked more like a magic trick than a goal. It was genuinely incredible, and the looks on the Scotland player's faces said it all. With 11 minutes of the game still to play, they knew they had lost, and they knew that it was thanks to one extraordinary, unforgettable minute of heart-stopping football.

16:37pm

At the newsagents on King Street in Dukinfield, the owner Mr Denton was becoming increasingly stressed out. He was waiting for both of his paper-boys to arrive and kept looking at his watch every few seconds, and then up at the door. He huffed loudly each time he did it, they were supposed to have been in at 4pm to deliver the final edition. But he knew full well that they were both watching the match and were bunking off.

But it wasn't all bad. If the two lads had showed up on time, they'd have been standing around waiting for the papers until half-four, and no doubt nicking Black Jacks and Flying Saucers, the two items in the 10p mix-up tray that every paperboy and girl in the area knew that he couldn't see from his side of the counter. Mr Denton had wondered for years why those two trays were always needing a top-up, until the day he caught one of his paperboys putting a fistful of them in his jacket pocket.

He huffed loudly again. The shop was dead this afternoon, it seemed that everybody was watching this bloody football match, and to hell with everything else. He was only here himself because his regular Saturday shop assistant had booked it off weeks ago, unbeknown to him at the time that it was because of the blasted football. Mr Denton took his little phone book out from under the till and looked up the names of the two paperboys. He lifted the phone and dialled the first number. It rang out, which caused him to huff loudly again. He then tried the second number, and again was left with no alternative but to exhale really loudly as he finally accepted that the lads were not for showing up today. At least not until the match had finished.

Looking at his watch once more, he worked out that the football match would be finishing in about ten minutes time. There was a good chance they'd turn up shortly after the final whistle. He hoped so anyway, the last thing he wanted to do was close the shop so he could drive around and deliver the papers himself.

Mr Denton decided to have a read of the Manchester

Evening News special edition that had just been dropped off, to help pass some time and take his mind off these bloody paper-lads messing him about. He was shocked by the photographs of Manchester, the damage which had been done, and the horror that was etched on the faces of the people in all the pictures.

"Poor bugger!" He said under his breath as he looked at the photograph of the bride running down the street, holding a little girl's hand. They both look petrified and the photograph really interested him, it put a human-interest angle on the story, making him think about his own daughter's wedding a few years ago and how the Denton family might have felt if something like this had wrecked their big day.

After reading the reports and looking at all the pictures, he checked his watch again. It was ten to five.

"I'll give it 'til five," he told himself, as the phone started ringing.

"Hello, Denton's."

"Yes, it's Mr Cartwright, on Chapel Street. He's not been."

"Ah, yes, hello Mr Cartwright. It's Mr Denton speaking, how are you today?"

"He's not been!" Said the elderly caller, cutting through the pleasantries.

"My apologies for that Mr Cartwright. Only, the paper's very late today because of what's gone on in Manchester. But you'll have it soon enough. Okay?"

"Rightio. Bye." With that, Mr Cartwright placed the phone down with a heavy clunk. Mr Denton knew all too well how grumpy people could be if their paper wasn't delivered on time. Especially Mr bleeding Cartwright, as he was referred to by the other staff at Denton's.

The shop bell rang as the door opened. It was one of Mr Denton's paper-lads, Darren.

"Ah! Who's this! Larry Let-down! That's who. Where the chuffing Norah have you been lad? Speak up!"

"Sorry, Mr Denton!"

"Sorry won't butter any bread! And what have I told you about leaving your bike in a heap on the pavement like that?

What if a blind man was walking out of the shop now? He'd fall over it, that's what!"

"But why would a blind man come into a paper-shop Mr Denton?" Asked Darren with a cheeky smile.

"Enough of your lip! You!" The newsagent gave the 13 year-old the hard-stare for a few seconds, before handing the bright orange bag over the counter which contained 47 copies of the Evening News.

"Now go on, fast as lightning! Your pal hasn't turned in, so there's a double round going if you're quick. Ride like the wind!"

"All I can think about is cracking open a can of freezing cold lager and pouring it straight down the back of my throat!" Miller was feeling the heat now, literally. He'd had to keep his poxy helmet on all day, and the heat that was trapped inside it was making him feel dizzy. The constant pouring of sweat and the dusty atmosphere all around resulted in a thick layer of powdery debris sticking to his face, his neck and his arms. He had never known his lips to be so dry, the heavy dust was making his eyes sting and his skin feel tight. He and all of the other emergency services workers who were trying to tidy the place up felt wretched, these were extremely uncomfortable conditions and the stupid bloody police helmets with their heavy padding inside didn't help matters. But, they'd all been ordered to keep them on as there was a very high risk of things falling from above today.

"I've had enough now. I'm just waiting for the message to stand us down."

Cleggy and Ellis were quiet. The mood had definitely dropped between the three, they were all exhausted, sun-burned and ready to call it a day. As the latest wheelbarrow of glass was filled and Cleggy lifted the handles and began pushing it towards the huge pile at the top of the street, Ellis put her shovel down and wiped her sweat away with the back of her hand.

"I bet I reek."

"You do. But no more than normal."

"Cheeky sod. So, what time do you think we'll get the order to stand-down?"

Miller was about to say something along the lines of 'it had better be bloody soon' when his and Ellis's radios crackled to life. "Control call to all early shift officers, and all off-duty officers phoned in on over-time, please complete your current tasks and head back to the station. Over."

"Thank God for that!"

"I second that!"

"Wait, is that Cleggy's?" Miller pointed to a police radio

which had been left on the window-sill of the shop they were working outside.

"Yes."

"Well, he won't have heard the message. Let's just piss off quietly and leave him at it!"

"Andy! You're so tight on him, it's well out-of-order. But come on, then."

Both of the officers looked along the street and saw that Cleggy had his back to the pair. He was still dumping the contents of the wheelbarrow into the huge pile of glass and rubble that he and other officers had been collecting together for the past few hours, instead of watching the football. This enormous pile was going to become somebody else's problem now. Cleggy hadn't looked round as Miller and Ellis slipped out of view down a back ginnel, laughing loudly as they made their way back towards Bootle Street police station.

"Aw, you're a right bastard! I love it!"

"This will get him back for what he did to you today, when he was telling you about his bird!"

Ellis laughed loudly. "Oh my God! What the hell!"

"Got to hand it to him, that was funny! Your face!"

"With each extra thing he said I was thinking he was taking the piss, but I just couldn't be sure! Eight kids with six dads, at twenty-three!"

"You should have twigged it there and then! But you just kept falling for it. So funny! You'll never make a detective, you."

"I know, but... imagine it was true and I'd said something?"

Miller laughed loudly and it echoed down the ginnel. Both of them were smiling widely, the day was finally coming to an end and it was desperately welcome.

"I proper miss working with you two, proper enjoyed today – despite the mental circumstances. I hope I'm put back on my old shift soon."

"What's going on with that? You were covering sick-leave weren't you? What's the officer got, a broken-back?"

"No, well, that was what I was told when I was put on

this shift. But I've since found out that I'm covering for somebody who's been suspended. Could be weeks, months even."

"That's shit."

"Tell me about it. But what you were saying, about me never making it as a detective…"

"What?" Miller stopped walking and faced his colleague. His only priority in the police was to work in CID. All this uniform work was a stop-gap to working in crime investigation. He had always dreamed of working as a detective, cracking cases and getting involved in criminal investigations. Dealing with the public on day-to-day police work was okay, but he was only doing this to get his hours done so he could apply for CID. He sensed that Ellis had a big announcement and he was desperate to hear more.

"My duty sarge on nights has told me that there's a fresh recruitment drive starting in September for various CID posts. Rooky DCs included."

"Honestly?"

"Straight up."

"Are you going for it?"

"I will if you do."

"Well I will be! No question about it."

"I am, then."

"Oh my God! This is the best news I've heard all day."

"Will Cleggy go for it as well?"

"Doubt it. He's not interested in CID, still wants to be a traffic cop."

"I've never understood that."

"Well, he reckons it's the only way he'll ever get to drive a Cosworth."

"Well, anyway, that's my news… I've got a really good feeling about CID. So, fingers crossed my sarge isn't just blagging my head because he knows I'm not keen on his shift."

"Nah, it'll be right. They've not recruited for two years. Sounds right. Oh my God, I'm proper excited now."

Ellis and Cleggy continued walking, making steady progress towards their nick when they heard heavy footsteps advancing quickly behind them.

"You pair of shit-heads!"

They turned round and saw Cleggy running towards them. "That was well snide!" He said as he reached them.

"Sorry mate," said Ellis. "But we heard somebody laughing really loudly and we thought it was your bird. Big Mandy."

"Tossers!"

"But it's alright, we knew it wasn't her because this one had a full set of teeth."

18:08pm

Andy Miller was in his car, heading away from Manchester. It felt brilliant to have the windows down and to feel the cool breeze rushing in through the window. The blast of air was cooling him down for the first time since he'd stepped out of the police station to attend the burglary shout at Stolen from Ivor ten hours earlier. He couldn't believe that was ten hours ago. It honestly felt like days, if not weeks ago. It was beyond his comprehension what had unfolded in the hours that followed. It was a crazy day, and he knew that he needed a bit of time to sit back and reflect on it all.

Sergeant Harris had been a diamond in the stand-down briefing. It was short and to the point, but the most loved Sergeant at Bootle Street had made himself even more popular with his officers thanks to his brief but sweet address to them at the end of that extraordinary shift.

"Well, everybody. The facts are this. 80,000 people were in the city centre this morning when you began your work in evacuating the area. The biggest bomb that has ever been planted on the British mainland has destroyed a large part of this city as well as every pane of glass within half a mile. Ten of my officers ensured that the public were moved out of harm's way more than an hour before the bomb exploded. The most important part of all is this. Nobody died. That's down to you guys, your hard-work, determination and professionalism. It was a miracle that nobody was killed today – and every single one of you men and women are that miracle. Give yourselves a round of applause, right now."

The mood had been ecstatic after this short but powerful speech. Sgt Harris had really made every single one of his officers feel valued and appreciated. It had been a hellish shift, for so many reasons. But to clock out knowing that all of that hard work and craziness had ended so positively was a terrific feeling.

The plan now was to get home, tell his mum and dad all about the day, have a shower and a freshen up and then ring a cab and get across to Karen and Bob's for the barbeque. Andy

Miller was planning to have a great many beers tonight. Even if he stayed the night, he was planning to drink so many beers that he'd still be unfit to drive in the morning.

"It's coming home! It's coming home!" Sang two pissed-up blokes in England shirts at the top of their voices as other cars beeped triumphantly at them. One was piggy-backing the other across the road while Miller waited at the traffic lights.

"I'm going home! I'm going home!" Sang the young PC under his breath as he waited for the lights to change to green, feeling just as jubilant as the two piss-heads, though he sensed that at least one of them would end up falling over and would require several stitches before their day was over.

"Aw for God's sake," said Miller as the lights changed and he looked in his rear-view mirror. The lower half of his face was bright red with sun-burn, whilst his forehead was marble-white where his helmet had shielded him from the sun. "I look like a bloody baby-bell."

19.35pm

The piquant aroma of the barbeque was wafting all around the local community by the time that Miller had arrived at Bob and Karen's house. The stimulating, unmistakable scent of sizzling sausages and burgers made him realise how hungry he was as he paid the cab driver. He walked straight round the back of the house and was greeted loudly by Bob, who was standing behind the cloud of smoke which was creating these amazing smells.

"Andy Miller! Welcome!"

"Alright Bob! You're making my mouth water!"

Without any further encouragement, Bob leaned over and handed a burger to his guest. "Salad and sauce is on the table behind you."

"Wow! Now that's what I call good service Bob! Cheers mate." Miller didn't bother with the sauce, he just took a big bite out of the burger. Bob laughed loudly.

"Bloody hell, you are hungry! Hey, I hope you've managed to avoid the score. I'm putting the match on from the beginning in a bit!"

Miller laughed loudly. The amount of sad-looking, inebriated men in kilts and ginger wigs and triumphant pissed-up England shirted morons that he'd encountered since leaving Manchester 90 minutes earlier had been a bit of a giveaway as to which way the score had gone. Then, when he'd arrived home, his dad greeted him by talking about the match before he'd even bothered to ask about the bomb.

Miller swallowed his food and replied with a smile. "Nah, I've not managed to avoid the news I'm afraid Bob!"

"Ah, that's a shame. Not a surprise, but a shame. Still, I'll put it on in a bit and we can all pretend."

"Nice one. I'll just go and stick this bag of meat in the fridge."

"No problem. I hope you're not full up off that burger. We've got half a cow and numerous pigs to get through here!"

"I'll find room, Bob. Don't you worry!"

There were lots of family and friends round, as well as

one or two of the neighbours. As a result, the garden was very busy with people. Cleggy had arrived just minutes before Miller and the beer was flowing freely. There was a great deal of excitement amongst many of the guests, the only conversation point was the bomb in town and many of the guests couldn't believe that three of the coppers who had been on duty in amongst it all were here. There was hope that after a few cans of lager, the coppers would be happy to talk about the things that had gone on in town and perhaps reveal some insider information.

Karen's dad had made a bee-line for Miller as soon as he stepped into the kitchen. They'd hit it off instantly at the passing out celebrations a few years earlier and had sat together at Karen and Bob's wedding. The two were laughing and joking like long-lost friends within minutes.

"God, look at my dad with Andy," said Ellis discreetly to Cleggy as they stood by the back door. "I always suspected that he wanted a son, but flipping heck, he's all over him."

Cleggy nearly spat out the lager that he's just taken a big swig of. "Yep. There's a real connection there between those two. You have every right to be worried."

"Well, I might cancel my surprise for Andy if he doesn't take his tongue out of my dad's ear!"

Cleggy looked interested. "What surprise is this?"

"What... Like I'm going to trust you! Piss right off mate!"

"Eh?"

"Listen, after that awful trick you played on me today, you're lucky you're even here, never mind hearing about any of my secrets."

"Oh, right! I can't believe you stood there, looking all interested in that."

"Knobhead."

"Anyway, come on. What's this surprise for Andy?"

"Okay, but don't say anything. Promise?"

"I swear on Big Mandy's grave!"

"I've bought him a bottle of fake tan for his forehead."

Cleggy laughed loudly as he looked into the kitchen and

noticed their friend's strange, two-tone complexion.

"I don't know what you're laughing at you mug. Yours is twice as worse!" Ellis laughed as she pointed at Cleggy's face, it was bright red from his neck up to his cheeks and then perfectly white up to his fringe.

"Aw bollocks! Are you serious?"

"It'll be fine. Just wear a balaclava. Nobody will know."

Ellis's abuse of her colleague was cut-short by Bob shouting from the barbeque.

"Karen, I think I just heard the door-bell."

"Oh!" Ellis started smiling as she headed around the side of the house.

Cleggy took a sip from his can and headed into the kitchen and stood beside Miller. Already, he had quite a crowd standing around him as he was telling a story about the day he'd had.

"So we're standing there, all you could see was broken glass everywhere, people covered in blood and you couldn't hear yourself think because of all the bloody alarm bells going off from every direction. I stood there thinking this can't be real, and just as I was thinking that, I looked down and right there, in a shop window that had just been blown out, there was about ten or twelve of those dancing sun-flowers. They were all jiving away and looking really happy. It was the craziest thing! It turns out, the noise from all the alarms was getting them in the mood for a rave!"

Miller's audience laughed at his surreal story and he used the opportunity to take a generous swig from his beer can.

"But yeah, it was quite a..." Miller suddenly stopped talking as he noticed Ellis talking to somebody in the back garden. He couldn't believe his eyes. It was the girl he'd saved from Tricky Mickey. And then from the German fans. He fancied her like mad and the sight of her confused him and his mind began wandering. His audience were all looking at him, waiting for him to finish his sentence but he was completely unaware.

"Go on, Andy..." Said Ellis's dad. Miller turned to look at him and remembered what he was saying. "Sorry, yes, so, anyway, we spent most of the afternoon clearing the glass up, bloody hard work. I'll sleep tonight, I'll tell you that!"

Cleggy saw that Miller was distracted and started talking about the funny hair-dresser who was reluctant to leave his shop in case his ladies ended up with a dodgy hair-do. As Cleggy began emulating the hair-dresser's funny mannerisms, a fresh wave of laughter resonated from the friends, neighbours and colleagues of Bob and Karen's. Miller saw his opportunity to step outside.

"We meet again!" Said Miller, smiling widely at the girl. "What are you doing here?" He asked. Ellis laughed.

"Well, I invited Clare along. She's miles from home in a strange city that's just been blown up. I thought she might like to meet some new people." Ellis was blushing violently as she spoke. She was such a shit liar. Miller was just glad he'd put his new Sergio Tacchini polo-shirt on.

"Well, that was very nice of you Karen!" Said Miller, completely aware that his friend and colleague had set him up on a date.

"To be honest," said Clare. "I've been brought here under false pretences. I think Karen is trying to set us up!"

Miller laughed as Ellis blushed again. "Anyway, I'd better go and see if Bob needs a hand. Clare, what are you drinking?"

"Oh, er, I'll have a lager, please."

"No problem. Can or bottle?"

"Bottle, please. Thanks."

Clare and Miller were left standing on the patio. They both realised exactly what was going on and laughed. A weird silence descended and Miller thought he'd better say something. "So..."

"Do you..."

They'd both had the same panicked urge to fill the silence and had both spoken at once, which made them both laugh and blush at the same time.

Ellis watched on as she gave Bob a kiss. "I love seeing you flipping burgers."

"Could have worked at McDonalds, me. Their loss! Who's that? Mate from work?" Asked Bob, wondering who the pretty young woman was.

"Oh, that's Clare, I don't really know her, only met her today. I've set her and Andy up on a date. I think the penny is just dropping now."

With that, Ellis walked away from her husband and headed into the kitchen. Bob didn't give his wife's bizarre answer a second thought as he continued flipping the burgers. He knew that she fancied herself as a bit of a match-maker, albeit with limited success so far. She'd set Bob's brother up with an old college friend, which had ended in a row about politics. Then, she'd tried to fix another friend up with one of the coppers at work, but that had ended badly when the policeman asked his date how many people she'd slept with as soon as they sat down. The worst one though was the time she'd tried to set Cleggy up with her best-friend, and he'd gone to the wrong restaurant. Both of them had sat there, in separate restaurants, thinking they'd been stood up. Karen's success rate so far had earned her the nickname "Cilla Cack."

Bob glanced over towards Miller and Clare and saw that they were laughing together. The chemistry between them looked excellent and he got the sense that maybe Karen had finally managed to get her match-making endeavours spot-on this time.

20:46pm

Professor Mackway-Jones had kept his word and had continued coming out of the hospital with updates for the media staff at regular intervals since the early afternoon. As he made his latest entrance on the steps of Manchester Royal Infirmary, he looked a lot more relaxed than he had done on any of his previous appearances.

"Good evening," he said, looking quite relieved to see that there were far fewer journalists and reporters at the foot of the steps than there had been previously. He was also pleased to see that the relentless sunshine which had been bugging his eyes each time he'd come outside was not so intense now.

It had been a long day for everybody concerned and the Professor was looking forward to heading off home soon himself. Despite the much smaller group of media personnel now, he noticed that the main broadcasters were all in attendance, the BBC, ITN and Sky News vans were still parked up across the car-park and the local radio and newspapers reporters were still waiting to hear the latest information.

"This will be the final update from me for today and I'd like to thank you all for being so supportive and understanding throughout the day. I feel that we have seen a very positive outcome from today's terrorist attack with regards to the patients that we have treated. As we switched our local hospitals into major incident centres this morning, we had been anticipating a great deal more trauma cases than we actually did see. As things presently stand, we have seen a total of two-hundred and twelve people today, the vast majority of whom have been, or are in the process of being discharged. We will be keeping nine patients in hospital over-night, one of whom is still being operated on at North Manchester General Hospital as I speak. I'm delighted to say that despite everything, we have not suffered any loss of life today. I'm sure that you will all agree with me that this staggering outcome is thanks to the excellent response to this incident from the police in the first instance, as well as the fire and rescue service and the ambulance teams who responded so brilliantly to the reports of injuries which followed the explosion at 11:17 this morning. There will be a further update at some point tomorrow, but I can confirm that the surgeons who are still operating are confident that the patient will make a positive recovery from the complicated injuries that were sustained as a result of the blast. Good evening."

With that, Professor Mackway-Jones nodded politely and headed back inside the hospital as the TV reporters made their summing-up comments to the cameras. The thrust of those comments was the excellent news that the biggest bomb that Britain had ever seen in peace-time had destroyed a huge part of Manchester, and that some-how, miraculously, there had been no loss of life.

Epilogue

Barbara Welch remained unconscious for three days following the blast. Despite the fact that she required more than 250 stitches to her face, Barbara made a full recovery from her extensive injuries, which required more than 50 hospital appointments, further surgery and many months of physiotherapy sessions. Barbara still finds small fragments of glass coming out of her head when she washes her hair. One of her colleagues who was sitting just behind her escaped the blast with a single cut.

Danny O'Neill slept through the bomb, so ill with the flu that he didn't surface again until the following Tuesday. When he did finally wake up, he was confused that the glass was missing from his bedroom window and that huge cracks covered every wall. The blast had vibrated through his bedroom so violently that the door wouldn't open fully as the frame was twisted. He did enjoy having reporters from the local news programme Northwest Tonight around to hear his story and to film footage of the damage. Damage that hadn't interrupted his sleep as he snored through the almighty blast 200 yards away from his bed.

Franklyn and Amanda managed to catch their honeymoon flight to Florida and returned to Manchester ten days later to a media frenzy. The press were desperate to know more about the bride and groom who'd been photographed running through the streets. The couple enjoyed making several national TV appearances and telling their incredible wedding day story. Sadly, by Christmas 1996, the marriage was in trouble and the couple split soon afterwards. Both are now remarried and are still living in Manchester.

Gazza's goal is still shown without fail on the "greatest goals of all time" montages on TV. Scotland fans still prefer not to talk about it.

It was almost a week before the last alarm bell stopped ringing in Manchester city-centre. When it was finally disabled, a huge cheer went up from all of the police officers, council officials and the hundreds of glaziers, scaffolders, construction workers and media staff who'd suffered the constant ringing in their ears non-stop through every day of work since being sent to Manchester to try and fix the place up.

It was quickly established that the western section of Manchester city-centre was going to be out of bounds for many weeks, if not months. The damage inflicted by the bomb was far greater than anybody had earlier anticipated. In glazing alone, the city needed a more than a million square metres of glass just to replace the broken windows. That was more glass than was actually available for purchase. Glazing companies from every corner of the UK were asked to load their surplus stock and get down or up or across to Manchester as quickly as they could. Demand was so great that glaziers from across Europe were asked to load their vans and make a journey through Calais with as much glass as they could bring with them. Many of the glaziers were still working on the job nine months later.

The demand for skips was also unprecedented. For the first week after the bomb went off, the entire city centre had more skips parked up than cars. The skies over Manchester were quickly filled with dozens of gigantic cranes, and they still haven't left yet. The clean-up from the bomb heralded the start of a rebuilding programme which would still be in progress 23 years later, when this book was being written.

A year before the IRA bombed Manchester, the city was awarded the Commonwealth Games, beating London in the prestigious competition to hold the event. Urban and economic regeneration of Manchester had been planned as part of the bid, and £200 million pounds of National Lottery funds were already in place to finance it, along with a grant of £100 million pounds from central government.

The Commonwealth Games went ahead as planned in 2002 and were hailed an enormous success. The transformation of the city in the seven years between the award of the games and the Queen's opening ceremony was a truly inspirational example of how great things can be achieved on a monumental scale. Not only did Manchester deliver on all of the ambitious regeneration plans for the games, but the powers-that-be also managed to rebuild a large part of its city-centre which was destroyed by 1.5 tons of explosives, which in context, is the equivalent to 30 bags of building sand. It remains the biggest peace-time bomb that has ever been detonated in Great Britain and it amazes many Mancunians that a lot of people around the UK have never even heard about it. The football grabbed all of the headlines that day, ultimately thanks to the fact that there were no fatalities.

Today, Manchester is one of the world's busiest and most cultured cities, attracting visitors from all over the globe. These visitors are attracted to the city because of the famous friendly northern welcome, the music that the city has produced, the universities and colleges, the arts and media, the sports stars it produces and its vibrant, exciting city-centre. Manchester was a great city, long before that bomb went off, and it is still a great city today.

It infuriates a lot of people that nobody was ever jailed for planting that bomb. Mr Fox, the dodgy guy who bought the getaway car and the truck from the used car-sales showroom in Peterborough was never charged, nor were his accomplices who delivered the bomb at 9.20am. GMP came very close several times, but various political problems and legal arguments prevented any charges being brought. It is largely down to the peace process that nobody was jailed for the worst act of vandalism that any British city has ever seen, an act which cost one and a half billion pounds to put right.

The Belfast Agreement, which was a major political development in the Northern Ireland peace process, was signed by all of the political parties on Good Friday, 1998. The Troubles, as they had been known, ended that day, largely thanks to the determined efforts of Mo Mowlam in bringing all of the opposing sides together and working out a positive way forward. One of the deciding clauses of the agreement was that Northern Ireland would finally have its own devolved powers and would no longer be controlled administratively by Westminster. Another major breakthrough was the agreement that the ugly and intimidating barb-wired check-points at the Northern Ireland border, which were heavily patrolled by armed British soldiers, would be torn down and the soldiers, their guns and their intimidating presence would be sent back to England.

It wasn't perfect for all sides, but it was certainly progress. Progress that ultimately brought about peace. It also prevented GMP from jailing the men that detectives were convinced were behind the Manchester truck-bomb attack. The Troubles, as awful as they had been, were over. The car-bombs, the petrol-bombs, shootings and beatings which had plagued both sides of the Irish sea for so long were finally over after more than 10,000 bombs and 3,000 deaths.

21 years after the Good Friday agreement was signed, the old horrors of the 60's, 70's, 80's and 90's returned to the streets of Belfast at 11pm on the 18th April 2019. Lyra McKee, a 29 year-old journalist from Londonderry was standing behind armoured vehicles, reporting on rioting when she was shot dead. This appalling crime sent shockwaves around the world and rocked the UK. But most powerfully, the communities in Northern Ireland felt this heinous crime the hardest, the people who had thought that those dark days were gone for good. In one, shocking incident which ended in the pointless, brutal and tragic death of a much-loved young woman from the local community, the Good Friday agreement appeared to have been ripped up and a return to the horrors of the past looked inevitable.

Lyra was one of the UK's best-known up-and-coming journalists, who had signed a two-book deal with publishing giants Faber, just weeks before her death. The mood in the weeks which followed her tragic murder became a message of hope which has resonated very loudly from the vast majority of people in Northern Ireland. They have all made it clear that they will not allow their lives to return to the misery which had plagued them through The Troubles. One thing which certainly became clear from this tragic incident was the resounding message that the people of Northern Ireland, particularly those too young to truly know the misery that The Troubles brought, were not looking to retaliate. The hope that surrounded the previous 21 years of peace still exists and this tragic murder has only renewed and refreshed that sense of hope.

Richard Leese, the council Leader who was just weeks into his job as the most senior politician in Manchester when the attack occurred remains in his post 23 years later. He has overseen the extraordinary rebuilding of Manchester and has been a driving force in the outstanding makeover which has been witnessed. When the bomb went off, very few people lived in Manchester city-centre. Today, more than 25,000 live in the new high-rise apartment blocks and refurbished mills and renovated warehouses inside the city-centre, boosting Manchester's economic and employment growth to previously unimaginable levels. His consistent achievements as the Leader of Manchester City Council through these progressive and transformational times have been recognised as well. He is called Sir Richard Leese CBE these days.

Much has been made in this story about the fact that nobody died on June 15th 1996, a fact which inspired the title for this book. But there were many things which happened that day which qualify as a miracle. Imagine if the traffic warden had placed the parking-ticket on the windscreen a little too heavy-handedly. Imagine if the big recovery truck had been at its base and came to remove the Ford Cargo when requested, ten minutes before the warning was phoned through to Granada TV. Imagine if PC Gary Hartley who found the bomb, had opened the Cargo truck's door to investigate further. Imagine if a little scally had spotted the truck parked up with its hazards on and decided to nick the radio.

Any one of these scenarios would have resulted in the deaths of hundreds, potentially thousands of people who were minding their own business on the surrounding streets and in the nearby shops. 80,000 people were in the vicinity of that truck and it is thanks to fate, and the excellent reaction to the warning by the uniformed services that everybody involved lived to tell the tale.

Tragically, it's not strictly true that nobody died as a result of the bomb. In March 2015, father-of-two Stuart Packard from Essex was diagnosed with mesothelioma, a deadly cancer caused by exposure to particles of asbestos. Stuart sadly died in October of that year, aged just 40 years old. Stuart had worked as a security guard around the Longridge House and Arndale bomb-site in the weeks following the blast, and was exposed to asbestos during this time, as the demolition of the worst affected buildings got under-way in haste. Mesothelioma is usually seen in people of retirement age, it is very rare that somebody so young suffers from the brutal disease. Stuart is the only person to have died as a result of the IRA bomb in Manchester. He left his wife of twenty years, Julie and their two children Isla and Kian, who were just five and ten when he died in a hospice, almost twenty years after the blast.

Some people claim that the IRA did Manchester a massive favour with that bomb. Barbara Welch thinks differently, and so do the 211 other people who were hurt, and the thousands more who witnessed the horror and the carnage and were emotionally scarred by the terror and panic they'd encountered that day. Many more people will never forget the long hours between hearing about the bombing and learning that their loved ones were safe. To say that the IRA did Manchester a favour on the 15th of June 1996 is an insult to everybody who was affected that day, to every emergency service worker, every good Samaritan and to every politician who worked tirelessly to keep Manchester open for business whilst a quarter of it was rebuilt. The IRA caused injuries, misery, pain and stress to thousands of people who lost homes, jobs, businesses and livelihoods. That's not a favour.

Manchester is the place where the Industrial Revolution began, where the first steam-powered mill was built. It is the place where the first passenger railway line was laid, where the first computer was created, where the atom was split, where 25 Nobel prize winners come from, where the world's first public library was built, the first artificial waterway was created, the city where the first international art festival was held, the place where Emmeline Pankhurst set up the Suffragette movement. Trade Unions were born here. Roget's Thesaurus was written here. The first bus route set off from here. This was the place that engineered the first fresh water supply for its citizens and it is the place that provided the first municipal park. It's the city that has created the best music and television, it is known globally as the number one football city. It also contains Britain's only UFO landing strip, proof if any were needed that this city always thinks ahead.

Manchester is a place so rich in success and major achievements that we could easily be here for another 100,000 words to look over the highlights.

If some moron ever tries to tell you that the best thing that ever happened to Manchester was a massive IRA bomb being dumped there, you should smile politely and tell them that they are talking shite.

The End.

If you enjoyed Miracle on Corporation Street, you will probably enjoy catching up with Andy Miller in the present day. These days Andy is head of Manchester's Serious Crimes Investigation Unit, in the popular DCI Miller series.

Miller 1 is "One Man Crusade"
Miller 2 is "Neighbours From Hell"
Miller 3 is "Road To Nowhere"
Miller 4 is "Gone Too Far"
Miller 5 is "The Final Cut"
Miller 6 is "Proof of Life"
Miller 7 is "Nothing To Lose"

Printed in Great Britain
by Amazon